American Constitutional History

Also by Jack Fruchtman

Author

The Supreme Court and Constitutional Law: Rulings on American Government and Society
The Political Philosophy of Thomas Paine
Atlantic Cousins: Benjamin Franklin and His Visionary Circle
Thomas Paine: Apostle of Freedom
Thomas Paine and the Religion of Nature
The Apocalyptic Politics of Richard Price and Joseph Priestley

Editor

Common Sense, Rights of Man, and Other Essential Writings of Thomas Paine
A Life in Jewish Education: Essays in Honor of Louis L. Kaplan
Britain in the Hanoverian Age, 1714–1837: An Encyclopedia (co-editor)
An Eye-Witness Account of the French Revolution by Helen Maria Williams: Letters Containing a Sketch of the Politics of France

American Constitutional History

A Brief Introduction

Second Edition

Jack Fruchtman
Professor Emeritus
Towson University
Towson, Maryland

WILEY Blackwell

This second edition first published 2022
© 2022 John Wiley & Sons, Inc.

Edition History
John Wiley & Sons, Inc. (1e, 2016)

Registered Office
John Wiley & Sons, Inc., 111 River Street, Hoboken, NJ 07030, USA

Editorial Office
111 River Street, Hoboken, NJ 07030, USA

For details of our global editorial offices, customer services, and more information about Wiley products visit us at www.wiley.com.

Wiley also publishes its books in a variety of electronic formats and by print-on-demand. Some content that appears in standard print versions of this book may not be available in other formats.

Library of Congress Cataloging-in-Publication Data
Names: Fruchtman, Jack, author.
Title: American constitutional history : a brief introduction, second edition / Jack Fruchtman, Professor Emeritus, Towson University, Towson, Maryland.
Description: Second edition. | Hoboken, NJ : John Wiley & Sons, 2022. | Includes bibliographical references and index. | Contents: Ideological origins of the new republic -- Representative and constitutional democracy -- Nationalization of the constitution and executive power -- Commerce, nullification, and slavery -- Civil War and Reconstruction -- Rights and privileges -- The development of substantive due process -- Civil rights after Reconstruction -- The re-emergence of executive power -- Advocates and enemies of social welfare -- The growth of civil liberties -- The civil rights movement -- Expanding presidential power -- Federal commerce power and economic regulation -- Rights, liberties, and judicial doctrines -- The struggle for equal rights and criminal justice -- The continued growth of executive power -- Epilogue : the 2020 Presidential Campaign and its aftermath. | Summary: "The new republic began in 1781 after the ratification of the Articles of Confederation and continued when the Americans replaced the Articles with the United States Constitution 7 years later. In 1789, the people elected their first federal government. Over the next 15 years, the founding generation made substantive formal changes: in 1791, the states adopted the first 10 amendments, known collectively as the Bill of Rights, followed by two others in 1795 and 1804. The United States doubled its geographic size in 1803 when the Jefferson administration purchased the Louisiana territory from France. The new republic endured slavery, even as some states began its gradual elimination in the 1780s. Most Americans focused on modifying their new government and its powers while declining to resolve the future of slavery. To avoid contention and disunion, the delegates to the constitutional convention did not address it. The words "slavery" or "slave" appear nowhere in the document. Some abolitionists like Benjamin Franklin - a former slave owner himself - John Adams, Alexander Hamilton, and Benjamin Rush attempted to raise the issue, but their efforts failed. Later leaders like William Lloyd Garrison, who founded the abolitionist paper, The Liberator, in 1831 and was co-founder of the Anti-Slavery Society, were active throughout the period. It was not until the end of the Civil War that slavery finally ended. The period also saw the enhancement of the Supreme Court's authority when Chief Justice John Marshall issued his unanimous opinion in Marbury v. Madison in 1803. Marshall wrote into the Constitution that the judges' duty was to interpret the document and to overturn all laws that conflicted with that interpretation. New institutions were created, such as the Bank of the United States, and the Court unanimously approved Congress's authority to create it. George Washington was the first president to sign an executive order while James Monroe was the first to issue a signing statement, indicating his ideas of legislation and how he intended to enforce it" -- Provided by publisher.
Identifiers: LCCN 2021035757 (print) | LCCN 2021035758 (ebook) | ISBN 9781119734277 (paperback) | ISBN 9781119739784 (ePDF) | ISBN 9781119734291 (ePub) | ISBN 9781119734307 (oBook)
Subjects: LCSH: Constitutional history--United States.
Classification: LCC KF4541 .F78 2022 (print) | LCC KF4541 (ebook) | DDC 342.7302/9--dc23
LC record available at https://lccn.loc.gov/2021035757
LC ebook record available at https://lccn.loc.gov/2021035758

Cover image: © rdegrie/Getty Images
Cover design by Wiley

Set in 10.5/13.5pt ITCGalliardStd by Integra Software Services Pvt. Ltd, Pondicherry, India
10 9 8 7 6 5 4 3 2 1

Again for Clara, Juliette, Sophia, Elsa, and Nicholas and in memory of Arnie Reisman

Contents

Acknowledgments

Five political scientists and historians have inspired the organization of this book as revealing how the Constitution evolved through a series of republics. None of them have developed the idea of six republics. Bruce Ackerman, who is also a law professor, Stephen Skowronek, Theodore Lowi, Richard Cortner, and Michael Lind have all argued that while the Constitution is virtually unchanged since the ratification of the Bill of Rights in 1791, the document did indeed evolve through distinct periods. I am grateful to them for their observations and analyses, which have informed my own thinking, but which also differs from theirs in many respects.

I wish to thank former Dean Terry A. Cooney of the College of Liberal Arts and former Provost Timothy Chandler, both of Towson University, for granting me a year-long sabbatical to work on and complete the manuscript. Discussions about American constitutional history have been invaluable to me as I formulated my thinking about the Constitution's evolution. I thank my colleagues Cynthia Cates, H. George Hahn, and Richard Vatz for raising questions and stimulating debate about the Constitution. I will always be indebted to John Pocock and the late J. Woodford Howard Jr. of the Johns Hopkins University whose work has long been a model to all who write about history, politics, and governing. In addition, I would like to recognize Stephens Broening, Herbert Goldman, Xerxes Mehta, and the late Judge Allen Schwait for engaging me in conversation and debate over the years about the nature and meaning of the Constitution.

I also appreciate the support that John Wiley & Sons have given me, especially my editor for the first edition, Peter Coveney, who supported this project and Jan East who edited it. I am grateful to the three anonymous reviewers of my manuscript, whose observations helped make the book more accessible to readers. Finally, I could not have completed this work without the support and devotion of my wife, JoAnn, whose lifelong companionship has been invaluable. All errors are of course my own.

The second edition covers the period from 2015 to 2021, including the controversial and bitter presidential election of 2020 when the current president, Donald J. Trump, claimed that he won, despite losing the popular vote by more than 7 million votes and the electoral vote, 306 to 282. Trump continued to espouse his charges of election fraud throughout 2021.

The edition also includes the addition of three new Supreme Court justices: Neil Gorsuch who succeeded the late Antonin Scalia; Brett Kavanaugh who took Anthony Kennedy's seat after his retirement; and Amy Coney Barrett who joined the Court after the death of Ruth Bader Ginsburg. The addition of these justices guaranteed a conservative majority for the near future if they voted in concert with Chief Justice John R. Roberts Jr. and Justices Clarence Thomas and Samuel Alito.

Additions to Part 5 comprise several important decisions the Court made after 2015, including affirming same-sex marriage and a woman's right to an abortion under certain circumstances. The justices also continued to guarantee an individual right to own and carry a firearm and the central place of religious liberty in American society. It also reiterated its constitutional and statutory support of the Affordable Care Act (Obamacare).

A major feature of the Trump administration from 2017 to 2021 was the continued, then rapid, surge in the power of the president that began during the Reagan administration. President George W. Bush and his vice president, Dick Cheney, espoused the theory of the unitary executive, meaning that presidents may protect the nation without congressional or judicial oversight. President Barack Obama began his two terms in 2009 stating that he planned to have a more cooperative relationship with Congress until he found that he had to work alone by signing executive orders or with members of his own party to pass laws he promoted. President Trump, who was the first president to enter office with no background in government or the military, claimed time and again that Article II of the Constitution allowed him to do whatever he wanted. He sought to halt immigration from both the southern border by advocating the construction of a wall and Muslim countries by signing an executive order that the Supreme Court eventually upheld. He supported the addition of a citizenship question on the forms determining the 2020 decennial census. He was the first president in American history to have been impeached twice by the House of Representatives, although the Senate declined to convict him both times. His relationship with the Senate was especially important: he ensured that its leaders followed his decisions, especially in passing the 2017 Tax Cut and Jobs Bill that enhanced the financial interests of corporations and wealthy individuals.

The Senate process known as budget reconciliation took on increased importance. Senate rules allow for a phenomenon known as the filibuster, which means that debate on a bill would not stop until a supermajority voted to halt it (stopping debate this way is called "cloture"). The filibuster, which originally meant an uprising or rebellion, is a Senate rule that began in the early twentieth century to slow or prevent legislation from assisting minorities and preserving Jim Crow laws that legally segregated Blacks from whites in places of public accommodations. Today, the supermajority stands at 60 votes, and then to start it, a senator proclaims a filibuster. No other action is necessary whereas originally a senator had to speak, sometimes for hours, to halt debate. The record holder is Senator Strom Thurmond of South Carolina who spoke for 24 hours, 18 minutes, to tie up a civil rights law. In 2021, some senators advocate its elimination or reform by lowering the vote threshold to 55 or a return to a "talking" filibuster. A change in the rule would take a simple majority vote.

Budget issues are excluded from the filibuster: in that case, a simple majority of senators may stop debate through the budget reconciliation process. The Senate, however, may use it only two or three times a year. The Senate used it to pass Obamacare in 2010, a tax cut bill in 2017, and a 2021 stimulus bill to help Americans out of work due to the Covid-19 pandemic.

I again thank the editors and staff at John Wiley & Sons for supporting the publication of the second edition. It has been a pleasure to work with my editor Andrew Minton, copy editor Helen Kemp, editorial coordinator Sophie Bradwell, and content refinement specialist Kanimozhi Ramamurthy. Special thanks to Jennifer Manias for her support of this second edition.

Prologue

The United States Constitution is the oldest continuous national republican document in existence today. It was not the first. Republics, or mixed regimes as they are also known, existed long before the Americans crafted theirs in 1787. Most did not last very long. In the ancient world, the Roman republic collapsed when it degenerated into empire. During the Renaissance, the Florentine republic in Italy survived a mere 14 years, from 1498 to 1512. It dissolved when the powerful Medici family, which had once ruled Florence, re-established a dictatorship. In the classical republican tradition, republics were fragile political organizations. The critical balance between the various branches of government could easily crumble when one or two dominated the others. The Americans modeled their constitution on the British government with its one-person executive and two-part legislature. For them, the British failed to create a true republic, because a hereditary monarch led the executive branch and hereditary aristocrats controlled the upper chamber, the unelected House of Lords. Meantime, large landowners controlled the House of Commons and only a few men possessed the right to vote. The Americans believed that after separating from the British Empire they could create a true republican structure where citizens participated in decision-making and enjoyed the peaceful transitions of power.

The Constitution created a democratic republic, not a democracy. In a democracy, citizens vote directly on government policies, while, in a republic, they elect representatives to develop policies on their behalf. Vestiges of democracy remain in America. They include the New England town meeting where residents directly vote on issues, such as whether the town should purchase a new police cruiser. The ballot initiative, also called the referendum, exists today in over forty states, allowing voters to make specific policies, such as whether a state should repeal its capital punishment law. Most laws in the United States today, however, are passed by representatives elected by the citizens. This system comprises the republic.

The Americans wanted their new government to represent every person, including those ineligible to vote such as women, making it a democratic republic. The Constitution addresses "persons," not "citizens" or "voters" when it guarantees a structure, rights, and liberties. It reserves direct elections only for the House of Representatives because many delegates to the constitutional convention, including James Madison, believed that ordinary citizens failed to have the requisite education, intelligence, or common sense to decide who should be a senator or president. They initially devised a system of indirect election for those offices. The people elected state legislators who then chose United States senators, a procedure that changed only in 1913 when the states ratified the Seventeenth Amendment. In presidential elections, the people vote for a special group of people, known as Electors. They alone vote directly for the president. Today, Electors still choose the president, an increasingly controversial process.

Since the Constitution's ratification over 235 years ago, Americans have formally added only 27 amendments. Congress still makes the laws, the president enforces them, and the courts interpret their constitutional validity. Formal changes to the document have typically occurred during or just after political or social crises. A few examples will suffice. The first 10 amendments, known collectively as the Bill of Rights, emerged in 1791 as a direct reaction to the Constitution's ratification process. Many state ratifying conventions argued in favor of adding a bill of rights, which occurred within two years of ratification.

The Twelfth Amendment in 1804 resulted from the highly contested 1800 presidential election. The Constitution initially provided that candidates for president and vice president run separately for office. The candidate with the highest number of electoral votes became president, the second highest vice president. This arrangement worked in the first three elections, despite the outcome in 1796 when men from different parties became president, John Adams, a Federalist, and vice president, Thomas Jefferson, a Republican. However, when Jefferson ran for president in 1800 with Aaron Burr as his vice-presidential running mate, the electoral vote ended in a tie between the two candidates. To avoid this from reoccurring, the Twelfth Amendment allowed presidential and vice-presidential candidates to run together on the same ticket.

The most striking examples materialized during and after the Civil War when the Thirteenth in 1865 ended slavery, the Fourteenth in 1868 ensured the equal protection of the laws, and the Fifteenth in 1870 guaranteed the right to vote for the newly freed Black slaves. The Nineteenth Amendment in 1920 extended the vote to women in national elections, a consequence of many years of contentious advocacy for the right. With the adoption of the Twenty-Second Amendment in 1951, the states created a two-term limit for presidents after Franklin D. Roosevelt won four presidential elections from 1932 to 1944. Years later, in 1971, the war in Vietnam paved the way for lowering the national voting age to eighteen with the ratification of the Twenty-Sixth Amendment.

The Constitution is notoriously difficult to amend. Over the years, members of Congress have proposed tens of thousands of amendments, but few have passed the stringent requirements set out in Article V: two-thirds of both houses of Congress must approve an amendment or the same two-thirds could call a constitutional convention to propose one, and then three-fourths of the states must ratify it. Among the failed amendments are those guaranteeing equal rights to women, balanced federal budgets, term limits for members of Congress and allowing prayer in the public schools, outlawing abortion, and prohibiting flag desecration. While 27 amendments have altered several constitutional provisions, the document has really changed only 13 times since 1804.

The founders modified and tinkered with their work as the new government was becoming settled, first in New York City, then Philadelphia, and finally Washington, DC. The founding generation added the first 12 amendments within 15 years after the document was ratified: the Bill of Rights in 1791; the Eleventh Amendment in 1795, overruling a decision by the Supreme Court to forbid citizens of one state to sue another state; and the Twelfth Amendment in 1804. These are really part of the original document in that the same generation proposed and ratified them. Finally, two amendments, the Eighteenth (1919) prohibiting the manufacture, distribution, or transportation of alcoholic beverages and the Twenty-First (1933) repealing the Eighteenth, effectively canceled out each other.

While American constitutional history comprises the story of these formal alterations, it is even more an account of informal changes. This is where constitutional interpretation comes in. The wording of the document is often vague and imprecise. It demands that people interpret the meaning of its words, like due process of law, equal protection, and cruel and unusual punishments. The First Amendment declares that "Congress shall make no law … abridging the freedom of speech." Was it left only to Congress to protect free speech? Did this mean the states could abolish it? What does "no law" mean: literally no law whatsoever, so that free speech is an absolute value that must be protected at all cost? What does "abridge" mean? No universal agreement has ever been reached when it comes to any provision – by the justices of the Supreme Court, the members of Congress, or the president.

This is why it is important to learn how the branches of government have interpreted the Constitution's words and spirit. Numerous informal changes have transformed their meaning: some are due to a president's decisions, especially in military affairs and national security, to Congress in the realm of lawmaking, or to the Supreme Court in deciding cases. Differing interpretative approaches have sometimes been a matter of partisan politics and political ideology, but more importantly it has been the result of competing values among liberals and conservatives in response to various events. When can the president act alone without congressional or judicial oversight? What is the appropriate relationship between the federal and state governments? What is the proper balance between liberty and security in a democratic order? What is the best way to pursue equality? How does religious faith figure in American society and government? These and other questions like them have faced all three branches since the Constitution's ratification over the past 235 years plus.

The Supreme Court, the president, and Congress have all changed the Constitution's meaning as they make public policy. Presidents issue executive orders, sign executive agreements, and claim unilateral authority, especially in matters of national security and military affairs. They have used "signing statements" to set forth their reasons for not enforcing a law even after they have signed it. While Congress may not delegate its authority to another branch of the government, it possesses the authority to change or repeal existing laws. Finally, Supreme Court justices have long held that precedent, known formally as the doctrine of *stare decisis* ("let the decision stand"), is an important principle to ensure legal continuity and stability. They have also stated that it is not an inexorable command whenever they overrule earlier decisions. In 1943, they held that states and local school districts could not require students to recite the pledge of allegiance as a matter of religious freedom or conscience. The decision overruled one from just three years earlier when the Court held that school districts did have such power. Congress and the states too may overrule Supreme Court decisions by adding a constitutional amendment to the Constitution, as they did when the states adopted the Eleventh Amendment in 1795. In 1913, the Sixteenth Amendment empowered the federal government to collect a tax on incomes, overruling two earlier Supreme Court cases that held that a federal income tax was beyond Congress's taxing power.

The structure of the book

The American republic today reflects the constitutional changes that have taken place formally and informally over the past two centuries. It has evolved through a series of clearly identifiable stages. In the new republic, the framers implemented their principles into practice, often tinkering with changes that developed into the first 12 amendments. Overshadowing everything was the institution of slavery, which increasingly became a contentious issue in the slave republic as the nation hurdled toward division and ultimately civil war. The aftermath of that horrendous struggle, in a period known as Reconstruction, led to new ideas as the United States entered the industrial age and the world of the free market. Manufacturing and the rise of the railroads contributed to the idea that government must avoid regulation as much as possible. At the same time, a countervailing ideology called for governmental intervention to help wage earners, farmers, and women. These reformers promoted wage and hour laws, unionization, and equal rights for women.

The welfare state took hold in America after the Depression of 1929 with the coming of the New Deal. New national entitlement programs and the drive for legal and social equality were hallmarks of the era in Franklin D. Roosevelt's presidency. They included Social Security, minimum wage and maximum hour laws, and even the regulation by the US government of local businesses. In the 1950s and 1960s, leaders of the civil rights movement like Dr. Martin Luther King Jr. and others stimulated a reconstituted vision of the Constitution as a guarantor of rights and liberties for minorities, including African Americans and women. This struggle, often known as a Second Reconstruction, opened a new debate over affirmative action programs to help minorities enter mainstream life in society. Others argued affirmative action was reverse discrimination.

The book is divided into five parts, one for each phase of the American republic. These phases are not hardbound and rigid. The new republic was also a slave republic and free market advocates have flourished well into the twenty-first century. Social reformers supported government-sponsored welfare and labor laws during the free-market republic, and supporters of civil rights advocated changes in the nineteenth century just as they did during the civil rights movement and today. Each of the five parts begins with a summary and a description of the formal constitutional amendments ratified by the states. The chapters that follow highlight the Constitution's evolution through three major developments: government regulation of the economy, individual and civil rights, and executive power. A short summary concludes each part. The goal is to show how the Constitution has evolved through formal amendments and informal decisions by the president, the Congress, and the Supreme Court.

Part 1

The New Republic, 1781–1828

The Constitution's first three articles set forth the structure of the new government with three separate and coequal branches: a Congress, divided into two houses, to make laws; a president to enforce them; and a Supreme Court to interpret them. The structure reflected the classical republican tradition, which envisioned a mixed regime where power was divided to avoid tyranny and to promote a public spirit among the people.

The Classical Republican Tradition

The framers' vision of a republic hearkened back to ancient Greek ideas about political organization. In one of his most celebrated works, *The Politics*, Aristotle, the fourth-century BCE philosopher, was concerned with the most practicable rather than the ideal state. He observed that society was naturally divided into three social classes: royalty, nobility, and the common people. In terms of governmental decision-making, this division falls into the categories of the one, the few, and the many. Only one ruler, a king or prince, comes from the royal class, a few from the aristocracy, and many from the people. In government, each class corresponds to a political body organized along these lines:

American Constitutional History: A Brief Introduction, Second Edition. Jack Fruchtman.
© 2022 John Wiley & Sons, Inc. Published 2022 by John Wiley & Sons, Inc.

	Rule by the One	*Rule by the Few*	*Rule by the Many*
Society:	Royalty	Nobility	Common People
Government:	Monarchy	Aristocracy	Democracy

To ensure that government represents all three classes, the political structure must guarantee that each has a role in making decisions and setting policy. The mixed regime, or republic, balances the three elements to ensure that citizens participate in decision-making, if only indirectly through representatives.

Early republics defined citizens as only male property owners and excluded all others. Landowning citizens possessed a stake in society; they were public spirited and had the desire and qualifications to participate in decision-making. No one held office for a long period of time, because when citizens rotate in and out of office they avoid corrupting influences. The great Renaissance theorist Niccolo Machiavelli argued in his *Discourses on Livy* that this public spiritedness promoted virtue (*virtú*), the highest ideal a republican citizen could achieve. Rooted in the Latin *res publica*, the term *republic* literally means the "public thing." In the eighteenth century, the framers used the word republic, or *res publica*, to refer to the "common good," the "public good," or the "good of all." Three examples from history illustrate how the republic and the balance of the mixed regime work in practice: ancient Rome; Renaissance Florence; early modern England. In each, the mixed regime combined all three forms of government. They supplied the republic with what Aristotle and Machiavelli thought was the most practicable way to achieve the common good. The structure followed this scheme:

	The One	*The Few*	*The Many*
Rome:	The Consuls	The Senate	The Council
Florence:	*Consigliere de justicia*	The Senate	The Great Council
England:	The King	House of Lords	House of Commons

While Americans believed that this pattern provided a model, many of them also thought that Britain did not have a true republic because of its hereditary king and nobility. Six months before the formal break with Britain in 1776, pamphleteer Thomas Paine wrote that its two remaining ancient tyrannies, the king and the Lords, dominated the "new republican materials" in the Commons. "The two first, by being hereditary," he contended, "are independent of the people; wherefore in a *constitutional sense* they contribute nothing towards the freedom of the state."

The Americans' first constitution, the Articles of Confederation (1781–1788), did not follow the historic pattern of the classical republic (Box 1). Only one branch existed, a Congress, which had no authority to raise revenue.

Box 1   The Articles of Confederation, Agreed to by Congress November 15, 1777; ratified and in force, March 1, 1781, excerpts

Preamble
To all to whom these Presents shall come, we the undersigned Delegates of the States affixed to our Names send greeting.

Whereas the Delegates of the United States of America in Congress assembled did on the fifteenth day of November in the Year of our Lord One Thousand Seven Hundred and Seventy seven, and in the Second Year of the Independence of America, agree to certain articles of Confederation and perpetual Union between the States of New Hampshire, Massachusetts-bay, Rhode Island and Providence Plantations, Connecticut, New York, New Jersey, Pennsylvania, Delaware, Maryland, Virginia, North Carolina, South Carolina and Georgia, in the words following, viz:

Articles of Confederation and perpetual Union between the States of New Hampshire, Massachusetts-bay, Rhode Island and Providence Plantations, Connecticut, New York, New Jersey, Pennsylvania, Delaware, Maryland, Virginia, North Carolina, South Carolina and Georgia.

Article I. The Stile of this Confederacy shall be "The United States of America."

Article II. Each state retains its sovereignty, freedom, and independence, and every Power, Jurisdiction, and right, which is

> not by this confederation expressly delegated to the United States, in Congress assembled.
>
> Article III. The said States hereby severally enter into a firm league of friendship with each other, for their common defense, the security of their liberties, and their mutual and general welfare, binding themselves to assist each other, against all force offered to, or attacks made upon them, or any of them, on account of religion, sovereignty, trade, or any other pretense whatever.
>
> The Articles of Confederation 1777 / Independence Hall Association / Public domain

The government also lacked an independent judiciary. After some Americans saw its shortcomings, they reconsidered the structure of their republic. After a rancorous debate, they ratified the Constitution in 1788, paralleling the ancient Roman Republic and its political heirs:

	The One	*The Few*	*The Many*
United States:	The President	The Senate	The House of Representatives

The Congress, with its bicameral legislature, and the president had links to the people through the electoral process, though mostly indirectly. The framers also created an unelected, unaccountable judiciary independent of the other two branches. The judges served terms "during good behavior," which means they remained in office until they retired, resigned, died, or were removed by Congress through impeachment. Congress could never lower the judges' compensation to influence their decisions. Americans thus engaged in a political experiment in ratifying a constitution that they hoped would achieve the good of all.

The framers divided power horizontally between the executive, legislative, and judicial branches of the national government in a scheme called the separation of powers. While classical republicanism promoted the separation of powers, the eighteenth-century French theorist, Baron de Montesquieu (1689–1755), strongly advocated it in *The Spirit of the Laws*. The framers were as familiar with Montesquieu's work as they were with Aristotelian and Machiavellian republican ideas. In Federalist 47, one of the essays designed to inspire the ratification of the new Constitution, James Madison noted that "the oracle who is always consulted and cited on this subject, is the celebrated Montesquieu."

The new American republic also divided power vertically between the states and the national government in a structure known as federalism. The states retained the authority to make laws regulating behavior within their own geographic territory. The delegates who signed the Constitution on September 17, 1787, were certain that no one branch of government and no state or federal entity could dominate the others. They thought that divided power ensured that just and fair laws would pass, the president would sign them, and the courts would ensure their constitutionality. It has not always worked out that way: presidents often take unilateral steps beyond their constitutional authority; Congress sometimes passes unconstitutional laws; and the Supreme Court decisions are final unless overturned by an amendment or overruled by a future Court opinion.

John Locke, Deism, and Religious Liberty

The classical republican tradition and Montesquieu's doctrine of the separation of powers formed part of the principles of the American republic. The influential ideas of John Locke (1632–1704) also contributed to the framers' understanding of government. Locke, an English political philosopher and statesman, provided the rationale for the overthrow of the Stuart monarchy in England in 1688 and the rise of parliamentary supremacy. While very few copies of his *Second Treatise of Government* (1689) turned up in America in the eighteenth century, his views were important to the development of Anglo-American political thought.

Locke posited a genial, pre-government state of nature when human beings mostly lived in peace. The few who failed to understand the needs and desires of their fellow human beings lived beyond the law of nature as outlaws. Men's responsibility was to destroy those who violated the peaceful state of nature, but this was an inconvenient duty. To overcome these inconveniences, the people entered into a social contract and gave up some of their natural rights in exchange for the security that government offered them. A legitimate government protected the people's possessions and their rights of life, liberty, health, and happiness. Natural rights were thus transformed into civil rights and civil liberties. Locke especially wanted to protect property rights. He developed an early form of the labor theory of value, which maintained that a person had the right to enjoy the fruits of his own labor. Government based on these principles was good.

Locke also set forth a theory concerning revolution. When government became oppressive and deprived its citizens of their civil rights and liberties, it broke the social contract. The people, in turn, have a right to change it, even by force, to create a new contract. The opening lines of the Declaration of Independence reflected this Lockean view of revolution: "When in the course of human events it becomes necessary for one people to dissolve the political bands which have connected them with another, and to assume among the powers of the earth the separate and equal station to which the laws of nature and of nature's God entitle them, a decent respect to the opinions of mankind requires that they should declare the causes which impel them to the separation." Jefferson, the principal author of the document, pointed to three of the four rights that Locke had addressed: life, liberty, and the pursuit of happiness. Some commentators have assumed that the latter was a euphemism for "property" or wealth, or at least its pursuit.

The reference to the laws of nature and nature's God in the Declaration reveals Jefferson's religious views. He did not believe in a personal God to whom he could pray for salvation, health, or riches. Like many of the American founders, he was a deist, who believed in Enlightenment reason and science. Deism holds that God exists only as a creator who had instilled free will in human beings. After he created the universe, God relied on human beings to improve or destroy it. Benjamin Franklin, George Washington, James Madison, and Alexander Hamilton were deists. John Adams was more orthodox in his Christianity.

The idea that God instilled in human beings a longing for freedom was rooted in early American history. It was embodied in the idea that freedom is as much a spiritual condition as it is a political and social one. The Puritan impact on New England colonies was profound. Obedience to state authority, especially to the established church, ensured a moral and righteous citizenry. John Winthrop, the seventeenth-century Puritan minister and governor of Massachusetts Bay Colony, understood this when he was on board ship in 1630 headed to

America, the "New Israel." He famously sermonized that "we shall be as a City upon a Hill," or else the Almighty would bring down His wrath. Fifteen years later, he told his flock that natural liberty differed from moral liberty. The former was the liberty "to do evil," whereas the latter was liberty "to do only what is good." To perform good deeds meant that the citizens had to adhere to the officially established church, its dogma, and teachings. Christian liberty demanded that citizens submit to the laws of the secular authority and, consequently, the will of God.

Not all religious leaders followed these precepts. Notably, Winthrop expelled Roger Williams from Massachusetts Bay in 1636 for heresy. Williams, a Baptist, believed in religious liberty. He moved south to found Rhode Island, a new colony, specifically underscoring the importance of the separation of church and state. William Penn, a Quaker who founded Pennsylvania as "a Holy Experiment" in 1681, mirrored Williams's beliefs in religious freedom. Penn's colony was to be a refuge for those seeking political and religious liberty. Quakers became so politically powerful in Pennsylvania that they controlled the colonial legislature until the mid-eighteenth century.

Although principles of religious liberty spread throughout the new American republic, most states, even after the ratification of the First Amendment's establishment clause, maintained officially established churches, some well into the nineteenth century. In the 1780s, Thomas Jefferson and James Madison fought against the establishment of the Anglican Church in Virginia. Jefferson initially drafted his bill, the Virginia Statute for Religious Freedom, as early as 1777 as a member of the Virginia legislature. It failed to pass until Madison reintroduced it by attacking tax revenues used to support the state-established Church. His powerful arguments in "Memorial and Remonstrance Against Religious Assessments," published anonymously, underscored the importance of religion as a private affair between man and God within the church and the family. It was not a matter for the public square of politics and government. In 1786, the Virginia assembly finally passed Jefferson's bill while he was serving in France as America's ambassador, and the doctrine of the separation of church and state became a foundation of the American republic.

1
Ideological Origins of the New Republic

The new republic began in 1781 after the ratification of the Articles of Confederation and continued when the Americans replaced the Articles with the United States Constitution seven years later. In 1789, the people elected their first federal government. Over the next 15 years, the founding generation made substantive formal changes: in 1791, the states adopted the first 10 amendments, known collectively as the Bill of Rights, followed by two others in 1795 and 1804. The United States doubled its geographic size in 1803 when the Jefferson administration purchased the Louisiana territory from France.

The new republic endured slavery, even as some states began its gradual elimination in the 1780s. Most Americans focused on modifying their new government and its powers while declining to resolve the future of slavery. To avoid contention and disunion, the delegates to the constitutional convention did not address it. The words "slavery" or "slave" appear nowhere in the document. Some abolitionists like Benjamin Franklin – a former slave owner himself – John Adams, Alexander Hamilton, and Benjamin Rush attempted to raise the issue, but their efforts failed. Later leaders like William Lloyd Garrison, who founded the abolitionist paper, *The Liberator*, in 1831 and was co-founder of the Anti-Slavery Society, were active throughout the period. It was not until the end of the Civil War that slavery finally ended.

The period also saw the enhancement of the Supreme Court's authority when Chief Justice John Marshall issued his unanimous

American Constitutional History: A Brief Introduction, Second Edition. Jack Fruchtman.
© 2022 John Wiley & Sons, Inc. Published 2022 by John Wiley & Sons, Inc.

opinion in *Marbury* v. *Madison* in 1803. Marshall wrote into the Constitution that the judges' duty was to interpret the document and to overturn all laws that conflicted with that interpretation. New institutions were created, such as the Bank of the United States, and the Court unanimously approved Congress's authority to create it. George Washington was the first president to sign an executive order while James Monroe was the first to issue a signing statement, indicating his ideas of legislation and how he intended to enforce them.

The Articles of Confederation and the Constitutional Convention

Five years after the Continental Congress passed the Declaration of Independence, the states adopted the Articles of Confederation, though Congress had acted from 1776 as if this had already occurred. Because the new government lacked sufficient authority to create a uniform legal system, the states were supreme. The Articles placed all power, limited though it was, in a single-house Congress. There was no separate executive, but only a "president" who chaired a temporary congressional committee when Congress recessed. Nor did the Articles provide for a judiciary. Congress itself was the nation's highest tribunal.

The problems with the Articles lay embedded in one of the main themes outlined in the Declaration. Jefferson ended the document with the resounding words that "these United Colonies are, and of Right ought to be Free and Independent States ... and that as Free and Independent States, they have full Power to levy War, conclude Peace, contract Alliances, establish commerce, and to do all other Acts and Things which Independent States may of right do." The use of the term "states" was significant. A state, as the founders understood it, signified a nation of people organized under one government in a defined territory. Many leaders of the new 13 states believed their states were independent, not only of Britain, but of each other, except for maintaining unity to combat Britain in the Revolutionary War. Accordingly, apart from Connecticut and Rhode Island, which simply adopted their existing colonial charters as their new constitutions, each state prepared new documents for internal governance. Because those two states were originally "corporate" colonies, they only had to revise their charters to eliminate British parliamentary supremacy and mandatory review of these laws by British officials in the Privy Council in London.

Other leaders, like Virginia's Patrick Henry, favored the Articles, because it preferred state supremacy over the new national government. The document amounted to a treaty between the states, an alliance of convenience undertaken due to the war with Britain. Unity was not, however, the goal beyond defeating Britain. "Each state retains its sovereignty, freedom and independence," the Articles announced, "and every Power, Jurisdiction and right, which is not by this confederation expressly delegated to the United States, in Congress assembled." The United States Confederation seemed to have an existence only "in Congress assembled." Without the authority to raise revenue, Congress had to rely on the generosity of the states to send monetary "gifts" to keep the government in operation. Without a national leader, no executive enforced its laws. Without a national judiciary, the states resolved all civil and criminal actions.

Meantime, the states were subject to fierce interstate competition, even potential warfare, over water and mineral rights and boundaries. James Madison, Alexander Hamilton, and George Washington thought that a weak United States made it especially vulnerable to outside influence, attack, and even conquest. They strove to strengthen the new government when a group of entrepreneurs wanted to open the Potomac River to navigation. To begin the process, as a private citizen, Washington invited some Virginia and Maryland citizens to meet at his home at Mount Vernon to find ways to establish better communication between the two states. A representative from Pennsylvania later attended. Madison saw this as an opportunity to discuss the future of the Confederation and persuaded the Virginia legislature to appoint commissioners to meet with their counterparts in Annapolis in September 1786 to address improvements to the United States government.

The attendance at the Annapolis meeting shows how divided the states were. Only five sent representatives: New York, New Jersey, Pennsylvania, Delaware, and Virginia. Four others appointed commissioners, but none attended. Apparently, Maryland, Connecticut, South Carolina, and Georgia were uninterested. After the meeting, Hamilton, who represented New York, drafted a report to the Confederation Congress. He wrote that the commissioners unanimously championed a future meeting of delegates from all the states to strengthen the republic by amending the Articles. Although the Annapolis commissioners were mainly concerned with the breakdown in commercial relationships among the states, Hamilton carefully noted that other problems might also surface. He closed the report with a request to

Congress to authorize the states to send delegates to Philadelphia the following May to discuss the matter.

The constitutional convention met eight months later and throughout the summer of 1787. Congress charged the delegates with reporting all proposed amendments to it. Under the Articles, Congress's acceptance of an amendment required the unanimous consent of the states. Convention delegates in Philadelphia elected George Washington, the most popular man in America, to preside over the proceedings. Not only was he the hero of the victory over Britain, but he was also regarded as America's savior, "the father of his country." Madison took notes every day and rewrote them every night. Franklin served as a delegate from Pennsylvania. Jefferson did not attend. He was serving in France as the American representative or minister. John Adams also was not present: he was the American minister to Britain.

Unlike the Annapolis convention, every state – except for Rhode Island – sent representatives to Philadelphia. As it turned out, Rhode Island became the last state to ratify the Constitution, and then only after the first federal government was already operating. Its ratifying convention adopted the Constitution by a narrow vote of 34 to 32. Some delegates who did attend occasionally left because they were either uninterested or had to attend to their businesses or professional duties. This was true especially of the New York delegation. Two of the three delegates immediately became disillusioned and left. The third, Alexander Hamilton, returned to his law practice in New York City for much of the summer. Once the process began, the delegates decided against proposing amendments to the Articles and instead crafted an entirely new document. Although Congress could have simply rejected it because the delegates had disregarded their charge to recommend amendments, congressional members decided to forward the new document to the states for consideration and ratification (Box 1.1).

The new Constitution was founded on a series of compromises, especially the longest, Article I, regarding Congress. Two key issues involved the legislative branch. First, the question of how to divide power in a democratic way when the more populous states like Virginia, New York, and Pennsylvania dominated. Delegates from these large states thought representation should be based on population: Madison's Virginia Plan. Smaller states like Maryland, Delaware, and New Jersey, however, possessed far less voting power in terms of population. The New Jersey Resolutions essentially kept the same scheme created by the

Articles of Confederation when each state could elect between two and seven delegates, but the states had only one vote. The second issue concerned slavery. Given the prevalence of large slave populations in mostly southern states, the question was whether slaves should be counted in apportioning the House of Representatives. If so, the South would numerically dominate the House and the election of the president, given that electoral voting is based on a combination of the number of senators, two from each state, plus the number of representatives in the House.

Box 1.1 The Constitution of the United States, the first three articles, excerpts

Preamble
We the People of the United States, in Order to form a more perfect Union, establish Justice, insure domestic Tranquility, provide for the common defence, promote the general Welfare, and secure the Blessings of Liberty to ourselves and our Posterity, do ordain and establish this Constitution for the United States of America.

Article I, Section 1
All legislative Powers herein granted shall be vested in a Congress of the United States, which shall consist of a Senate and House of Representatives.

Section 8
The Congress shall have Power To lay and collect Taxes, Duties, Imposts and Excises, to pay the Debts and provide for the common Defence and general Welfare of the United States; but all Duties, Imposts and Excises shall be uniform throughout the United States;

To borrow Money on the credit of the United States;

To regulate Commerce with foreign Nations, and among the several States, and with the Indian Tribes;

To establish an uniform Rule of Naturalization, and uniform Laws on the subject of Bankruptcies throughout the United States;

To coin Money, regulate the Value thereof, and of foreign Coin, and fix the Standard of Weights and Measures;

To provide for the Punishment of counterfeiting the Securities and current Coin of the United States;

To establish Post Offices and post Roads;

To promote the Progress of Science and useful Arts, by securing for limited Times to Authors and Inventors the exclusive Right to their respective Writings and Discoveries;

To constitute Tribunals inferior to the supreme Court;

To define and punish Piracies and Felonies committed on the high Seas, and Offences against the Law of Nations;

To declare War, grant Letters of Marque and Reprisal, and make Rules concerning Captures on Land and Water;

To raise and support Armies, but no Appropriation of Money to that Use shall be for a longer Term than two Years;

To provide and maintain a Navy;

To make Rules for the Government and Regulation of the land and naval Forces;

To provide for calling forth the Militia to execute the Laws of the Union, suppress Insurrections and repel Invasions;

To provide for organizing, arming, and disciplining, the Militia, and for governing such Part of them as may be employed in the Service of the United States, reserving to the States respectively, the Appointment of the Officers, and the Authority of training the Militia according to the discipline prescribed by Congress;

To exercise exclusive Legislation in all Cases whatsoever, over such District (not exceeding ten Miles square) as may, by Cession of particular States, and the Acceptance of Congress, become the Seat of the Government of the United States, and to exercise like Authority over all Places purchased by the Consent of the Legislature of the State in which the Same shall be, for the Erection of Forts, Magazines, Arsenals, dock-Yards, and other needful Buildings; – And

To make all Laws which shall be necessary and proper for carrying into Execution the foregoing Powers, and all other Powers vested by this Constitution in the Government of the United States, or in any Department or Officer thereof.

Section 9

The Migration or Importation of such Persons as any of the States now existing shall think proper to admit, shall not be prohibited by the Congress prior to the Year one thousand eight hundred and eight, but a Tax or duty may be imposed on such Importation, not exceeding ten dollars for each Person.

The Privilege of the Writ of Habeas Corpus shall not be suspended, unless when in Cases of Rebellion or Invasion the public Safety may require it.

No Bill of Attainder or ex post facto Law shall be passed.

No Capitation, or other direct, Tax shall be laid, unless in Proportion to the Census or enumeration herein before directed to be taken.

No Tax or Duty shall be laid on Articles exported from any State.

No Preference shall be given by any Regulation of Commerce or Revenue to the Ports of one State over those of another: nor shall Vessels bound to, or from, one State, be obliged to enter, clear, or pay Duties in another.

No Money shall be drawn from the Treasury, but in Consequence of Appropriations made by Law; and a regular Statement and Account of the Receipts and Expenditures of all public Money shall be published from time to time.

No Title of Nobility shall be granted by the United States: And no Person holding any Office of Profit or Trust under them, shall, without the Consent of the Congress, accept of any present, Emolument, Office, or Title, of any kind whatever, from any King, Prince, or foreign State...

Article II, Section 1

The executive Power shall be vested in a President of the United States of America. He shall hold his Office during the Term of four Years, and, together with the Vice President, chosen for the same Term, be elected, as follows

Each State shall appoint, in such Manner as the Legislature thereof may direct, a Number of Electors, equal to the whole Number of Senators and Representatives to which the State may be entitled in the Congress: but no Senator or Representative, or Person holding an Office of Trust or Profit under the United States, shall be appointed an Elector...

Article III, Section 1
The judicial Power of the United States, shall be vested in one supreme Court, and in such inferior Courts as the Congress may from time to time ordain and establish. The Judges, both of the supreme and inferior Courts, shall hold their Offices during good Behaviour, and shall, at stated Times, receive for their Services, a Compensation, which shall not be diminished during their Continuance in Office.

Section 2
The judicial Power shall extend to all Cases, in Law and Equity, arising under this Constitution, the Laws of the United States, and Treaties made, or which shall be made, under their Authority.

Article I-III / U.S. Constitution / Public domain

To resolve these two main issues, the delegates agreed to major compromises to ensure that the Convention stayed together. If the delegates failed to deal successfully with either one, the Convention could have dissolved. The first compromise concerned the structure of Congress's bicameral legislature. The House, elected every two years, represented the people. Each state possessed congressional districts of approximately equal numbers of people. Article I, Section 2, suggests that all the people in the district should be counted, not only registered voters: "Representatives ... shall be apportioned among the several states ... according to their respective numbers." To emphasize this point, when the Fourteenth Amendment was ratified in 1868, Section 2 stated that "Representatives shall be apportioned among the several states according to their respective numbers, counting the whole number of persons in each state, excluding Indians not taxed." These ideas reflected the classical republican ideal that electoral districts should be more or less equal in population or voters and that elections should be frequent. The Senate, meantime, represented the states, not the people or its voters. Each state was to have two senators no matter its geographic location or population size. Senators sat for six years, a long term, but the delegates agreed that the length was necessary for a body theoretically more deliberative than the House. Senate elections were undemocratic, because state assemblies, not the people, elected them, a procedure that lasted until 1913 when the Seventeenth

Amendment was ratified. Indirect election of senators reflected most delegates' view of human nature. As Madison famously wrote in Federalist 55, human passions and emotions always trump human reason: "Had every Athenian citizen been a Socrates, every Athenian assembly would still have been a mob," he wrote.

The second compromise involved slavery. Southern delegates thought that the census should include all slaves while northern delegates, many of whom were abolitionists, opposed including slaves. Northerners argued that slaves were neither free nor voters but mere property. The delegates finally agreed that for census purposes slaves would count as three-fifths of a person. This compromise not only held the convention together but also greatly influenced Congress and presidential elections during the nation's first half century. Virginia, which had fewer white voters than Massachusetts, maintained a larger congressional delegation than Massachusetts by counting three-fifths of the slaves there. After Jefferson won the presidency in 1800, he was often called "the negro president," because his enemies thought that the three-fifths compromise guaranteed his election. Of the first seven presidents, five were from the South, four of whom were Virginians. A third compromise also involved slavery. The Constitution empowered Congress to pass laws concerning the return of fugitive slaves, which it did in 1793, and to refrain from ending the slave trade until 1808.

Articles II and III also reflect the delegates' negative view of human nature. The people indirectly elected the president, just as they did senators. The Constitution provides that Electors, specially chosen to meet approximately one month after the popular vote, shall make the final choice. The Constitution does not mention an "Electoral College." That term came about in the early nineteenth century. Congress codified it into law in 1845. Because of its placement and brevity, Article III concerning the judiciary appears almost as an afterthought. The shortest of the articles, it lays out only one Supreme Court and all other courts that Congress decides to create. The Court's original and appellate jurisdictions indicated that most of its work was to hear appeals, except when foreign ambassadors, public ministers, or a state were litigants. For these, it possessed original jurisdiction, meaning that litigants could file actions directly in the Supreme Court. The people did not elect the federal judges, including Supreme Court justices. The president nominated a candidate and then the Senate alone confirmed or rejected the nomination by a simple majority.

Article IV addresses the states and what they may and may not do regarding the federal government. Section 4 demands that every state must guarantee that it has "a republican form of government." The article does not specify the structure of that government. It does not even demand that state governments had to be modeled on the US government. A state may have a unicameral legislature as, for example, Nebraska currently does, or, if it had two legislative houses, the makeup of both may reflect the size of the population. Article IV also includes a privileges and immunities clause, which states that a citizen from one state traveling in another state shall enjoy the same privileges and immunities of those residing in the state the citizen is visiting, but the Constitution does not define these "privileges and immunities." Finally, a provision requires each state to recognize the laws of the other states, the so-called full faith and credit clause: "full faith and credit shall be given in each state to the public acts, records, and judicial proceedings of every other state."

Article V sets out amendment procedures. Congress may propose an amendment when two-thirds of both houses agree and then three-quarters of the states ratify it. Alternatively, the states themselves may call a constitutional convention, though it would once again take a two-thirds vote in both houses of Congress. Ratification would follow, requiring, again, three-quarters of the states to ratify it. Article VI contains a provision forbidding religious tests for federal officeholders.

Unlike the Articles, which require the unanimous vote of the states to ratify an amendment, the Constitution provides for the people in each state to elect special ratifying conventions to vote on the new document. The people in conventions, not their representatives in state legislatures, decided the document's fate. On September 17, 1787, 39 of the original 55 delegates signed the Constitution. Those who declined to sign believed that the powers vested in the three branches of government were too strong and centralized. They thought that the document excessively diminished the power of the states, the true representatives of American democracy and its people. Such concentrated power, they argued, led to tyranny. This argument opened the struggle over ratification that pitted the Constitution's supporters, the Federalists, against their opponents, the Anti-Federalists.

Anti-Federalists, like Patrick Henry, feared the very wording of the first three articles, which comprised bundles of power.

- Article I: "All legislative powers granted herein shall be vested in a Congress."
- Article II: "The executive power shall be vested in a President."
- Article III: "The judicial power of the United States shall be vested in one supreme court, and in such inferior courts as the Congress may from time to time ordain and establish."

Each article used the imperative form of the verb "to be," *shall*. The Constitution commands that all legislative powers or the executive power or the judicial power shall, not may or might, be vested in these branches of government. The state governments seemed to be left only with residual power when compared with what they possessed under the Articles of Confederation. Anti-Federalists were concerned that the states seemed to be only political appendages to the new national government. Moreover, they feared that the lack of a bill of rights might lead to a future despotism.

Article I also includes several provisions concerning what it authorizes Congress to do (Section 8), as well as limitations on that power; that is, what the document prohibits Congress from doing (Section 9). Congress could tax and spend, regulate commerce among the states, and declare war. It could also create a military force and devise the rules of war. It could suspend habeas corpus in the event of an invasion or rebellion. Article II, concerning presidential power, is vague in terms of what presidents may or may not do. As Section 2 states, presidents "execute" or enforce the law and serve as the commander in chief of the armed forces, though the Constitution notes only "the army and navy." Presidents negotiate treaties, while two-thirds of the Senate must consent before they are ratified. Presidents also appoint executive branch personnel and nominate judges, but only with Senate approval by a simple majority. They receive ambassadors and inform Congress of the state of the union.

The Constitution does not specify term limits for any office. The president, senators, and representatives must stand for re-election when their terms are ending, but they need not step down until they decide to do so or when they are defeated. The House of Representatives, by a simple majority, may impeach presidents if they have committed "high crimes and misdemeanors," which the Constitution does not define. The Senate then, by a two-thirds vote, may remove the president from office. Although Hamilton thought that presidents and senators should be elected for life, re-election indirectly promised possible life terms for elected federal officials. Jefferson, for one, despised Hamilton's views, calling him "a monocrat." Like Jefferson, Anti-Federalists thought that presidents could possibly be elected and re-elected for life, making them little more than elected monarchs. The Twenty-Second Amendment (1951) limited the president to two terms in office.

Anti-Federalists also feared the new federal judiciary. Article III announces that the Supreme Court and presumably whatever lower courts Congress creates would have authority to rule on all cases and controversies that come before the United States. It created an independent judiciary that was neither related nor beholden to the legislative or executive branches. First, all federal judges serve "during good behavior," which meant life terms: service until they died, retired, or resigned, though Congress could remove them through impeachment. Second, Congress could never lower their salaries nor could Congress use its taxing and spending power to control judicial outcomes. There would be no threats to force judges to rule the way Congress wanted. The main oversight that Congress had over the Supreme Court was its authority to make exceptions to its jurisdiction, a power rarely used, the impeachment of individual justices, or the passage of constitutional amendments.

Article VI contains the supremacy clause, which states that the Constitution and the laws and treaties of the United States shall be the "supreme law of the land." The Anti-Federalists believed this clause totally undermined state sovereignty. Moreover, they disliked the provision that demanded that the states be bound by the Constitution no matter what their state legislatures may say to the contrary. They also opposed the ratification process set out in Article VII. Only nine of the 13 states were needed to bring it into effect, not the unanimous vote of all states, which the original Articles required. With that, the battle over ratification began.

Ratification and the Bill of Rights

Supporters of the new document, the Federalists, advocated ratification, because they thought that the Constitution provided needed order and stability. It centralized power in a strong national government with Congress as the key lawmaker. One of the biggest states, New York, was a stronghold of Anti-Federalism. Alexander Hamilton, a

Federalist, feared that if his state of New York failed to adopt the new document, others might well follow suit. Should that transpire, proponents would be unable to attract affirmative votes from the necessary nine states to secure ratification. To sway the New York state convention, Hamilton recruited fellow New Yorker John Jay and Virginian James Madison to address these and other issues to persuade the New York convention to ratify the new document. All three men were prominent statesmen. Madison, known by historians as the "father of the Constitution" because of his work during the constitutional convention, was later elected the fourth president of the United States. Hamilton served as the nation's first and youngest-ever secretary of the treasury. Jay, an eminent lawyer and diplomat, became the first chief justice of the United States and later governor of New York.

Publius, the collective pseudonym Hamilton chose for the series, signed all the essays. The name referred to Publius Valerius Publicola, the renowned sixth-century BCE Roman statesman and republican leader. Of the 85 essays, known collectively as The Federalist Papers, Jay wrote five, with the remaining 80 split between Hamilton (51) and Madison (29). The essays soon appeared periodically in several New York newspapers, analyzing the virtues of the Constitution, and were later collected in book form. Madison's fellow Virginian, Thomas Jefferson, called the Papers "the best commentary on the principles of government which ever was written."

Anti-Federalists, in the meantime, undertook their own propaganda campaign, hoping to keep the Articles in place. Led by the powerful New York governor, George Clinton, and others, they fought ratification. Their camp included some at the convention who declined to sign the Constitution, prominent leaders like Virginia's George Mason and Edmund Randolph, a future attorney general of the United States. Both were Virginians. Mason is known in history as "the father of the Bill of Rights" for his advocacy of a list of rights protected by the Constitution. Luther Martin, an able though often drunk Maryland lawyer, also refused to sign. He later argued cases before the Supreme Court. Elbridge Gerry of Massachusetts, whose name is forever linked to the practice of gerrymandering election districts for political party gain, became a vocal Anti-Federalist.

Still, the Constitution became effective on June 21, 1788, when the ninth state ratified it. Two important states failed to do so until after that date: New York by a close vote of 30 to 27 and Virginia with a slightly better majority of 89 to 79. With a great deal of perseverance, the founding generation formed a "more perfect Union," as the Constitution's Preamble promised. The Constitution overcame its predecessor's economic and political deficiencies. The framers designed it to balance the authority of the state and federal governments and to allow the federal government to raise revenue and enforce its laws. One of the most important national laws passed under the Articles of Confederation but recognized as part of federal law under the new document, was the Northwest Ordinance of 1787. This measure imposed common-law principles on the new nation's frontier, namely that voters in the territories were equal with one person having one vote. A second important law was the Judiciary Act of 1789, which created the lower federal courts and laid out the Supreme Court's jurisdiction, notably to hear appeals from state appellate courts involving federal or constitutional issues. The third law, a collection of several acts known as the Decision of 1789, specified the first three executive departments: state, treasury, and war.

Meantime, Anti-Federalists, later known as Republicans, were still disgruntled. They argued that the document did not guarantee rights and liberties. Hamilton argued, notably in Federalist 84, that the Constitution itself was a bill of rights (Box 1.2). Many state conventions, however, rejected this view and demanded that the first Federal Congress adopt amendments to guarantee rights and liberties. One of the most vocal supporters of a bill of rights along with George Mason was Thomas Jefferson, who advocated his position while serving as the American minister in France. Jefferson eventually persuaded his friend and Virginia colleague, James Madison, who led the battle in the House of Representatives to pass 12 amendments. The states ratified only 10 of them on December 15, 1791. The two that failed addressed the size of the House and the pay for its members. Those that were ratified added guarantees of free speech, a free press, freedom of religion, and other rights and liberties. The proposal concerning congressional pay eventually became the Twenty-Seventh Amendment in 1992 after it was revived in the 1980s.

Box 1.2 Federalist 84, 1788, excerpt of Alexander Hamilton

The truth is, after all the declamations we have heard, that the Constitution is itself, in every rational sense, and to every useful purpose, A BILL OF RIGHTS. The ... constitution of each State is its bill of rights. And the proposed Constitution, if adopted, will be the bill of rights of the Union. Is it one object of a bill of rights to declare and specify the political privileges of the citizens in the structure and administration of the government? This is done in the most ample and precise manner in the plan of the convention; comprehending various precautions for the public security, which are not to be found in any of the State constitutions. Is another object of a bill of rights to define certain immunities and modes of proceeding, which are relative to personal and private concerns? This we have seen has also been attended to, in a variety of cases, in the same plan.

Alexander Hamilton 1788 / Federalist 84 / Public domain

The First Amendment, originally the third submitted to Congress, sets out five important individual rights. These include two religion clauses: the right of religious liberty and the prohibition of the national government to establish a religion. It also provides for free speech, a free press, freedom of assembly, and the freedom to file grievances with the government. The common-law tradition allowed for a free press and free speech, but not without limits. Seditious libel, for example, was excluded: this meant that criticism of the government and its officials may be punishable by a fine and/or imprisonment. Madison hoped to forestall the implementation of this common-law idea in what became the First Amendment by proposing more wide-ranging language: "The people shall not be deprived or abridged of their right to speak, to write, or to publish their sentiments; and the freedom of the press, as one of the great bulwarks of liberty, shall be inviolable." Instead, the common law was preserved in the vagueness of the final language: "Congress shall make no law respecting the establishment of religion, or prohibiting the free exercise thereof; or abridging the freedom of speech, or of the press; or the right of the people to peaceably to assemble."

Seven years after the ratification of the Bill of Rights, in 1798, Congress under Federalist control passed the Alien and Sedition Acts that President John Adams, a Federalist, signed into law. The Alien Act empowered the president to deport any non-American citizen whom he believed was dangerous to American national security. The more far-reaching Sedition Act was based on the common-law principle of seditious libel. Under the act, the government arrested and tried many critics of the Adams administration who claimed that Adams sought to transform the United States into a British-style government. The administration feared that France was planning to invade the United States and turn it into a French republic, as it had with Holland and Switzerland, and thought limits on speech and the press would protect the nation.

Some public officials believed that many Americans like Thomas Jefferson sympathized with France and its 1789 revolution. In fact, he did. Adams thought that they ignored the horrors of the French Revolution, which had resulted in the Reign of Terror from 1793 to 1794 and the executions of thousands of innocent people. Because the nation was in imminent danger of a French invasion, Adams and Congress agreed to the deportation of dangerous aliens and incarceration and fines for those found guilty of seditious libel. The Sedition Act provided for imprisonment for up to two years, a fine of up to $2000, or both, after speaking and publishing words that a court found to be seditious libel.

Several editors faced prosecution. One was Benjamin Franklin Bache, Franklin's grandson, who edited a Philadelphia paper highly critical of the Adams administration. After his indictment, Bache died in a yellow fever epidemic before trial. James Thomson Callender, an editor and pamphleteer in Richmond, who was a spokesman for Jefferson, claimed that Adams's "reign" was "one continued tempest of malignant passions." Supreme Court Justice Samuel Chase presided over his trial when justices acted as federal trial judges. He sentenced Callender to nine months in jail and a $200 fine. Thomas Cooper, born in London and educated at Oxford, emigrated to America and became a follower of the Jeffersonian Republicans. He attacked the Adams administration and spent two years in jail with a fine of $400. He later served as president of what is now the University of South Carolina.

Not all trials involved editors. US Representative Matthew Lyon was imprisoned for publishing a letter in the *Vermont Journal* that attacked Adams for having "an ungrounded thirst for ridiculous pomp, foolish adulation, and selfish avarice." Justice William Paterson sent him to jail for four months and fined him $1000. Lyon was re-elected to the

House of Representatives from his jail cell. In all, 25 people were arrested, 15 indicted, and 10 convicted under the law. Madison and Jefferson opposed the Alien and Sedition Acts. Unlike Hamilton, who believed in the supremacy of the new national government over the states, the two Virginians argued that the Constitution created a union of sovereign states. They saw the acts as a mechanism to silence Jeffersonian critics of the Adams administration's pro-British, anti-French policies.

Jefferson attacked the Sedition Act anonymously in his Kentucky Resolutions, published in November 1798. A month later, Madison's Virginia Resolutions appeared in print, also anonymously. They argued that the power to control sedition remained with the states, not the federal government. The states possessed the authority to judge, Jefferson wrote, "how far the licentiousness of speech and of the press may be abridged without lessening their useful freedom." The states thus possessed the authority to reject federal laws if the Constitution did not specifically empower Congress to pass it in the first place. These resolutions were a late eighteenth-century version of later debates over the doctrine of nullification. Jefferson's original draft of the Kentucky Resolutions included the states right of "nullification" of all federal laws. His editors deleted it. Congress later repaid the fines that the courts had imposed on those convicted under the Sedition Act, which expired in 1801.

Seditious libel remained a federal offense under common law until 1812 when the Supreme Court held that the common law did not make it a crime. Some states continued to try those engaged in seditious libel. Ironically, as president, Jefferson encouraged the prosecution of those who criticized him and his administration. Perhaps the most famous case took place in 1804 in New York when Jeffersonians prosecuted a Federalist editor, Harry Croswell, for seditious libel. Though convicted, despite the eloquent defense of his counsel, Alexander Hamilton, he received no sentence. A year later, he won a new trial, but by then Hamilton was dead of the gunshot wound inflicted by Vice President Aaron Burr in their famous duel in Weehawken, New Jersey.

The remaining nine amendments protected the individual against the national government. The ambiguously written Second Amendment led to a long debate over whether gun ownership was an individual or collective right: that is, whether it protected gun owners' right to purchase, carry, and own a firearm (the individual right) or whether the right was linked to the raising of a militia to protect the community (the collective right). The Third Amendment addressed the problem of British soldiers who seized the homes of American colonists without their express permission. To forestall the US government from imitating this practice, the amendment simply prohibited it in peacetime and required Congress to act in a time of war.

The next three amendments addressed those suspected of committing a crime. The search and seizure provisions of the Fourth Amendment overcame the issuances of general warrants. This was a remnant of a British legal practice, which had ended in Britain in 1763 but the British government maintained in its colonies. A general warrant allowed law enforcement officers to search places, often print shops, and make arrests of those suspected of crimes without specifying a particular person or place. The amendment required a judge or magistrate to first issue a search warrant, but only based on "probable cause," and to specify the place to be searched and the objects or persons to be seized.

The Fifth, like the First Amendment, comprised several provisions. It required a grand jury to issue an indictment before the accused went to trial: the exception was during wartime. It prohibited double jeopardy, meaning that the United States may not try a person twice for the same crime. It contained the first of two due process clauses (the second one binds the states in the Fourteenth Amendment), which forbid the United States from depriving any person of life, liberty, or property without "due process of law." The phrase "due process of law" has its roots in the Magna Carta of 1215. That thirteenth-century document suggested that due process rights encompass a long history of English legal conventions. It required "a process" in a criminal proceeding involving many of the guarantees in the Fourth, Fifth, and Sixth Amendments. The Fifth also included the takings clause, which prohibited the federal government from seizing private property except for public use and paid for with "just compensation," a phrase left undefined.

The Sixth Amendment included five provisions: juries for criminal trials, which must be speedy (a term not defined) and in a public place; trials must take place where the alleged crime took place; prisoners have a right to know the charges against them; they have the right to confront the witnesses who testify against them and to call witnesses in their defense; and they enjoy the right to have an attorney or legal "counsel" represent them in a court of law. The Seventh guaranteed a jury in civil trials if the monetary value of the suit is over $20, a figure Congress has raised to $75,000, according to the current Rules of Federal Procedure. The Eighth Amendment prohibited the federal government from making criminal suspects pay "excessive" bail to obtain their release. The term "excessive" was undefined. Nor can the United States inflict "cruel and unusual" punishments on persons convicted of a federal crime. This last provision has stimulated a storm of controversy over whether capital punishment is "cruel."

As Hamilton noted in Federalist 84, the framers found it impossible to identify every possible civil right or liberty. The Ninth Amendment opened the door to the addition of rights not included: "The enumeration in the Constitution, of certain rights, shall not be construed to deny or disparage others retained by the people." For some commentators and historians, the language is so broad it means nothing. Finally, the Tenth, or states' rights, Amendment emphasized the federal nature of the new governing structure: "The powers not delegated to the United States by the Constitution, nor prohibited by it to the States, are reserved to the States respectively, or to the people." This provision, along with the foundation established by Madison and Jefferson in their Virginia and Kentucky Resolutions, inexorably led to the states' rights battles of later years.

2

Representative and Constitutional Democracy

The essence of representative government lies in the legal fiction that legislators pass and executives enforce laws as if the people themselves passed and enforced them. The theory holds true, despite the initial indirect election of US senators and presidents by Electors. A good example of representative democracy in action occurred in the electoral crisis that erupted during the 1800 presidential election. Historians have long noted that the election demonstrated that the new nation made a peaceful, democratic transition that year from one political party to another, from Federalist to Republican. It was not an easy power shift, because at the time presidents and vice presidents were elected separately. Electors voted for two candidates and the one with the highest number of electoral votes became president. The vice president was the candidate with the second highest number of votes.

In the first two elections, no problems arose, because the Electors in 1789 and again in 1792 unanimously chose George Washington, the only American president ever to achieve the honor. Matters changed when political parties emerged during the Washington administration as conflicts grew between Republicans and Federalists. Thomas Jefferson, as secretary of state, advocated states' rights, along with James Madison in the House. They were opposed by Alexander Hamilton, as secretary of the treasury, and Vice President John Adams who were determined to create a strong national government. In 1796, the Federalists faced the Jeffersonian Republicans. The result was an anomaly when a Federalist

American Constitutional History: A Brief Introduction, Second Edition. Jack Fruchtman.
© 2022 John Wiley & Sons, Inc. Published 2022 by John Wiley & Sons, Inc.

president, John Adams, served with a Republican vice president, Jefferson. Four years later, the election ended with a tie between the two Republican candidates. Jefferson was the presidential candidate, and Aaron Burr the candidate for vice president. As the Constitution required under Article II, Section 1, the tie went to the House of Representatives, which, voting by states, elected Jefferson after 36 ballots, when one member, James Bayard of Delaware, changed his vote. The result was the passage and ratification of the Twelfth Amendment in 1804, which provided for the election of presidential and vice-presidential candidates together on the same ticket.

While the executive and legislative branches are separate, they must work together to fulfill their obligations to the people. Congress makes the laws, and the president must veto or sign and enforce them. On the other hand, both houses of Congress, by a two-thirds vote, may override, or nullify, a president's veto. In this regard, Madison in Federalist 51 spoke of how the Constitution diffuses power so that no one branch predominates over the others. No two branches may unite to overpower the third. This process demonstrates how the framers envisioned a workable representative democracy.

Meantime, the judicial authority encompasses neither lawmaking like Congress nor enforcing the law like the president. Nor are the judges accountable to the people through the electoral process. Moreover, the language of Article III is vague concerning how much power the federal courts possess. Since 1791, the courts have demonstrated that, in addition to being a representative democracy, the United States is also a constitutional democracy due to the role of the judges. The framers set forth two basic goals for federal judges when they heard cases. First, they oversee the actions of the other two branches of government to ensure that they do not unconstitutionally delegate their powers to the other branch. Congress may not pass laws that transfer any of its powers to the president and vice versa.

Second, judges must make certain that the president, Congress, and the state governments do not interfere with the people's rights and liberties. Although no right or liberty is absolute, including fundamental ones like those embodied in the First Amendment, the people may express their political opinions and publish them. Neither Congress nor a state government may deprive them of those rights without a compelling reason. Should a dispute arise over whether the government may limit speech, that dispute would likely go to a court of law for a final determination. The judges, perhaps even the Supreme Court justices, will ultimately decide the matter. This accounts for the workings of a constitutional democracy, that is, when unelected and unaccountable judges decide whether state or federal officials, who were democratically elected, have unconstitutionally restricted the people's rights and liberties.

The nation's first constitutional crisis occurred in 1793 when Alexander Chisholm, a creditor's executor living in South Carolina, sued the state of Georgia for failing to pay for goods delivered during the American Revolution. Justice James Iredell, a Federalist from North Carolina who strongly believed in states' rights, initially dismissed the suit when riding circuit in Georgia. Chisholm appealed to the Supreme Court under the theory that federal courts had jurisdiction over "Controversies ... between a State and Citizens of another State." The Court issued its decisions in the first decade of the republic with the justices writing *seriatim*, meaning that each justice wrote his own opinion.

James Wilson, who had served as a delegate to the constitutional convention and to the Pennsylvania ratifying convention, wrote for the Court in *Chisholm v. Georgia*, its first important constitutional decision, that a citizen of one state could in fact sue another state in federal court. His opinion attracted the majority. Here, the Court interpreted a constitutional provision and applied its view. Unelected judges acted as independent agents to determine the reach of Article III regarding an individual's right to sue a state. Iredell's dissent was so vigorous that the states ratified the Eleventh Amendment just two years later in 1795, the first time an amendment overruled a Supreme Court decision. The Eleventh Amendment barred such civil actions. Representative democracy, in this instance at least, overcame constitutional democracy. As the history of the nation shows, this has not always been the case.

Also in 1793, the justices declined to issue advisory opinions when one of the other two branches of government submitted questions to them. Secretary of State Thomas Jefferson asked the Court some 29 questions concerning an interpretation of the 1778 treaty between the United States and France. Chief Justice John Jay's response was pointed: the doctrine of the separation of powers outlined in the Constitution gave the Court no authority to issue advisory opinions but only to resolve disputes between parties.

Judicial Review, Judicial Duty

A question left unanswered in the Constitution is whether the Supreme Court can negate federal and state laws or the actions of federal and state officials, including the president of the United States. As the court of last resort, its authority has roots in the English common-law tradition of judge-made law. English judges long objected to laws passed by Parliament or decrees issued by the king, but they had little or no authority to invalidate them. Sometimes when they tried to do so, they were dismissed or, worse, executed. With the rise of parliamentary supremacy after the Glorious Revolution of 1688, Parliament became the highest lawmaking authority in the realm. When Anti-Federalists read Article III of the proposed Constitution, they feared that the Supreme Court would be able to nullify laws passed by democratically elected assemblies. A New Yorker, who wrote under the pseudonym "Federal Farmer," argued in 1788 that "the judges under this constitution will control the legislature, for the supreme court are authorised in the last resort, to determine what is the extent of the powers of the Congress; they are to give the constitution an explanation, and there is no power above them to set aside their judgment."

Meantime, some framers, especially Alexander Hamilton, were adamant that the primary duty of the judges was to determine the constitutionality of laws that Congress or state legislatures passed. Two months after the Federal Farmer article appeared, he wrote in Federalist 78 that the judiciary possesses neither the power of the sword, as does the president, nor the purse, as does Congress. The judges' independence makes them peculiarly reliable and objective. Their "duty it must be to declare all acts contrary to the manifest tenor of the constitution void." Hamilton did not mean only the specific words or provisions of the Constitution, but its "manifest tenor," certainly an open-ended term. The judges' responsibility was to resolve disputes that arose between the Constitution's words and spirit and a public official's action or a state or federal law. In 1796, the Court made its first Hamiltonian-inspired decision when it reviewed a federal tax law in *Hylton* v. *United States*. There, the justices validated a federal tax on carriages, but indicated that they could have very well have voided it. Two years later, in *Calder* v. *Bull*, Justice Samuel Chase noted that the Court had the authority to overturn all laws that conflicted with fundamental principles or a constitutional provision.

In 1803, the Court directly embraced its duty to review state and federal legislation and actions. Chief Justice John Marshall's famous opinion in *Marbury v. Madison* focused on the judge's duty to declare unconstitutional acts null and void. The case began in February 1801, when just before leaving office President Adams nominated an eminent Maryland landowner and banker, William Marbury, along with 41 others, to serve as justices of the peace in the District of Columbia. The Federalist-controlled Senate confirmed all the nominees, including Marbury, and Adams signed their commissions. Most soon took office, but four did not. One was Marbury whose commission was not delivered to him.

While the secretary of state was authorized to deliver these commissions, John Marshall, then serving in that office, failed to do so. The reason was that Adams had nominated Marshall, a distant cousin of Thomas Jefferson, to be chief justice, and he was moving to that new office. Before he left the state department, he affixed the Great Seal of the United States on the four commissions and asked his clerk, his brother James, to deliver them. However, James did not deliver any of them. After Jefferson took office in March 1801, he ordered his acting secretary of state, Levi Lincoln, and later attorney general, to hold onto them. By the time Jefferson's permanent secretary, James Madison, arrived in Washington to take office, Marbury petitioned the Supreme Court to issue a writ of *mandamus,* a court order requiring an official to carry out his duty: in this case, to force Madison to deliver the commission.

Marbury relied on Section 13 of the Judiciary Act of 1789. The section noted that the Supreme Court mainly heard appeals in cases that have a constitutional or federal issue at its core. In very specific areas, the Court had original jurisdiction, which meant that it may hear a case in its first instance without first having a lower court trial. These include disputes between states and those involving ambassadors, public ministers, and consuls. Article III did not address whether the Court may issue writs of *mandamus* under original jurisdiction, but Section 13 suggested it did. Section 13 thus seemed to expand the Court's original jurisdiction, and Marbury relied on that interpretation to file his suit. Marshall disagreed and voided the section.

The case focused precisely on the judges' duty to invalidate laws they found violated some provision of the Constitution. For Marshall, the answer was clear. Echoing Hamilton's Federalist 78, he noted that "it is emphatically the province and duty of the judicial department to say what the law is" (Box 2.1). Judicial review was not merely the authority of the judges to rule on the constitutionality of the laws but their responsibility as judges. With its historic political intrigue setting Marshall against Jefferson, the chief justice believed the case was about Congress's attempt to redefine the Supreme Court's jurisdiction. Marshall's decision halted the action. He wanted to avoid a direct confrontation with Jefferson because he knew he could not win the battle. The Court stood to lose prestige and authority if the president simply disregarded any order requiring Madison to deliver Marbury's commission. In the end, he avoided a confrontation with the president by ruling that Section 13 was "repugnant" to the Constitution.

Box 2.1 Federalist 78 (Alexander Hamilton) and *Marbury* v. *Madison* (1803) (John Marshall), excerpts

By a limited Constitution, I understand one which contains certain specified exceptions to the legislative authority; such, for instance, as that it shall pass no bills of attainder, no *ex post facto* laws, and the like. Limitations of this kind can be preserved in practice no other way than through the medium of courts of justice, whose duty it must be to declare all acts contrary to the manifest tenor of the Constitution void. Without this, all the reservations of particular rights or privileges would amount to nothing.

Federalist 78 (Alexander Hamilton), 1788

It is emphatically the province and duty of the judicial department to say what the law is. Those who apply the rule to particular cases, must of necessity expound and interpret that rule. If two laws conflict with each other, the courts must decide on the operation of each. So if a law be in opposition to the constitution: if both the law and the constitution apply to a particular case, so that the court must either decide that case conformably to the law, disregarding the constitution; or conformably to the constitution, disregarding the law: the court must determine which of these conflicting rules governs the case. This is of the very essence of judicial duty.

Chief Justice John Marshall, *Marbury* v. *Madison* (1803)
Adapted from Alexander Hamilton, Federalist 78 and John Marshall, *Marbury* v. *Madison*, 1803

As early as the sixteenth century, English courts had declared laws "repugnant" when determining whether laws passed by American colonial assemblies violated the laws of England. In 1796, Lord Chief Justice John Holt, referring to the colonies as plantations, noted the following: "all Lawes Byy-Laws Usages or Customes att this tyme or which hereafter shall bee in practice or endeavored or pretended to bee in force or practice in any of the said Plantations which are in any wise repugnant to the before mentioned Lawes or any of them." When repugnancy arises in colonial laws, they were "illegal, null and void" even if they were reasonable. His duty was to resolve the conflict in favor of England, not the colonies. Marshall thus resolved the conflict between Marbury and Madison in favor of the Constitution. When the Court speaks, therefore, it speaks the law and changes the meaning of the Constitution. It has the same binding force of law as if a legislature had passed a bill and an executive enacted it. At the same time, Marshall enhanced the strategic power of the Court for the next 220 plus years.

On the one hand, the decision was well within Jefferson's belief in "departmentalism" or "coordinate review." Jefferson argued that the president ought to interpret laws having to do with the executive branch just as Congress should interpret laws concerning the legislative. *Marbury* focused only on the Court's jurisdiction, so the justices had final authority to interpret constitutional provisions involving the judiciary. Over time, the doctrine of judicial review has been universally accepted, though often criticized. As many commentators have noted, the Court's invalidation of a law that a popularly elected legislature enacted is undemocratic. On the other hand, others have argued that the role of the Court only ensures that laws literally in conflict with a constitutional provision should not stand. Still others hold that the role of the Court is to make certain that a despotic majority may not eliminate minority rights and liberties.

Some historians have contended that Marshall should have only engaged in statutory construction to rule that Section 13 did not extend the Court's original jurisdiction. It merely clarified that jurisdiction. If one state sued another state, it could ask for a writ of *mandamus* directly from the Court. And some have argued that Marshall's opinion established "judicial supremacy" over the Constitution and the law. Still others have insisted, as Marbury's attorneys did, that the case was actually brought via the Court's appellate jurisdiction, because Marbury was appealing Madison's refusal to deliver his commission. An "appeal," as we know it today, was quite different from appeal in the eighteenth century. Alexander Hamilton, in Federalist 81, explained that the members of the constitutional convention defined the term "appellate" in its broadest sense. An appeal might then well be based on a ministerial decision, not a judicial one. If that were the case, Marshall would have had to grant the writ and order Madison, who was acting ministerially, to deliver the commission. At the time, however, the term "public minister" was relegated to foreign ambassadors and consuls, not officeholders.

Economic Policy in the New Republic

The early Court also explored whether the document protected property rights, known in the English common-law tradition as vested rights. Vested rights figured in the ideals of natural rights philosophy that identified some rights as so fundamental that government could never control or restrict them, including the right to own private property. This is reflected in the takings clause in the Fifth Amendment. Government could seize private property only for public use and only in exchange for "just" compensation. If a state legislature passed a statute that interfered with private property, the Court could declare that it violated a basic tenet of constitutional government.

In 1798, in *Calder* v. *Bull*, the Court reviewed a decision by the Connecticut legislature to allow a rehearing to probate a will. After a state court ruled that the will was invalid, the loser asked the legislature to invalidate that ruling and order a new hearing. A second review led to the probate court upholding the will. Those who would have profited by the first decision then appealed to the Supreme Court, claiming that the legislature had passed an *ex post facto* law in violation of Article I, Section 10, and that the court had unconstitutionally deprived them of their property. The Supreme Court unanimously held that *ex post facto* laws applied only to criminal, not civil, actions, and that only state courts could resolve conflicts between state constitutions and state laws. The Court also carefully preserved the right of federal courts to engage in judicial review.

One justice, Samuel Chase, explicitly raised the doctrine of vested rights in his opinion. "An act of the legislature (for I cannot call it a *law*) contrary to the *great first principles* of the social compact, cannot be considered a *rightful exercise* of legislative authority" when it comes to potential loss of property rights. "A law that takes property from A, and gives it to B: It is against all reason and justice, for a people to entrust a Legislature with such powers; and therefore, it cannot be presumed that they have done it." To do so would deprive a person of his property, his vested rights. The framers accordingly acknowledged the right of private property by prohibiting Congress from laying direct taxes and guaranteeing the return of fugitive slaves.

Article I, Section 10, also includes the contracts clause, which prohibits states from "impairing the obligation of contracts" between two parties. While the contracts clause does not specify whether it includes private and public contracts, the Marshall Court in two important cases resolved that issue. In *Fletcher* v. *Peck*, the issue was whether the Constitution protected the sale of land by Robert Fletcher to John Peck. The land was part of the 35-million-acre parcel that the Georgia legislature sold in 1795 to an array of companies in exchange for bribes and stock options. The land included today's entire states of Mississippi and Alabama. Because the deal was so obviously corrupt, the people of Georgia the next year voted all the legislators out of office. The new assembly rescinded the deal except for a few thousand acres that it set aside in anticipation of future monetary issues.

Peck's purchase was part of this remainder parcel. Both Fletcher and Peck were stockholders in the New England Mississippi Land Company, which had been involved in the original bribery scheme, though no evidence implicated either Fletcher or Peck. Most likely, they simply wanted to know whether their deeds were good. They believed that they owned the land but were uncertain as a result of the action by the new Georgia legislature. They therefore orchestrated the case to test their ownership. As Peck lived in Boston and Fletcher in New Hampshire, Peck filed suit in federal district court because of diversity of residency. Fletcher received a favorable ruling from the lower courts but appealed to the Supreme Court to obtain a final ruling on the legislature's repeal of the land grants.

John Marshall, who delivered the unanimous opinion of the Court in 1810, determined that the contracts clause overrode the legislature's action and that Fletcher owned the land when he sold it to Peck. Peck "has paid his money for a title good at law; he is innocent, whatever maybe the guilt of others, and equity will not subject him to the penalties attached to that guilt. All titles would be insecure, and the intercourse between man and man would be very seriously obstructed, if this principle be overturned." Marshall seemed almost apologetic when he noted that he did not mean to show disrespect for the Georgia legislature and its actions in 1796. And yet, the federal Constitution prohibited that state from impairing the contract into which Peck had innocently entered with Fletcher. "If an act be done under a law, a succeeding legislature cannot undo it. The past cannot be recalled by the most absolute power."

Georgia had impaired the two men's contract. Its action, echoing *Marbury* just seven years earlier, was "repugnant to the Constitution." At the same time, Marshall carefully noted that the contract between Peck and Fletcher was a vested right. The doctrine of vested rights, as Chase wrote in 1798 in *Calder*, preserved Peck's deed to the land as an act of good faith and innocence. The contracts clause barred states like Georgia "from passing a law whereby the estate of the plaintiff in the premises so purchased could be constitutionally and legally impaired and rendered null and void."

Nine years later, Marshall took an even sharper view by applying the doctrine of vested rights to a corporate charter that George III had issued before the Revolution. The chief justice acknowledged that the contracts clause as an expression of vested rights was so powerful that it preceded the Constitution. The case concerned the governance of small Dartmouth College in Hanover, New Hampshire. In 1754, Eleazar Wheelock, a Congregational minister, established a school to train missionaries to convert Native Americans to Christianity and to provide tribal members with educational opportunities. Fifteen years later, George III chartered and incorporated the college. The charter named Wheelock president for life and authorized the creation of a self-perpetuating 12-member board of trustees. The charter also empowered the president to name his own successor.

In 1779, Wheelock died and his son, John, succeeded him. Over time, John became increasingly autocratic in dealing with the trustees. In 1816, the board dismissed him. To resolve the impending upheavals in the college, the governor encouraged the state legislature to seize the college and create a new board of trustees of 21 members, all appointed by the governor. It authorized the college's treasurer, William Woodward, to take possession, temporarily at least, of all college property, including its seal. The former trustees were determined to maintain George III's charter. They hired Daniel Webster, a college alumnus and member of the Supreme Court bar who was one of the nation's great political orators, to demand the immediate return of all property as a violation of the contracts clause. Webster's argument was eloquent and emotional. Dartmouth was "a small college and yet, there are those who love it … I care not how others may feel, but, for myself, when I see my Alma Mater surrounded, like Caesar in the senate-house, by those who are reiterating stab on stab, I would not, for this right hand, have her turn to me, and say *et tu quoque, mi fili* [and you too, my son]."

Marshall, as usual, wrote the Court's opinion in *Trustees of Dartmouth College* v. *Woodward*, focusing on the original contract from 1769 and concluding with a paean to the doctrine of vested rights. The instrument the king had signed was a contract under the Constitution. The original contract prevailed because the corporation survived. The state could not impair a corporate charter that the king had granted. "It is a contract for the security and disposition of property. It is a contract, on the faith of which real and personal estate has been conveyed to the corporation. It is then a contract within the letter of the constitution and within its spirit also." In nullifying the original structure, the legislature substituted its will for that of the college founders who created the institution. That was "repugnant to the constitution of the United States."

Marshall's decisions in *Marbury*, *Fletcher*, and *Dartmouth College* permanently confirmed the Court's duty to declare constitutional principles at the local, state, and federal level. His most powerful statement came the same year as the college case in *McCulloch* v. *Maryland* in 1819, an opinion that reflected his nationalist views. The case focused on whether a state government could impose a tax on the US government.

McCulloch v. *Maryland* raised issues that the ratification of the Constitution did not settle: where does state sovereignty begin and end and what does it mean when Article VI proclaims that the Constitution and laws of the United States are the supreme law of the land? While Marshall did not resolve these questions with finality, he established that in a contest between national and state governments, the national government wins. The debate itself continued until the end of the Civil War when it was finally, but not conclusively, settled, even though today Americans still hear demands for "states' rights."

The Second Bank of the United States was a highly controversial institution from the moment the first bank was incorporated in 1791 during Washington's first administration. Hamilton, as secretary of the treasury, was the primary mover behind the bank because of his beliefs in a strong, fiscally sound central government. He thought he could achieve good economic planning by establishing a national bank along the lines of the Bank of England, which had emerged a hundred years earlier. A bank was necessary for a variety of reasons. It provided a foundation for the new national government's duty to tax in that it was a place to store the revenue. It gave the government credibility to secure loans from foreign countries. It allowed the treasury department to manage the government's finances in a rational manner based on sound financial principles.

Hamilton argued that, although Congress did not possess a specific power to create a corporation like a bank, the government could establish one anyway to carry out its new administrative functions and conduct its business. In 1790, he submitted to Congress his *Report on a National Bank*: "It is not denied that there are *implied*, as well as *express* powers, and that the former are as effectually delegated as the latter … That it follows, that as a power of erecting a corporation may as well be *implied* as any other thing; it may as well be employed as an *instrument* or *means* of carrying into execution any of the specified powers, as any other instrument or means whatever." In other words, as an implied rather than express power, the Constitution's necessary and proper clause authorized Congress to create a bank.

Hamilton's opponents included James Madison, then serving in the House of Representatives, and Jefferson, the secretary of state. As a legislator, Madison could speak freely when the bill incorporating the new bank came before the House for consideration. For his part, Jefferson, as a member of Washington's cabinet, could only write the president a private memorandum condemning it. Madison argued that the bank was not a means to create fiscal soundness, but an end in itself, an institution that, once established, allowed the national government to do anything it wanted. "The proposed bank could not be called necessary to the Government; at most could be convenient." As an alternative, Madison suggested that the federal government might use the existing commercial banks or none at all. Jefferson, in his note to Washington, feared that the new bank would intrude on the states' authority and increase the power of the national government. If a power is not specifically granted to the national government, it remained with the states. "The incorporation of a bank, and the powers assumed by this bill, have not, in my opinion, been delegated to the United States by the Constitution."

In other words, the debate became a classic example of the struggle between state and federal governments. When the bank's 20-year charter expired in 1811 during Madison's first term, Congress declined to renew it because of a combined effort by the Republicans and the owners of private banks and state officials who thought it was competitive with state-chartered financial institutions. The law allowed private citizens to deposit their money in it. Four years later, even Madison and the retired Jefferson advocated its re-establishment due to the debts the United States incurred during the War of 1812. This became the Second Bank of the United States, and the institution under consideration in *McCulloch* v. *Maryland* (Box 2.2).

Because it competed with the local banks, Maryland levied a tax on it, requiring it to issue its notes on specially stamped paper that Maryland sold at an annual cost of $15,000. The state then added an additional amount for each note printed. After James W. McCulloch, the bank's cashier, refused to pay the tax, Maryland sued him in Baltimore county court. When McCulloch lost, he appealed to the state's court of appeals, where he lost yet again. At that point, McCulloch, represented by Daniel Webster and William Pinckney, appealed to the Supreme Court, while Maryland engaged Luther Martin and former Supreme Court Justice Joseph Hutchinson to argue its case.

Box 2.2   *McCulloch* v. *Maryland* (1819), excerpt

Among the enumerated powers, we do not find that of establishing a bank or creating a corporation. But there is no phrase in the instrument which, like the articles of confederation, excludes incidental or implied powers; and which requires that everything granted shall be expressly and minutely described. Even the 10th amendment, which was framed for the purpose of quieting the excessive jealousies which had been excited, omits the word "expressly," and declares only, that the powers "not delegated to the United States, nor prohibited to the states, are reserved to the states or to the people;" thus leaving the question, whether the particular power which may become the subject of contest, has been delegated to the one government, or prohibited to the other, to depend on a fair construction of the whole instrument. The men who drew and adopted this amendment had experienced the embarrassments resulting from the insertion of this word in the articles of confederation, and probably omitted it, to avoid those embarrassments. A constitution, to contain an accurate detail of all the subdivisions of which its great powers will admit, and of all the means by which they may be carried into execution, would partake of the prolixity of a legal code, and could scarcely be embraced by the human mind. It would, probably, never be understood by the public. Its nature, therefore, requires, that only its great outlines should be marked, its important objects designated, and the minor ingredients which compose those objects, be deduced from the nature of the objects themselves. That this idea was entertained by the framers of the American constitution, is not only to be inferred from the nature of the instrument, but from the language. Why else were some of the limitations, found in the 9th section of the 1st article, introduced? It is also, in some degree, warranted, by their having omitted to use any restrictive term which might prevent its receiving a fair and just interpretation. In considering this question, then, we must never forget that it is a constitution we are expounding.

Chief Justice John Marshall
McCulloch v. *Maryland* 1819 /
U.S. Department of Justice / Public domain

In his opinion for the Court, Marshall posed two questions. The first was whether Congress possessed the power to incorporate a bank. If the Court's answer were negative, the case was over, and Maryland wins. If not, a second question arose: did Maryland have the right to tax a federal corporation? In response to the first query, Marshall investigated the original meaning of the Constitution. He noted that Article I, Section 8, laid out all the powers of Congress, but nowhere did it say it could create a bank or any corporation. The people, however, must not expect a constitution to lay out every contingency and possibility: constitutions are unlike ordinary statutes. "A constitution, to contain an accurate detail of all the subdivisions of which its great powers will admit, and of all the means by which they may be carried into execution, would partake of a prolixity of a legal code, and could scarcely be understood by the human mind." Constitutions and laws are different, and "we must never forget that it is a constitution we are expounding."

While the Constitution nowhere mentioned banks and corporations, it did include the necessary and proper clause. This provision suggested that Congress possessed residual power "to make all laws which shall be *necessary* and proper for carrying into execution the foregoing powers." If Congress could raise taxes, coin money, and engage in other monetary and financial activities, it may well conclude that it was "necessary" to find a corporate entity to house revenues. Marshall devoted a ton of words to investigating the word *necessary*. "A thing may be necessary, very necessary, absolutely necessary, or indispensably necessary." Congress's duty was to determine whether banks or corporations were necessary considering its extensive powers. The clause "is made in a constitution intended to endure for ages to come, and, consequently, to be adapted to the various crises of human affairs." Congress, therefore, in answer to the first question, possessed the power to create corporations, including the Second Bank of the United States.

In addressing the second question of whether Maryland could tax the bank, Marshall looked to Article VI's supremacy clause, which emphasized that the Constitution, the laws, and treaties of the United States "shall be the supreme law of the land." The answer to question two was simple: "that the power to tax involves the power to destroy; that the power to destroy may defeat and render useless the power to create; that there is a plain repugnance" to what Maryland was attempting to achieve. The US government was supreme over the states. If Maryland could tax the bank, it could also tax other federal entities such as the mail, the mint, the patent office, the papers of the custom house, and even the judicial process. And with that, the Court unanimously ruled in McCulloch's favor.

Madison and Jefferson supported the Court's unanimous ruling for *McCulloch*, although they were skeptical of Chief Justice Marshall's expansive view of the national government's power. They were persuaded that if he continued to rule as broadly as he did, Congress and the national government would eventually absorb most of the political power in the nation with only a residue left to the states. The growing power of the national government over the states fueled the anger and tensions in the growing sectional differences between North and South, ultimately sparking the outbreak of the Civil War after Abraham Lincoln's 1860 election to the presidency and the secession of South Carolina and 10 other states.

Five years after ruling in *McCulloch*, for the first time the Court interpreted the commerce clause in a dispute that once again involved a matter of state and federal law. And again, the case, like *McCulloch*, demonstrated Marshall's nationalist outlook. Article I, Section 8, empowers Congress "to regulate commerce with foreign nations, and among the several states, and among the Indian tribes." Like most provisions in the document, it was not self-defining. The framers were unhelpful in making clear just how far this power extended. Marshall, in another unanimous decision, fixed that problem by giving meaning to the phrase "interstate commerce:" Congress's authority was limited to commerce that passed through more than one state. At the same time, he used absolutist language when it came to how far the power extended.

The issue arose when the New York State legislature granted a monopoly to Robert Livingston and Robert Fulton to operate passenger steamboats across the Hudson River. The two men, in turn, licensed Aaron Ogden to provide exclusive ferry service on steamboats from New York to New Jersey. Meantime, Thomas Gibbons also transported passengers on steamboats from New York to Elizabethtown, New Jersey, under a 1793 federal law that had regulated boats "employed in the coasting trade and fisheries." Ogden sued Gibbons for interfering with his monopoly. The New York courts agreed with him that the 1793 federal law did not cover steamboats, but only coasting or sailing vessels. They also said that Congress had passed no law regulating steamboats. Gibbons appealed to the Supreme Court.

Box 2.3 *Gibbons* v. *Ogden* (1824), excerpt

The [federal commerce] power, considered in itself, is supreme, unlimited, and plenary. No part of any sovereign power can be annihilated. Whatever portion, then, of this power, was not granted to Congress, remains in the States. Consequently, the States have exclusive authority to promote science and the arts, by all other modes than those specified in the constitution, without limitation as to time, person, or object; and the Legislature is the sole judge of the expediency of any law on the subject.

Chief Justice John Marshall
Gibbons v. *Ogden* 1824 / U.S. Department
of Justice / Public domain

In *Gibbons* v. *Ogden*, again for a unanimous Court, Marshall ruled that the New York law interfered with Congress's authority to regulate interstate commerce (Box 2.3). The 1793 federal law superseded Ogden's monopoly granted to him by New York's legislature. Here, Marshall noted the extent of Congress's interstate commerce power. No state could ever infringe on federal power. Congress's authority was based on a broad definition of commerce. It is "intercourse," meaning that it was more than mere buying and selling but included navigation and transportation. He then used unconditional language to hold that Congress possesses the power "to regulate; that is, to prescribe the rule by which commerce is to be governed. This power, like all others vested in Congress, is complete in itself, may be exercised to its utmost extent, and acknowledges no limitations, other than are prescribed in the Constitution." Congress's interstate commerce power is "plenary ... as absolutely as it would be in a single government." Marshall's words were absolute: "complete," "unlimited," and "plenary" made clear that national commerce power in interstate transactions remained under federal, not state, authority.

3

Nationalization of the Constitution and Executive Power

The president's main domestic duty is to enforce the laws that Congress makes after he and his predecessors sign them. Madison and Hamilton differed over whether Congress or the president should be the most powerful agent of government. Madison preferred the legislature, whereas Hamilton the executive. In Federalist 51, Madison argued that "in republican government, the legislative authority, necessarily predominates." Most of the Constitution's framers agreed, given the placement in and length of Article I of the Congress and their fear of an executive who might resemble King George III. Madison's statement had a positive and negative meaning. It was positive because the legislature theoretically reflected the people's will. It was negative because legislatures might oppress the minority. The check on Congress was the president's veto. But Congress could then mount a two-thirds vote in both houses to override it. Meantime, Hamilton's view was different. In Federalist 70, he promoted "a vigorous executive" and stated that "energy in the executive is a leading character in the definition of good government." Some commentators have concluded that Hamilton expounded the theory of the unitary executive, the principle that the president, as the chief executive and commander in chief of the armed forces, may act alone in matters of military and national security policy when he was not answerable to congressional or judicial oversight. Presidents also issue executive orders, which have the authority of law, but may easily be overturned by their successors.

American Constitutional History: A Brief Introduction, Second Edition. Jack Fruchtman.
© 2022 John Wiley & Sons, Inc. Published 2022 by John Wiley & Sons, Inc.

The Constitution roots military command under civilian control. The check on the president is that Congress, not the executive, possesses the power to declare war. This procedure contrasted with the British convention of the king deciding when to send troops into battle. Although the Constitution demanded that Congress has the exclusive power to declare a war, it is silent about whether the president has a duty to ask Congress to review his decisions regarding national security. In Federalist 70, Hamilton noted that a president may have to react immediately in times of crisis: "Decision, activity, secrecy, and dispatch will generally characterize the proceedings of one man in a much more eminent degree than the proceedings of any greater number; and in proportion as the number is increased, these qualities will be diminished." A strong president was critical to protect "the community against foreign attacks."

After George Washington became president, he encountered the first major crisis of his administration, the 1792 uprising among whiskey distillers in western Pennsylvania, a series of events known as the Whiskey Rebellion. Distillers in the area were furious at an excise tax on distilled spirits that Hamilton proposed, and Congress enacted, to raise revenue. This was America's first "sin" tax. Until this enactment, the government collected its revenue through tariffs and import taxes, but these levies promoted smuggling, tax evasion, and even attacks on government tax collectors. Some Americans viewed the whiskey tax as a reassertion of tyrannical power, akin to the hated taxes that Britain imposed on the colonies just before the American Revolution. The Stamp Act and Townshend Duties forced Americans to pay taxes over which they had no say, and Hamilton's new excise seemed to repeat recent history. Several revenue collectors were attacked, beaten, tarred and feathered, especially in western Pennsylvania.

To put down the rebellion, Washington acted on the constitutional principle that the president "shall take Care that the Laws be faithfully executed," as prescribed in Article II, Section 3. He federalized the militia of the state, a power he exercised under Article I, Section 2. He initially hoped that a presidential proclamation demanding the citizens of the west to abide by the law would quell the resistance even if they opposed it. He hesitated to use military force. To call out the militia to put down a domestic rebellion smelled to some of British tyranny. When the rebels kept harassing tax collectors and even threatened constitutional government, in 1794 the president succumbed to Hamilton's importunities to act with military force.

On September 9, he wrote that "if the laws are to be trampled upon with impunity and a minority is to dictate to the majority (a small one too), there is an end put, at one stroke, to republican government." One month later, Washington personally led 12,000 militiamen to the west, the first time an American president directly led troops into battle. When they reached Carlisle, Washington had second thoughts and ordered Hamilton and Virginia governor Henry Lee to take command of the troops. Washington returned to Philadelphia, then the capital. The militia halted the rebellion, and its leaders were arrested, tried, and convicted. Public opinion supported the president's actions in crushing the rebellion, for his forthrightness in acting and then offering clemency to the participants. It was a stroke of executive genius.

Jefferson's view of executive power initially differed from that of Hamilton and the second president, John Adams. During the early years of the republic, he proclaimed that Hamilton and Adams were monarchists who failed to appreciate republican principles and would transform the American republic into a tyranny. Fearful of power, Jefferson argued until his election that presidents must rely on Congress to support their actions. Moreover, Jefferson was aware that Article I stated that Congress held the power of the purse, which meant that only the legislative branch could decide whether to purchase additional US territory. Moreover, Article IV stated that only Congress "shall have Power to dispose of and make all needful Rules and Regulations respecting the Territory or other Property belonging to the United States." In other words, the president neither controlled territory coming into the United States nor had a voice in the creation of new states. Only Congress did.

Jefferson's views dramatically changed when he took office in 1801. First, on his own initiative, he sent American frigates to the coast of North Africa, then called the Barbary Coast, when the Pasha of Tripoli demanded $225,000 in bribes to prevent pirate attacks on American shipping (in 2021 dollars, the amount is over $4.7 million). Congress empowered Jefferson to use his executive authority "to protect our commerce and chastise their insolence – by sinking, burning or destroying their ships and vessels wherever you shall find them." The result was the undeclared First Barbary War in 1801–1805, which led to several successful American raids on Barbary ports and the eventual capture of the Tripolitan city of Derna (in today's modern Libya).

Second, in 1801, Jefferson learned through Secretary of State James Madison that France had purchased from Spain nearly half of its North American colonies. Jefferson feared that France intended to re-establish its empire right at the doorstep of the new United States. The report led him to think that this action would drive the Americans into a closer relationship with Britain, France's traditional enemy. He had always been sympathetic to France, especially in his historic conflict with Hamilton, who as treasury secretary had argued that despite French support of the Americans during the Revolutionary War, the Americans had more in common with the British than the French. Now France appeared to be the threat. Napoleon envisioned a French republic spreading its ideology and power throughout Europe. This vision, along with his catastrophic attempt to destroy the slave revolt in San Dominque (today, modern Haiti) led by Toussaint Louverture, soon drove France toward bankruptcy. Napoleon was suddenly willing to sell the Louisiana territory to the United States.

Jefferson knew that he had to act quickly before Napoleon changed his mind or found additional sources of revenue elsewhere. In agreeing to the purchase, Jefferson became an imperial president who wanted to create in America "an empire of liberty" (his words). He knew he was acting on soft constitutional grounds by excluding Congress. He and Madison drafted an amendment to the Constitution that would empower the president to make the purchase, a move that was politically and personally clumsy. By then, he had already made the purchase, and now he was asking Congress to agree to allow him to complete something he had already done. They dropped the idea of an amendment. Instead, they asked Congress to ratify the purchase as a treaty, which passed the Senate by a vote of 21 to 7, comprising the most aggressive executive action to date. It had more far-reaching consequences than Washington's suppression of the whiskey rebels 10 years earlier. The land, which cost a mere $15 million, or around a quarter of $1 billion in twenty-first-century terms, doubled the size of the new nation. The United States acquired the entire Midwest section of the country: north to south from Canada to the Gulf of Mexico and east to west from the Mississippi to the Rocky Mountains. It opened the way for the government to begin its expansion to the Pacific Ocean.

Ironically, Jefferson opposed Hamilton's bank in 1791 and Washington's treaty with Britain, known in history as the Jay Treaty, in 1795. He thought that both overstepped executive authority. They were Federalist plots to aggrandize executive authority. But not now, because "by enlarging the empire of liberty, we multiply its auxiliaries, and provide new sources of renovation, should its principle at any time degenerate in those portions of our country which gave them birth," an extraordinary statement of nearly unrestrained executive power from a man who earlier had despised that power. To consolidate the new territory, soon after the purchase, he authorized Meriwether Lewis, his personal secretary, and frontiersman and draftsman William Clark to survey the new lands beyond the "great rock mountains" to consolidate his empire of liberty in what would eventually become the contiguous 48 states.

Another moment in unitary executive action occurred during the presidency of James Monroe, a follower of Jeffersonian Republican ideas and, like Jefferson and Madison, a Virginian. In 1803, along with Robert Livingston, the American minister in Paris, Monroe signed the deal with France culminating in the Louisiana Purchase. As president from 1817 to 1825, he grew displeased and worried about foreign incursions into the Western Hemisphere. He was anxious about Russian operations on the northwest coast and, perhaps more dangerous to American security, the growing desire of reactionary European states, united in the Holy Alliance, to re-establish their colonies in North America. After consulting with Jefferson and Madison, Monroe accepted the advice of Secretary of State John Quincy Adams to take unilateral action against foreign powers in the Western Hemisphere. In his seventh annual message to Congress in 1823, he enunciated his views in what became known as the Monroe Doctrine. The United States had recognized several new Latin American states that had recently achieved independence from Spain. Monroe promised that the United States would not interfere in European affairs and would look with great displeasure on attempts by any European nation to draw the new nations into their political sphere. Congress did not support his declaration with enabling legislation so these were the words of the president alone.

Although the term "Monroe Doctrine" did not come into common usage until the 1850s, it was clear that he believed that presidents had unitary power in matters of foreign policy and national security. The president's powers were vested in him as commander in chief and to execute the laws faithfully. "We owe it, therefore, to candor and to the amicable relations existing between the United States and those powers to declare that we should consider any attempt on their part to extend their system to any portion of this hemisphere as dangerous to our peace and safety. With the existing colonies or dependencies of any European power we have not interfered and shall not interfere." The United States was prepared to defend its geographic integrity and protect its national interests in the region.

Monroe was also the first president to prepare a so-called signing statement. Until the presidency of George W. Bush (2001–2009), signing statements had limited consequences. After a president signed a law, the statement might lay out his understanding of the meaning of the law and how he intended to enforce it. After Congress passed a law in 1822 with respect to a reduction in the size of the army and a process of appointing officers, Monroe issued a signing statement. The appointment of officers was entirely a presidential matter and had nothing to do with Congress. If Congress and not he appointed officers, "such a construction would not only be subversive of the obvious principles of the Constitution, but utterly inconsistent with the spirit of the law itself." He alone possessed the appointment power of military officers.

The new republic began with the demise of the first American government under the Articles of Confederation and the emergence of a "more perfect union" promised by the new Constitution. The struggle over ratification stimulated a great deal of quarrelsome debate between pro- and anti-constitutionalists known as Federalists and Anti-Federalists. Their differences prompted the first federal government to add the first 10 amendments in 1791 once the states ratified them and the rise of the first political parties.

The party apparatus did not formally develop until conflicts broke out during Washington's first administration, pitting Secretary of the Treasury Alexander Hamilton against Secretary of State Thomas Jefferson. Hamilton believed in a strong national government and manufacturing as the basis of the American economy while Jefferson contended that the states must maintain their primacy in the new federal structure and that agriculture, not manufacturing and finance, promoted citizen virtue. A striking development in party politics occurred during the Adams administration when Congress passed and the president signed the Alien and Sedition Acts in 1798, which Jefferson and his ally Madison attacked in their Kentucky and Virginia Resolutions.

They claimed that state officials need not enforce federal laws with which they disagreed.

The Supreme Court found that its duty was to declare unconstitutional all laws and actions by public officials when they violated any provision of the document. The landmark decision of *Marbury* v. *Madison* in 1803 established the power and responsibility of the Court to be the last word on constitutional questions. A decade and a half later, the Court ruled in *McCulloch* that, despite the views of Madison and Jefferson, the federal government was supreme in matters of legislative power. A fiery debate ensued over state's rights versus federal power, first in matters having to do with tariffs but then, and more importantly, slavery. Did the states have the power to decide whether to maintain slavery or was it a federal question? The nullification controversy that erupted in the 1820s over the issue, coupled with the question of whether slavery ought to accompany the new states joining the Union, led to the increasing dilemma America faced in the slave republic.

Part 2
The Slave Republic, 1789–1877

Slavery was prevalent throughout the years of the new republic, but the debate over its continued existence took on new urgency after 1820. The heated dispute that erupted over its abolition culminated in the secession of 11 states, a five-year brutal Civil War, and then Reconstruction. In the southern colonies, slave populations represented a substantial proportion of the total number of inhabitants. In 1770, these included Maryland (32 percent), Virginia (41 percent), North Carolina (35 percent), South Carolina (a whopping 61 percent), and Georgia (45 percent). In the Chesapeake region, tobacco, a labor-intensive crop, promoted slavery. Given the cost of the production of tobacco, free labor only added to profits. Some plantation owners like Thomas Jefferson and George Mason demanded the retention of the institution, while philosophically condemning it. They accepted slavery as a matter of economic necessity and moral responsibility. Slaves, they argued, were so inferior that they lacked the innate ability to survive without the paternalistic protection of the superior white race. Abolition would be a personal and immoral disservice to them. Worse, it would mean economic disaster for plantation owners. They thus claimed that they alone should decide how and when to end slavery without northern intervention.

Northern colonies were not immune to slavery. Eighteenth-century New York had the highest percentage of slaves at 12 percent of the

American Constitutional History: A Brief Introduction, Second Edition. Jack Fruchtman.
© 2022 John Wiley & Sons, Inc. Published 2022 by John Wiley & Sons, Inc.

population. Even Pennsylvania, despite its anti-slavery Quaker residents and rhetoric, engaged in the slave trade and slave markets. After he purchased the *Pennsylvania Gazette* in 1728, Benjamin Franklin, himself a slave owner, regularly placed advertisements seeking the return of runaway slaves alongside articles written by abolitionists like the Mennonites and Quakers. Many preachers inspired by the renewed emphasis on religious revivalism, which was sparked by a movement known as the Great Awakening, argued against slavery.

The American Revolution helped motivate anti-slavery efforts when many slaves served in the Continental Army. By the end of the century, leaders of the American Revolution like Alexander Hamilton, John Adams, Dr. Benjamin Rush, and Benjamin Franklin, who had renounced the institution and freed his slaves, joined these efforts. Franklin and Rush became the first and second presidents, respectively, of the Pennsylvania Abolition Society. In 1777, Vermont became the first to pass an emancipation law, followed by Pennsylvania in 1780, with a gradual one. New York was next in 1799, and then made it mandatory in 1828. New Jersey passed a gradual law in 1804, the last northern state to do so before the Civil War.

North–South sectional differences and states' rights arguments characterized the 1820s and 1830s. Southern states, largely agricultural, relied on slave labor to support a plantation system that produced staple crops like cotton and tobacco. Northern states also produced agricultural goods, but the region also possessed a growing manufacturing and industrial sector that did not entail Black slave labor. South Carolina Senator John C. Calhoun supported the most extreme form of state's rights when he announced the doctrine of nullification, echoing the reasoning behind Madison and Jefferson's 1798 Virginia and Kentucky Resolutions in opposition to the Alien and Sedition Acts. Nullification asserted the right of the states to disregard federal law. Initially, it centered on two tariff acts (1828 and 1832), but it soon exploded onto the issue of slavery and its spread to new territories.

In 1836, Texas slaveholders, mainly to preserve the institution, revolted against Mexico, which had abolished slavery. Texas was admitted to the Union in 1845 as the 28th state, precipitating the Mexican War the following year when a dispute arose over where the border should lie. President James Polk, Andrew Jackson's protégé, with a broad concept of presidential authority, claimed land to the Rio

Grande River, while Mexico asserted it owned land north of there to the Nueces River. After Polk ordered General Zachary Taylor into the disputed territory, war broke out and lasted until 1848. With the US victory, the nation vastly expanded to include what are now southwest states of Texas, Arizona, New Mexico, California, Nevada, Utah, and western Colorado. Congressional abolitionists tried to keep slavery out of newly acquired territory from Mexico by adding an amendment to the appropriations bill that funded the acquisition of this territory. The amendment is known as the Wilmot Proviso, sponsored in the House by Representative David Wilmot of Pennsylvania. Southern Democrats in the Senate stymied the attempt. The debate demonstrated that the Jeffersonian view of slavery – that it was an evil though necessary institution, which would eventually die out – was no longer salient. The position now was that slavery was absolutely fundamental to the southern agricultural economy. It included the racist idea that slaves were less than human and could never live as freemen. The institution was for their benefit.

By the late 1820s, Chief Justice John Marshall's influence had greatly diminished, especially as he confronted new colleagues on the Court. Justice Joseph Story's *Commentary on the Laws of the United States* established him as an intellectual giant and Marshall's equal. After Marshall's death in 1835, Jackson nominated his former attorney general and secretary of the treasury, Roger Brooke Taney, a former Maryland slaveholder, to succeed him. Taney, who took office the following year, remained on the Court until his own death in 1864. While many cases during his tenure dealt with economic and financial questions, his historical reputation primarily rests on the 1857 *Dred Scott* decision, which contributed to America's path to civil war by identifying slaves as mere property and non-citizens.

Presidential authority increased during Andrew Jackson's imperial presidency, but then grew dramatically during the Civil War when Abraham Lincoln was president. It then declined during Reconstruction when Congress became ascendant. A fierce nationalist, Jackson wanted to ensure that American-made goods enjoyed competitive advantages over foreign-made ones. He supported the Tariff Act of 1828, signed in the waning days of John Quincy Adams's administration. Jacksonian Democracy, with its emphasis on popular sovereignty, commercial enterprise, and the common man, faced a backlash when the new Whig party complained of Jackson's imperious behavior, often referring to him as "King Andrew." After the Court decided *Worcester* v. *Georgia* in 1832, denying states the authority to interfere with federally recognized Indian tribes, an angry Jackson was overheard to say, "John Marshall has made his decision, now let him enforce it." Or so journalist Horace Greeley reported.

Lincoln took steps without congressional authority during the Civil War to suspend habeas corpus, the right of a prisoner to know why law enforcement or military officers have detained him. A judge might release him if he found no good reason to hold him. Lincoln also allowed his commanders to create military tribunals to try those whom they believed were either sympathetic to the southern cause or were working to promote the South's victory over the Union. Even as the war raged on, he began the process of reconstructing the Union. Vice President Andrew Johnson, a staunch war Democrat who was the only southerner to remain in the Senate after Tennessee's secession, succeeded Lincoln following his assassination in 1865. He continued Lincoln's policies, only to encounter a far more radical Congress that personally weighed in against him. When southern Democrats re-emerged as a political force in Congress in 1877, at the conclusion of Ulysses S. Grant's presidency, Reconstruction finally ended.

Constitutional Amendments

For 60 years, the states ratified no amendments to the Constitution. During and after the Civil War, they quickly added three for the first time since 1804: the Thirteenth (1865), Fourteenth (1868), and Fifteenth (1870, the same year Congress created the Department of Justice). These amendments transformed the Constitution, and some historians call the period "the Second American Revolution." Perhaps noteworthy was that the southern states that had made up the Confederacy had to give up slavery and ratify the amendments as a requirement for returning to their normal relationship with the Union. Reconstruction demanded military conquest and then occupation and civilian control from Washington.

The most straightforward of the post-Civil War amendments was the Thirteenth, which abolished slavery throughout the United States.

Like many others, the Fourteenth comprised a variety of provisions that included a definition of US citizenship and three statements prohibiting actions by the states. First, it stated that anyone who "born or naturalized in the United States, and subject to the jurisdiction thereof, are citizens of the United States and of the State where they reside." Naturalization meant that the federal and state governments recognized that foreigners who assumed US nationality possessed citizenship rights and privileges equal to those born in the United States. They could vote in elections and hold federal, state, and local offices.

Second, the amendment presented three constraints on the states: the privileges and immunities, the due process, and the equal protection clauses. The first two repeat language located elsewhere in the Constitution but with different implications. Article IV, Section 2, contains a privileges and immunities clause. It holds that "the Citizens of each State shall be entitled to all Privileges and Immunities of Citizens in the several States." The courts have interpreted this clause to bind the states to treat all citizens equally, no matter their state of residence. This means that Maryland citizens traveling to Pennsylvania receive the same treatment from Pennsylvania state authorities as if they resided in that state, though they may not hold office or vote. They may enter into contracts, and if they are tried in a criminal court, they receive no harsher treatment simply for being out-of-state residents.

The Fourteenth Amendment prohibited states from making or enforcing "any law which shall abridge the privileges or immunities of citizens of the United States." Two important differences separate this statement from the one in Article IV, Section 2. The first is the replacement of the conjunction "and" in Article IV with "or" in the amendment. For most constitutional scholars, this difference is of little notice. The more important one is that Article IV addresses state citizenship whereas the amendment reflects national citizenship. Neither Congress nor the Supreme Court has ever defined the meaning of the terms "privileges and immunities."

The Fourteenth Amendment's due process clause prohibits states from depriving "any person of life, liberty, or property, without due process of law" whereas the Fifth Amendment's due process clause, like the Bill of Rights, binds the United States government. The two clauses now required both the federal and state governments to guarantee due process rights to their citizens when law enforcement officers charge them with a crime. In its American incarnation, procedural due process includes people's rights to know the charges against them, to cross-examine witnesses, to review evidence, to have a trial by jury, to have the assistance of counsel, and so on. In later years, the Court expanded the notion of due process to include substantive rights like the right to own property, to enter freely into contracts, and to enjoy privacy.

The Fourteenth Amendment also included the equal protection clause: no state "shall deny to any person within its jurisdiction the equal protection of the laws." This provision ensured the legal equality for the newly freed Black slaves in American courts.

Finally, the voting rights amendment, the Fifteenth, guaranteed to all citizens the right to vote, no matter their "race, color, or previous condition of servitude."

Congress was empowered by all three amendments to enforce their provisions.

4

Commerce, Nullification, and Slavery

Several economic issues – slavery, technological changes, and economic development – dominated the slave republic. The Supreme Court dealt with many of them, such as its 1837 decision concerning two Massachusetts bridge companies that built spans across the Charles River between Charlestown and Boston. *Charles River Bridge Company* v. *Warren Bridge Company* focused on the tension between community responsibility and private property. The constitutional question again focused on the contracts clause. In 1785, the Charles River Bridge Company received a 40-year charter from the Massachusetts legislature for a toll bridge. Almost a half century later in 1832, the Warren Bridge Company received a second charter just 300 yards from the existing one. Once the company paid its construction costs, the new bridge would become a public entity without tolls. The Charles River Bridge Company sued Warren Bridge owners, alleging that the new span undermined the value of its contract with the legislature. Chief Justice Roger Brooke Taney, writing for a majority of five to two, ruled that Massachusetts entered into the original charter to provide for the public good and not the private interests of a bridge company. The Warren Bridge was also good for the community and did not interfere with the operation of the Charles River Bridge, which could still collect its tolls.

The same year, 1837, the Taney Court heard its first major interstate commerce case since Chief Justice Marshall's 1824 landmark *Gibbons*

American Constitutional History: A Brief Introduction, Second Edition. Jack Fruchtman.
© 2022 John Wiley & Sons, Inc. Published 2022 by John Wiley & Sons, Inc.

decision. In *New York* v. *Miln*, a six to one majority ruled as constitutional a state law requiring ship captains to provide a list of their passengers to public authorities and to post bonds for immigrants. In validating the law's constitutionality, Justice Philip Barbour, a Virginian who wrote for the Court, for the first time employed the doctrine known as state "police power," which entitles states to pass laws to ensure the safety, health, welfare, and morals of the people.

Another interstate commerce case arose in 1851 in *Cooley* v. *Board of Wardens of the Port of Philadelphia*. The issue was whether Pennsylvania could require specially trained pilots to guide all ships into or out of the Philadelphia port. The state fined Aaron Cooley's company after two of his captains failed to employ a pilot. Cooley claimed that the fee was an unconstitutional state tax on interstate commerce. The Board of Wardens, the governing entity of the port, argued that a 1793 federal law left pilot regulation to the states. Justice Benjamin Curtis, writing for a majority of seven to two, found no conflict between the 1793 act and the Pennsylvania law. Congress had left pilot regulation to the states until such time that Congress decided to regulate it. Congress had so far declined to do so.

Other Economic Rulings

While slavery and the Civil War dominated the United States in the 1860s, the Court also managed other issues concerning government economic regulations. In 1862 and 1863, Congress passed the Legal Tender Acts, making paper currency, known as greenbacks, the official means of monetary exchange. A woman by the name of Mrs. Hepburn attempted to discharge a debt owed to Henry Griswold by giving him the new currency. He wanted hard specie (gold or silver) and refused to accept the greenbacks. The Court of Errors agreed with him. Hepburn then appealed the case to the Supreme Court in 1870. By that time, Chief Justice Salmon Chase (1864–1873), who wrote the majority opinion in Hepburn's case, had succeeded Taney after his death. In *Hepburn* v. *Griswold*, Chase overturned the act and ruled that Congress's power to coin money did not include the authority to produce paper currency. One year later, a similar case moved the Court to overrule *Hepburn* by a bare majority after President Ulysses S. Grant nominated two Republican justices to join the Court. In *Knox* v. *Lee*, it now held that Congress did possess power to issue paper money.

Salmon Chase was an abolitionist and reformer from Ohio. Although he challenged and lost to Lincoln in the 1860 presidential election, Lincoln shrewdly appointed him his secretary of the treasury where he unhesitatingly enforced wartime laws involving taxes, greenbacks, and commerce. After Taney's death, Lincoln nominated him to be chief justice. One of his notable innovations was to refer to his office as "Chief Justice of the United States," a title not in the Constitution. During Chase's tenure, the Court overturned 10 federal laws, most having to do with Reconstruction, whereas from 1789 to 1864, the Court overturned only two acts of Congress: Section 13 of the Judiciary Act of 1789 and the already repealed Missouri Compromise of 1820.

Among Chase's most important decisions was a circuit court ruling that upheld the constitutionality of the Civil Rights Act of 1866 under the Thirteenth Amendment. The law declared that citizens "of every race and color" had the right to benefit from "all laws and proceedings for the security of person and property, as is enjoyed by white citizens." When the law was challenged, Chase ruled *In re Turner* that the act granted full legal equality to all citizens. This meant that all Americans, Black or white, possessed the equal right "to make or enforce contracts, to sue, be parties, and give evidence, to inherit, purchase, lease, sell, hold, and convey real and personal property." When a Black woman, a former slave, wanted to abrogate a work contract with her former owner and now current employer, Chase, sitting as judge on a circuit court in Maryland, concluded in 1867 that she could not only sue in federal court, but that she also had the full right to testify and cross-examine witnesses. The ruling established that Blacks and whites enjoyed legal equality. However, it did not address the more difficult question of social equality, which would mean the integration of public facilities like schools, taverns, hotels, theaters, and railroad cars. The case was not appealed to the Supreme Court.

Chief Justice Morrison Waite, who succeeded Chase in 1874 and served until his death in 1888, followed Taney's views of states' rights when deciding the *Granger Cases*. The issue centered on the states' regulation of the economy, specifically whether Illinois possessed the authority to set maximum rates on privately owned grain storage warehouses and elevators. Ira Munn refused to comply because he claimed that the law violated the commerce clause and the Fourteenth Amendment's due process clause. He based his argument on the principle that Illinois deprived him of his property without due process of law, echoing the doctrine of vested rights in its burgeoning new guise as substantive due process. In 1877, writing for a majority of seven to two in *Munn* v. *Illinois*, Waite, a wealthy Ohio attorney before he became chief, argued that although the regulation involved a private enterprise, the state's interest was economic stability and prosperity. The Granger Movement, after all, had its roots in independent Midwestern farmers who were promoting their business interests, and Waite was happy to accommodate them. A private enterprise, once "clothed with a public interest," ceased to be merely private. He compared grain elevators to a public utility subject to the police power of the states. They comprised businesses that were "carried on exclusively within the limits of the State of Illinois" and were open to the public even if they were privately owned. Justice Stephen Field dissented, complaining that the state had no authority to regulate a private industry. "No reason can be assigned to justify legislation interfering with the legitimate profits of that business, that would not equally justify an intermeddling with the business of every man in the community." No captain of industry could have articulated a better defense of private enterprise.

The Nullification Controversy

Meantime, the debate over the nullification of federal law in the states dominated the nation's attention, especially in economic matters. Although a southerner, Andrew Jackson promoted northern interests in supporting the Adams administration's Tariff Act of 1828. That law stimulated the mushrooming nullification controversy, especially in South Carolina, whose leader was the powerful orator, John C. Calhoun.

Calhoun once served in the South Carolina legislature and became a major voice for war against Britain in 1812, making him a spokesman for the so-called War Hawks. He was secretary of war under President James Monroe and then vice president under President John Quincy Adams. When he broke with Adams, he joined forces with Jackson, who defeated Adams in the 1828 election with Calhoun again winning the vice presidency, now as a Democrat. Calhoun was concerned that the tariff law favored the commercial and industrial North over the South's plantation economy that remained dependent on slave labor. Calhoun's secret, though vehement, opposition to the Tariff Act of 1828 (opponents called it the Tariff of Abominations) pitted him against Jackson.

Southerners claimed the tariff lowered the cost of cotton shipped abroad and increased the price of goods produced in northern states and sent for purchase in the South. He resigned the vice presidency to work openly against it. The South Carolina legislature elected him to the US Senate where he opposed the even higher Tariff Act of 1832. He was now determined to preserve the integrity of his state.

The nullification controversy turned white hot when just seven days after passage of the 1832 bill, South Carolina nullified it in light of a law that passed the legislature: the South Carolina Nullification Ordinance. State officials simply refused to collect the tariffs. Considering that action, Jackson submitted the Force Act to Congress, which authorized him to deploy troops to any state to enforce a federal law. In March 1833, Jackson and members of Congress reached a compromise with the nullifiers, and the crisis was averted.

While the tariff debate sparked heated discussions, the specter of slavery – its continuation or abolition – dominated the slave republic, especially in terms of governmental regulation of the economy. In 1842, in *Prigg* v. *Pennsylvania*, the Court affirmed congressional authority under the Constitution to pass the 1793 Fugitive Slave Law. Meantime, Senator Daniel Webster of Massachusetts, with whom Calhoun engaged in debate on the floor of the Senate, supported both tariff acts and vigorously opposed slavery. He also argued that preservation of the Union was more important than a sectional crisis. He supported the Compromise of 1850, which was intended to resolve several issues raised after the United States seized territory from Mexico following the Mexican War: the key issue was whether Congress could prohibit slavery in the new territories. Abolitionists, mainly Whigs and some northern Democrats, demanded that Congress admit these territories as free states; their opponents, southern Democrats, wanted Congress to permit slavery there. Under the Compromise of 1850, California joined the Union as a free state while New Mexico and Utah were admitted with no mention of slavery.

Many American leaders hoped that the Compromise of 1850, which was a series of separate bills, ended the controversy. It did not. Four years later, the Kansas–Nebraska Act repeated the same arguments, centering on the expansion of slavery into the western territories. That debate was complicated by disagreement over the location of the transcontinental railroad. Northerners wanted to locate the western end of the line in Chicago. Southerners demanded a southern route to St. Louis. Southern Democrats and some of their northern allies also fought against the admission of free states west of Missouri. Illinois Senator Stephen A. Douglas, chairman of the Senate Committee of the Territories and a Democrat, supported a bill, which eventually became the Kansas–Nebraska Act, leaving the final decision about slavery to territorial settlers in a scenario known as "squatter sovereignty." He naively thought that settlers in the Nebraska and Kansas territories would never choose slavery. But the drive for westward expansion complicated the debate even more. Douglas, like many Americans, believed deeply in an America that spanned the country from the Atlantic to the Pacific, leading one Philadelphia newspaper editor to write, famously, in 1853 about Manifest Destiny: "East by sunrise, West by sunset, North by the Arctic Expedition, and South as far as we darn please." Douglas had no truck for American Indians who had to be removed for the new rail line and American's westward movement. He called their tribal camps and reservations "barriers of barbarism."

The Kansas–Nebraska Act empowered Kansas to enter the Union by permitting slavery while banning it in Nebraska. As the Missouri Compromise of 1820 made slavery in either territory illegal – they were both above the 36° 30' parallel, that is, the southern border of Missouri – the new law contained an amendment repealing the provision in the Missouri Compromise prohibiting slavery above the 36° 30' parallel. For the first time, Congress opened the North to slavery. While Nebraska was thought to be too far north to become a slave territory, Kansas was not. The result was the horrible history known as Bloody or Bleeding Kansas as thousands of abolitionists and slavery proponents rushed to the territory and murdered each other to "persuade" the majority of the territory's residents to elect candidates sympathetic to their cause.

And yet, not all northerners in Kansas were abolitionists. Many simply wanted to be left alone. They despised plantations not because of slave labor but because they consumed so much land, leaving too little for them. Free Soil meant free land for free whites, not free Blacks. The result was that two governments – one pro-slavery, the other anti-slavery – claimed authority in Kansas. President Franklin Pierce recognized the pro-slavery government even after a congressional committee proclaimed that the rightful government was the abolitionist one. Southern members of the Senate demanded that the pro-slavery forces kill, maim, tar, and feather as many free-state men as they could. In response, the abolitionist John Brown and his sons arrived to kill pro-slavery forces.

The worst fighting took place in 1856 in Lawrence, Kansas. There, pro-slavery men burned down the Free State Hotel, killed many men, and pillaged and looted the town. Brown and his sons retaliated by brutally murdering five pro-slavery men. After a final massacre, the new territorial governor, John W. Geary, restored order, though fighting continued until the outbreak of the Civil War. The Senate finally accepted Kansas's application for admission to the Union in 1861, but only after the South seceded when southern senators could no longer block its admission as a free state.

Dred Scott

Amid this upheaval and bloodshed loomed *Dred Scott* v. *Sandford*, a Supreme Court decision that marked a haunting moment in American history. The case targeted the legal status of American slaves when the debate had already become murderously bloody over slavery's continuation or elimination. The Constitution with its fugitive slave clause (Article IV, Section 2) and the Fugitive Slave Acts of 1793 and 1850 required those who captured escaped slaves to return them to their owners. Until the 1830s and 1840s, many northerners agreed with southerners that slaves were not free even when masters took them into free territories. Abolitionists were revolted by this and often refused to return runaway slaves.

The events began in 1834 when Dred Scott's owner took him to Illinois and federal territory above the 36° 30′ parallel where slavery was forbidden by the Missouri Compromise. Scott sued for his freedom and won in two lower Missouri courts, which agreed that his residence in a non-slave location meant that he was free. After the Missouri Supreme Court overruled that decision, Scott appealed to the Supreme Court. During oral argument in 1856 at the height of the troubles in Kansas, Sanford's attorney (the clerk misspelled his name in the records) unexpectedly raised another issue, namely that Scott could never become free because the Missouri Compromise was unconstitutional.

Chief Justice Taney wrote the opinion of the Court denying Scott's claim (Box 4.1). As a slave of African ancestry, Scott was mere property or chattel and had no right to sue for his freedom in a court of law. Taney determined that the framers never originally intended that black slaves would be citizens. He claimed that he was not commenting on whether his conclusion was the right or wise policy or whether he agreed with it. He said that only the political branches make that determination. His duty was to interpret the Constitution "according to its true intent and meaning when it was adopted," a mid-nineteenth-century version of what in the next century would be termed the doctrine of originalism.

Box 4.1   *Dred Scott* v. *Sandford* (1857), excerpts

It is too clear for dispute, that the enslaved African race were not intended to be included, and formed no part of the people who framed and adopted this declaration; for if the language, as understood in that day, would embrace them, the conduct of the distinguished men who framed the Declaration of Independence would have been utterly and flagrantly inconsistent with the principles they asserted; and instead of the sympathy of mankind, to which they so confidently appealed, they would have deserved and received universal rebuke and reprobation.

Yet the men who framed this declaration were great men – high in literary acquirements – high in their sense of honor, and incapable of asserting principles inconsistent with those on which they were acting. They perfectly understood the meaning of the language they used, and how it would be understood by others; and they knew that it would not in any part of the civilized world be supposed to embrace the negro race, which, by common consent, had been excluded from civilized Governments and the family of nations, and doomed to slavery. They spoke and acted according to the then established doctrines and principles, and in the ordinary language of the day, and no one misunderstood them. The unhappy black race were separated from the white by indelible marks, and laws long before established, and were never thought of or spoken of except as property, and when the claims of the owner or the profit of the trader were supposed to need protection.

This state of public opinion had undergone no change when the Constitution was adopted, as is equally evident from its provisions and language. ...

The rights of property are united with the rights of person, and placed on the same ground by the fifth amendment to the Constitution, which provides that no person shall be deprived of life, liberty, and property, without due process of law. And an act of Congress which deprives a citizen of the United States of his liberty or property, merely because he came himself or brought his property into a particular Territory of the United States, and who had committed no offence against the laws, could hardly be dignified with the name of due process of law. ...

Upon these considerations, it is the opinion of the court that the act of Congress which prohibited a citizen from holding and owning property of this kind in the territory of the United States north of the line therein mentioned, is not warranted by the Constitution, and is therefore void; and that neither Dred Scott himself, nor any of his family, were made free by being carried into this territory; even if they had been carried there by the owner, with the intention of becoming a permanent resident.

Chief Justice Roger Brooke Taney
Dred Scott v. *Sandford* 1857 / U.S. Department
of Justice / Public domain

Taney noted that even the broad wording of the Declaration of Independence was useless to Scott when it proclaimed that "all men are created equal," because "neither the class of persons who had been imported as slaves, nor their descendants, whether they had become free or not, were then acknowledged as a part of the people, not intended to be included in the general words used in that memorable instrument." Blacks were "beings of an inferior order ... unfit to associate with the white race." They were slaves for their own benefit. A slave could be "bought and sold" like an "ordinary article of merchandise and traffic, whenever a profit could be made by it." A slave was a commodity like a donkey or mule.

In focusing on whether Scott became a free man when he traveled to a free territory, Taney reviewed the constitutionality of the Missouri Compromise despite its repeal by the Kansas–Nebraska Act. He aimed his arrow at the heart of the property argument, suggesting that the old common-law doctrine of vested rights prevailed. The states and the territories possessed the authority to determine for themselves whether they allowed their citizens to own slaves. Nothing in the Constitution empowered Congress to pass the Compromise. The only provisions relating to slavery and the slave trade lay embedded in Article I, Section 9, the earliest date that Congress could eliminate the slave trade (1808, although it continued illegally until the Civil War), and Article IV, Section 2, the fugitive slave provision.

When Congress decided that some states, some territories, above the 30° 36′ parallel were free, it violated the Fifth Amendment's due process clause. The lower trial courts deprived John Sanford of his property, his slave Dred Scott, without due process of law. An "Act of Congress which deprives a person of the United States of his liberty or property, merely because he came himself or brought his property into a particular Territory of the United States, and who had committed no offense against the laws, could hardly be dignified with the name of due process of law." In a single sentence, Taney linked the doctrine of vested rights to slave ownership.

Within 50 years, this statement, expressed in mid-nineteenth-century vested rights terms, became the doctrine of substantive due process. Taney argued that Sanford had been deprived of his substantive due process right to own property in a human being. The Missouri Compromise violated the Constitution despite its repeal in 1854. The nine justices filed nine opinions in the case. Six concurring opinions agreed that Scott, as a Black slave, possessed no rights. Only two justices dissented: John McLean, an Ohio Republican, and Benjamin Curtis, a Massachusetts Whig, the first justice to have earned a degree from a law school (Harvard). Abolitionists vigorously condemned Taney's opinion. Abraham Lincoln denounced the decision in one of his famous debates with Douglas while running unsuccessfully for the US Senate in 1858. "We propose so resisting it as to have it reversed if we can, and a new judicial rule established upon this subject."

The decision was later overruled by the Thirteenth and Fourteenth Amendments, ratified in 1865 and 1868, respectively. Increasing divisiveness among the North and South meant that civil war was now an unavoidable outcome. Meantime, two powerful presidents, Andrew Jackson and Abraham Lincoln, emerged in the era of the slave republic. Both increased executive authority until Lincoln's assassination when the power of the president declined in the wake of Andrew Johnson's presidency.

5

Civil War and Reconstruction

The two most powerful presidents in the slave republic were Andrew Jackson, who emerged based on his electrifying personality, and Abraham Lincoln, whose authority materialized as a consequence of the Civil War. With Jackson's election in 1828, the period displayed a growing sensitivity toward ordinary citizens in what is popularly called Jacksonian Democracy. Ordinary citizens, tradesmen, artisans, and craftsmen occupied a place of primacy in American society as the new president staunchly opposed the finery of the upper class and promoted the essential equality of all citizens. This was the reason he vetoed the 1832 bill that re-chartered the Second Bank of the United States. He believed the bank promoted the wealth of the elite and privileged classes and ignored the common man.

Historians describe Jackson as extremely polarizing in dealing with both friends and enemies. Orphaned at 14, he eventually gained sufficient education to be a lawyer. His military career in fighting the British, especially during the War of 1812, epitomized his strength of character. Called Old Hickory because of his toughness on the battle-field and habit of engaging in duels (at the time called "affairs of honor"), Jackson removed more American Indians from reservations than any other president. In line with earlier Jeffersonian agrarianism, he thought the best form of the republic developed when the people were rooted to the land and paid their debts in hard specie (gold and silver). While the bank held all US assets, the "people's money," it was

American Constitutional History: A Brief Introduction, Second Edition. Jack Fruchtman.
© 2022 John Wiley & Sons, Inc. Published 2022 by John Wiley & Sons, Inc.

not subject to congressional or presidential oversight. Private individuals like the powerful Nicholas Biddle, its president, controlled it. Jackson believed Biddle used the bank to finance political campaigns and twist elections to control the American economy. It fundamentally undermined the democratic order he wished to create.

When the Bank of the United States had four years left on its charter, Jackson ordered his secretary of the treasury, William Duane, to withdraw all federal deposits. He knew full well that without these funds, the bank would fail. Duane refused, claiming that only Congress had the authority to decide the matter. Jackson thought Duane was merely his agent and had to obey his orders. Jackson fired him in 1833, setting off a constitutional struggle with the Whigs, the party in opposition to the Democrats, over the removal powers of the president. The Whigs claimed that the "tyranny" of Andrew Jackson matched the tyranny of George III. Whereas previous presidents had removed cabinet members without Senate or other congressional approval, those had occurred only after wrongdoing, not partisan politics. Jackson took the removal power to a new level.

Senator Henry Clay of Kentucky argued that only Congress, especially the Senate, possessed the power of removal because the Senate was empowered to confirm all high officials like the treasury secretary. When the Senate censured Jackson, he ignored them and named his attorney general, Roger Brooke Taney, secretary of the treasury as a recess appointment. Taney immediately withdrew all funds from the bank and redeposited them in state-chartered banks. The bank was then re-chartered as a private entity but finally liquated in 1841. As a result of his action, Taney failed to win Senate confirmation as secretary. The Senate did, however, later confirm him as chief justice, but only after the 1834 by-election when the Democrats controlled the Senate.

Lincoln and War

After Jackson's presidency, the Whig Party was successful in the 1840 and 1848 presidential elections – William Henry Harrison and Zachary Taylor, respectively – but, by 1854, the Whigs faded as a new abolitionist party arose, the Republicans, whose first president was Abraham Lincoln. Following his election, the secession of the first seven states, led by South Carolina, culminated in the creation of the Confederate

States of America, which no nation ever recognized. Before Lincoln took office, outgoing President James Buchanan, with one month remaining in office, declined to act. Everything Lincoln did was wholly improvised to preserve the nation. He had to claim his own constitutional authority. Only later did Congress retroactively confirm most of his decisions and actions.

An early decision came in April 1861, when Lincoln ordered the blockade of southern ports after the Confederate government captured the US military post at Fort Sumter in South Carolina. The US Navy seized several ships owned by various American and foreign shipping companies that had ignored the boycott. By July, Congress reconvened and confirmed the president's declaration that the southern states had rebelled against the United States. The next month Congress agreed that he had acted correctly to blockade the ports. The shipowners claimed that the Navy had illegally seized their ships because the president lacked authority to blockade a port unless he had prior congressional authorization.

By a vote of five to four in the 1863 *Prize Cases*, Justice Robert Grier ruled in the president's favor. A former Pennsylvania lawyer, Grier, who had voted with Taney in *Dred Scott*, held that the United States must protect itself when one of the states wars against it. The president acted appropriately because a state of war existed between the United States and the seceded states when the first shots were fired at Fort Sumter. "This greatest of civil wars was not gradually developed by popular commotion, tumultuous assemblies, or local unorganized insurrections ... The President was bound to meet it in the shape it presented itself, without waiting for Congress to baptize it with a name." Dissenting, Justice Samuel Nelson, with Taney joining him, argued that no war existed until Congress declared it under its powers set out in Article I, Section 8.

Lincoln also undertook several actions without congressional consent, including increasing the size of the military forces and calling up the state militias. Perhaps his two greatest enhancements of executive authority were his decisions to suspend the right of habeas corpus and to allow commanders to form military tribunals in various regions of the country. In the early decades of the new nation, most jurists and legislators believed that Congress possessed sole authority in both areas. The Constitution declares in Article I, Section 9, that "the privilege of the Writ of *Habeas Corpus* shall not be suspended, unless in Cases of Rebellion or Invasion the public Safety may require it in the case of rebellion or invasion." Because Article I concerns Congress, the assumption is that only that body may suspend it. Moreover, Article III, which focuses on the judiciary, designates only one Supreme Court, and then adds that the creation of all other courts is the responsibility of "Congress … from time to time [to] ordain and establish."

Habeas corpus had long been part of the British common-law tradition whereby prisoners could ask a judge why they were being held. If the judge issued the writ, the jailor would have to bring prisoners before the judge to hear the factual basis for holding them. Lincoln claimed that although Congress in normal times possessed the sole power to suspend habeas corpus, he acted while Congress was not in session and his oath of office demanded that he "preserve, protect and defend the Constitution of the United States." But Lincoln feared that early Confederate military advances would lead to the capture of Washington, DC, a difficult development for him and the Union. Virginia was a hostile state, and the status of Maryland, just to the north, was uncertain. As a border state, Maryland never seceded, but its population had a great number of southern sympathizers.

The president became alarmed when in April 1861 some Baltimoreans, loyal to the southern cause, destroyed railroad tracks, bridges, and telegraph lines to prevent northern militiamen from Massachusetts, Pennsylvania, and elsewhere from reaching Washington. Maryland governor Thomas Hicks and Baltimore mayor George Brown, in an effort to keep the peace, declined to allow any northern troops to travel through Baltimore or anywhere else in Maryland. On April 27, Lincoln suspended the writ from Maryland to Philadelphia. He empowered his military commanders to arrest and to detain anyone they thought were disloyal to the United States or gave aid and comfort to the Confederacy.

After Congress reconvened in July of 1861, it affirmed the president's suspension of the writ, and asserted that all acts and proclamations by Lincoln were "approved and in all respects legalized and made valid … as if they had been issued and done under the previous express authority and direction of the Congress of the United States." Two years later, Congress passed the Habeas Corpus Act of 1863, delegating the power to the president to suspend the writ in cases of insurrection. With this authority, along with the Conscription Act of 1863, the president authorized district commanders in various states and territories to declare martial law if they believed that Confederate loyalists acted against the Union. Once in custody, these loyalists might have to appear before military tribunals, a development that formed the second extraordinary move the president made during the Civil War.

Because communication and transportation in most regions were poor, many commanders decided on their own whether to establish military tribunals. Three cases in particular, two of which became notable rulings, included those of John Merryman, Clement Vallandigham, and Lambdin Milligan. The first of these took place in September 1861. Lieutenant John Merryman of Baltimore sympathized with the Confederacy and raised troops for the South. He participated in stopping southbound trains from passing through Maryland. After his arrest in May 1861, he was imprisoned in Fort McHenry. Chief Justice Taney, at that time assigned to the circuit court in Maryland, heard his appeal for habeas relief and ordered the commander of the fort, General George Cadwalader, to release Merryman on a writ of habeas corpus. When Cadwalader refused, Taney issued an arrest warrant for Cadwalader, but the general would not allow the US marshal to enter the fort.

Powerless to act, Taney ruled on the case anyway, giving Lincoln a lesson in constitutional law. He held that the question of whether a person has a right to the writ is a matter for the courts, not the president, to decide. No commander possessed the right to arrest and to detain without charge "a person not subject to the rules and articles of war, for an offence against the laws of the United States, except in aid of the judicial authority, and subject to its control." After reading Taney's decisions, Lincoln posed this question to Congress in July: "Are all the laws but one to go unexecuted and the government itself go to pieces lest that one be violated?" (Box 5.1). In the end, he suspended habeas corpus all the way to Maine. After a federal judge eventually released Merryman on $40,000 bail, the United States never brought him to trial.

Another Confederate sympathizer, Clement Vallandigham of Ohio, openly criticized the federal government, claiming that the "that the present war was a wicked, cruel, and unnecessary war, one not waged for the preservation of the union, but for the purpose of crushing our liberty and to erect a despotism." It was "a war for the freedom of the blacks and the enslavement of the whites; and that if the administration had not wished otherwise, that the war could have been honorably terminated long ago." Vallandigham also charged the president with transforming the states into military districts and depriving the people of their liberty, rights, and privileges. General Andrew Burnside, commander of the Ohio district, declared that anyone who spoke sympathetically about the Confederacy might well face the death penalty if found guilty after a trial by military tribunal. This meant that free speech, as guaranteed by the First Amendment, was dead in wartime Ohio.

Box 5.1   President Abraham Lincoln, Address to a Special Session of Congress, July 4, 1861, excerpt

To state the question more directly, are all the laws, but one, to go unexecuted, and the government itself go to pieces, lest that one be violated? Even in such a case, would not the official oath be broken, if the government should be overthrown, when it was believed that disregarding the single law, would tend to preserve it? But it was not believed that this question was presented. It was not believed that any law was violated. The provision of the Constitution that "The privilege of the writ of habeas corpus, shall not be suspended unless when, in cases of rebellion or invasion, the public safety may require it," is equivalent to a provision – is a provision – that such privilege may be suspended when, in cases of rebellion, or invasion, the public safety does require it. It was decided that we have a case of rebellion, and that the public safety does require the qualified suspension of the privilege of the writ which was authorized to be made. Now it is insisted that Congress, and not the Executive, is vested with this power. But the Constitution itself, is silent.

Abraham Lincoln 1861 / Message to Congress
in Special Session / Public domain

After his detention, Vallandigham, a lawyer by profession, argued to no avail that he ought not to be subjected to a military tribunal because he was not a soldier. Instead, he deserved a trial in a civilian criminal court. Still, a tribunal found him guilty and sentenced him to detention in a military installation until the war ended. Vallandigham appealed to the Supreme Court, which unanimously ruled that it lacked jurisdiction under its Article III appellate powers to hear appeals from military tribunals. Vallandigham was stuck. Lincoln, unhappy with Burnside's extreme actions, commuted the sentence and banished Vallandigham to the Confederate states until the end of the war.

The Civil War case involving a military tribunal that perhaps had the longest lasting impact was that of Lambdin P. Milligan, a lawyer, a citizen of the United States, and a resident of Indiana; courts still cite his case in the twenty-first century. In October 1864, General Alvin

Hovey, the Indiana military commander, ordered Milligan's detention in a military prison for conspiring against the federal government by inciting insurrection, engaging in disloyal practices, and violating the laws of war. Tried by a military commission in Indianapolis, Milligan was found guilty of joining a secret society known as the Order of American Knights or Sons of Liberty whose purpose was to overthrow the US government. In addition, he had conspired to seize war materiel to liberate Confederate prisoners of war. After the military commission rejected Milligan's claim that the commission had no jurisdiction over him, he was found guilty and sentenced to death by hanging.

Milligan appealed to the federal circuit court for a writ of habeas corpus. He argued that at no time had he ever been in the military service of any state in rebellion and that he was a resident of Indiana, which was not a state in insurrection. Moreover, Indiana had open and functioning civilian courts that could have tried him. Because the appellate court was so deeply divided, the judges certified several questions for the Supreme Court. Among these were whether Milligan had a right to a writ of habeas corpus and whether the military commission had jurisdiction over him. In 1866, a year after the war ended, the Court unanimously ruled, in *Ex parte Milligan*, that the president lacked authority to use military tribunals to try civilians when the civilian courts were open and operating.

Justice David Davis delivered the opinion of the Court. Davis, a lawyer from Illinois, had served as a Republican Party campaign manager in the 1860 presidential election and, in return for his loyalty, Lincoln nominated him to the Court in 1862. He forcefully argued that even presidents were under the law and the Constitution. In his rebuke to the now-deceased president, he wrote, "The Constitution of the United States is a law for rulers and people, equally in war and in peace, and covers with the shield of its protection all classes of men, at all times, and under all circumstances." As a civilian, Milligan had been arrested for speaking his mind in a state that was not in rebellion against the United States. Moreover, Davis emphasized that the courts in Indiana were "always open to hear criminal accusations and redress grievances." General Hovey deprived Milligan of his right to a trial in a civilian court with a neutral judge and jury.

The most powerful statement came toward the end of Davis's acidic opinion. If the president of the United States or a military officer under his command deprived a citizen of the United States of their fundamental rights, "republican government is a failure, and there is an end of liberty regulated by law." Civil liberty and martial law "cannot endure together; the antagonism is irreconcilable; and, in the conflict, one or the other must perish." Great men like Washington and Lincoln might well know how to conduct themselves during perilous times like the Civil War or during an invasion. The United States, however, cannot count on having great men in office all the time. There may well come a time when "wicked men," "ambitious of power, with hatred of liberty and contempt of law," will subvert the very freedom and rights the Constitution guarantees.

On January 1, 1863, Lincoln announced the Emancipation Proclamation, freeing more than 3 million slaves in the states that had seceded from the Union. While the proclamation has become in American history a symbol of Lincoln's desire to end slavery, it does not reveal his earlier ambivalence that slaves should be freed slowly and then subject to colonization or forced emigration to Africa. With the proclamation, Lincoln announced his changed view: whenever southern slaves escaped to the North or to Union commanders, they would immediately and automatically be free. Former slave owners would not be compensated for their lost "property" and the liberated slaves would be free to live in America.

At the height of Reconstruction, Chief Justice Chase supported Lincoln's nationalist views in his 1869 opinion in *Texas* v. *White*. He characterized his views in the guise of the redundant-sounding doctrine of "dual federalism." Both the United States and the states occupied equal prominence in the Union, a sentiment echoed by Justice Samuel Miller later in 1873 in *The Slaughterhouse Cases* when he wrote that "it is quite clear ... that there is a citizenship of the United States and a citizenship of a state, which are distinct from each other and which depend upon different characteristics or circumstances in the individual." Now, having been restored to the Union, the state of Texas claimed ownership of state-owned securities that the Confederate Texas government had sold. In response, the securities' owners, George White and John Chiles, claimed that Texas had not yet rejoined the Union and thus had no standing to file a claim in federal court. Chase rejected White's argument, making the remarkable statement that the Constitution created "an indestructible Union, composed of indestructible States." The Confederate states had never left the Union but formed only an illegal consortium.

Reconstruction

By the time the Chase Court heard this case, the nation had already begun the long, arduous task of Reconstruction, which lasted until 1877. Reconstruction, the term commonly used to describe how the seceded states returned to a normal relationship with the Union, evolved through two primary stages. The first was the short-lived, presidential stage that centered on restoring the southern states to their pre-1860 relationship with the United States. The second was the longer congressional stage when the Radical Republicans controlled the House and Senate and rammed through several pieces of punitive law that the South loathed.

During the presidential period, ongoing disagreement raged over what precise legal status the southern states enjoyed. Lincoln held strong views about how the government should reconstruct the nation. A beginning point was Article IV, Section 4's Guaranty Clause, which provided that every state must have a republican form of government. Like Chief Justice Chase, Lincoln never recognized secession. He distinguished the states, which remained in the Union, from the unconstitutional Confederate governments that had illegally seized control of the South. In 1865, Lincoln announced his willingness to allow representatives from the so-called seceded states to take their seats in Congress. Moreover, he was also prepared to recognize a few of those states, such as Tennessee, Arkansas, Louisiana, and Virginia, after they held conventions to rewrite their constitutions to include provisions abolishing slavery. He also thought that citizens from the South who had not directly participated in secession could again exercise their right to vote and participate in politics.

After his assassination in 1865, Lincoln was succeeded by Andrew Johnson, who essentially agreed with this position. Congressional leaders like Representative Thaddeus Stevens of Pennsylvania and Senator Roscoe Conklin of New York had different ideas. They thought that with the victory of Union over the seceded states, the federal government could treat them like defeated, even conquered, enemies. Senator Charles Sumner of Massachusetts disagreed. He claimed that when they seceded, they returned to their former status as territories. Congress had the authority to readmit these territories into the Union. Congress then created the Joint Committee on Reconstruction to confront the president, reject his program, and develop its own plans based on the ideas of leaders like Stevens, Cockling, and Sumner. This meant that no southern delegates could sit in Congress. When Johnson angrily rejected these steps, he alienated Congress even more, driving moderate Republicans into the Radical camp. Worse, the punitive approach pushed the southern states to establish the so-called Black Codes that totally disenfranchised the newly freed slaves and rooted them to the soil under white property owners. Under the Codes, Blacks could not purchase land and they possessed no political or civil rights.

The Radicals won the 1866 by-election with veto-proof majorities in both houses. Now, presidential authority severely declined. Johnson faced an increasingly hostile Radical Republican Congress, which wanted the southern states to re-enter the Union with punishing requirements. Johnson thought that the Confederate states could normalize their relationship with the Union when they drafted new constitutions and ratified the Thirteenth Amendment abolishing slavery. To rally support for this policy, he went on a sweeping national speaking tour, but to no avail. He vetoed every Reconstruction act Congress passed, but every time both houses overrode his veto.

In 1865, Congress created the Bureau for Refugees, Freedmen, and Abandoned Lands (the Freedmen's Bureau), a relief agency for the newly freed Black slaves. Congress renewed it a year later when it became a major shield for Black citizens. Any individual denying civil rights to Blacks could face a military tribunal with no due process rights, such as a grand jury indictment or a trial by jury. Johnson vetoed the bill, but Congress easily overrode his veto. The Radicals argued that the Thirteenth Amendment's enforcement provision gave Congress the authority to pass it. Southerners and the president now claimed that the law violated the Fifth Amendment's due process clause, which stimulated Congress to pass progressive legislation like the Civil Rights Act of 1866, which established legal equality for all Black citizens. Again, the president vetoed the act, and again Congress overrode the veto. At that point, Johnson's control over Reconstruction effectively ended.

In 1867, Congress passed the Military Reconstruction Act, which transformed the South into military districts under army commanders. Johnson also vetoed that one, but once again Congress immediately overrode his veto. The act displaced the civilian governments that the Johnson administration had temporarily erected in those states. Congress demanded that all 11 southern states call constitutional conventions, disenfranchise all white leaders who had led the states in the

Confederacy, and enfranchise Black voters. Mississippi in 1867 and Georgia in 1869 tried to stop the federal government from enforcing this law as well as the Congressional Reconstruction Act in their states. They wanted to maintain civilian governments in their states, not those of the military commanders created by the Reconstruction Acts. When their challenge reached the Chase Court, the justices unanimously declined to issue an injunction, holding that the president had acted pursuant to acts of Congress. In *Mississippi* v. *Johnson*, Chief Justice Chase declared the Court would not interfere with a decision that was essentially political in nature, thus distinguishing a "ministerial" act by the president when he acted alone on his own constitutional authority and a "political" act when he enforced a congressional law, even if over his veto. Congress and the president had to resolve it, not the courts.

The following year, Congress passed the Fourteenth Amendment, and required the southern states to ratify it as part of the terms of their return to a normal relationship with the Union. Because three-quarters of the states must ratify amendments before they are added to the Constitution, the requirement meant that the amendment was a guaranteed addition to the Constitution. The irony was that though they required the seceded states to ratify the amendment, the Radical Republicans had all along refused to recognize them as states at all.

Soon, southern politics became a stronghold of northern immigrants and Black voters as new residents poured into the South. By the time the new Alabama constitution was ratified, for example, it enfranchised a total of 160,000 voters, 104,000 of whom were Black. Five other states had Black voting majorities. In July 1868, Congress readmitted seven states (Alabama, Arkansas, North and South Carolina, Georgia, Florida, and Louisiana), and added three more two years later (Mississippi, Virginia, and Texas), though Georgia had to be readmitted twice after Congress objected to its government. The final push came in 1870 when the Radical Republicans pushed through Congress, and forced the southern states to ratify, the Fifteenth Amendment, guaranteeing all citizens equal voting rights.

Meantime, as tensions and anger between Johnson and the Radical Republicans increased, the Republicans passed the Tenure in Office Act in 1867, which meant that the president could not remove a subordinate from office without Senate approval. The goal was to undermine Johnson's authority and reduce him to figurehead status. When Johnson fired Edwin Stanton, the secretary of war, because he was sympathetic to Republican Reconstruction plans, and replaced him with General Ulysses S. Grant, the Senate declined to approve the action. The president acted anyway, but instead of Grant, he appointed General Lorenzo Thomas to the position. The Republicans saw their chance to be rid of Johnson: impeach the president for violating the Tenure in Office Act and remove him from office.

At his impeachment hearing in the House, Johnson argued that the First Federal Congress had left the removal power to the president and pointed out that Andrew Jackson had singlehandedly removed William Duane as treasury secretary in 1833. Congress refused to budge, and Johnson became the first president in US history to be impeached by the House of Representatives, although the Senate refused to convict him and remove him from office. The Constitution requires the Senate to muster a two-thirds vote to remove the president, and it failed to convict the president by only a single vote.

One of the last acts that the Radical Republicans pushed through the lame-duck Congress, before the Democrats took their seats, was the Civil Rights Act of 1875 (Box 5.2). It went beyond the legal equality that the Civil Rights Act of 1866 had established and guaranteed social equality between the races. The new law was a public accommodations act that required all private businesses that opened their doors to the public – businesses like hotels, taverns, bars, theaters, restaurants, and such – to practice non-discrimination based on race. By that time, with Grant in the White House, however, the power of the Radical Republicans had faded. After March 1875, southern Democrats controlled eight states and had a majority in the House of Representatives, which they maintained for the next 10 years.

Box 5.2   The Civil Rights Act of 1875, excerpt

An act to protect all citizens in their civil and legal rights. Whereas, it is essential to just government we recognize the equality of all men before the law, and hold that it is the duty of government in its dealings with the people to mete out equal and exact justice to all, of whatever nativity, race, color, or persuasion, religious or political; and it being the appropriate object of legislation to enact great fundamental principles into law:

Therefore, Be it enacted by the Senate and House of Representatives of the United States of America in Congress assembled, That all persons within the jurisdiction of the United States shall be entitled to the full and equal and enjoyment of the accommodations, advantages, facilities, and privileges of inns, public conveyances on land or water, theaters, and other places of public amusement; subject only to the conditions and limitations established by law, and applicable alike to citizens of every race and color, regardless of any previous condition of servitude.

Civil Rights Act of 1875 /
U.S. Federal law / Public domain.

This state of affairs set the stage for the muddled results of the 1876 presidential election that pitted Democrat Samuel Tilden of New York against Republican Rutherford B. Hayes of Ohio. Tilden won the popular vote but Hayes the electoral vote, which is what mattered. After the appointment of 15 commissioners (five each from the Senate, the House, and the Supreme Court), the two parties reached a compromise. In exchange for Hayes's election as president (the commission awarded him 20 disputed electoral votes and he won the presidency by one vote), all northern troops would evacuate the South. Once Hayes withdrew troops from Louisiana and South Carolina, Reconstruction ended.

Meantime, as the nation faced the challenges of slavery, civil war, and reconstruction, it also had to deal with other issues involving rights and liberties.

6

Rights and Privileges

The first 10 amendments to the Constitution set forth an array of rights and liberties guaranteed to the American people against intrusion by the US government. An open question after their collective ratification in 1791 was whether any of them applied to the states. Chief Justice John Marshall decisively answered that question in 1833 when he ruled on an action that John Barron brought against the City of Baltimore and its city council. In 1815, the city began to improve the streets and byways, which resulted in the diversion of many streams. When it rained, sand and dirt poured into Baltimore's harbor. Barron, who operated a lucrative wharf, could no longer service the needs of large cargo ships as the sludge accumulated in the water around his wharf. He sued the city and the city council on the grounds that he had been deprived of his property without just compensation in violation of the takings clause of the Fifth Amendment. The court awarded him $4500 in compensation. The Maryland Court of Appeals overruled that decision, and the Supreme Court unanimously agreed.

In *Barron* v. *Baltimore*, Marshall asked Barron's counsel to address whether the framers originally understood that the Bill of Rights applied to local and state governments or only to the federal government. After hearing an unpersuasive claim, Marshall told the attorneys from Baltimore that he did not need to hear their argument and summarily ruled against Barron. "We are of opinion, that the provision in the Fifth Amendment to the Constitution, declaring that private property shall

American Constitutional History: A Brief Introduction, Second Edition. Jack Fruchtman.
© 2022 John Wiley & Sons, Inc. Published 2022 by John Wiley & Sons, Inc.

not be taken for public use, without just compensation, is intended solely as a limitation on the exercise of power by the government of the United States, and is not applicable to the legislation of the states." The application of various provisions of the Bill of Rights to the states was now settled until the ratification of the Fourteenth Amendment 35 years later. It took another 40 years after that, beginning in the late 1890s, for the Court to begin the slow process of selectively incorporating various provisions of the Bill of Rights and applying them to the states.

Barron was one of the last significant decisions of the Marshall Court. His successor, Roger Brooke Taney, dealt with an issue in 1849 involving Article IV that requires each state to have "a Republican Form of Government." As with many provisions, the phrase is not self-defining. States certainly must have an electoral process for state officials, but the provision did not set out detailed procedures such as the structure of government, voter qualifications, the size and shapes of electoral districts, or tax rates. For the first several decades, no constitutional issues arose over the meaning of a "republican form" of government. One emerged in 1842 when Rhode Island had two competing state governments. The state constitution limited the franchise to those who owned land worth at least $134. Rural conservatives thus controlled the governor's office and legislature. With the growth of the cities, especially because of the mill industry, urban dwellers demanded representation. When their demands were ignored, they called a constitutional convention. State officials then called their own constitutional convention. In 1842, two rival governments claimed legitimacy. The Dorr Rebellion was led by a Rhode Island lawyer who advocated universal manhood suffrage. Thomas Dorr and his sympathizers wanted to create a true "republican" form of government. The incumbent governor and legislature declared martial law. Dorr was arrested and tried for treason and then sentenced to life imprisonment in solitary confinement at hard labor.

Martin Luther, a Dorr supporter, then sued a government militiaman, Luther Borden, who broke into Luther's home to search it. Borden claimed the old charter gave him the authority to search the premises under martial law. The case that grew from this incident, *Luther* v. *Borden*, asked the Supreme Court to determine the nature of a "republican" form of government as guaranteed in Article IV. By an eight to one majority, Chief Justice Taney ducked the issue. He declined to define republican government. Only Congress could answer that question. Because the justices were unaccountable, unelected, and served life terms ("during good behavior"), the Court was unresponsive to popular sentiments. Taney thus gave rise to a new constitutional doctrine: the political question. The ultimate determination must come from the people themselves. It was a "political question to be settled by the political power."

Privileges and Immunities

If the justices dodged the issue in *Luther* because it posed a political question, they faced a more difficult problem in meaningfully interpreting the first section of the Fourteenth Amendment, which overruled *Dred Scott*. The section defined US citizenship in broad terms, making no distinction between races or previous condition of servitude. Anyone born or naturalized in the United States is a citizen of the United States and the state in which they reside. The most controversial part of the amendment was not the definition of citizenship but the phrases in the second sentence. Three provisions, as noted previously, assert that "no state shall make or enforce any law which shall abridge the privileges or immunities of citizens of the United States; nor shall any State deprive any person of life, liberty, or property, without due process of law; nor deny to any person within its jurisdiction the equal protection of the laws."

Interpreting the meaning of the first of these major clauses especially was no easy matter. Its drafters in Congress, led by Representative John Bingham of Ohio, believed that its force lay in the privileges and immunities clause, which nearly repeated, almost word for word, Article IV, Section 2: "the citizens of each state shall be entitled to the Privileges and Immunities of citizens in the several states." Neither Congress nor the Court had ever outlined the meaning of the phrase "privileges and immunities."

Most commentators refer to a passing statement Justice Bushrod Washington, George Washington's nephew, made in 1823 when he sat as a circuit court judge in New Jersey. The case involved a law that prohibited non-residents of New Jersey from collecting oysters in the state. In upholding the law, he outlined what he thought might cover some of a citizen's privileges and immunities, such as general ones like the "protection by the government and the enjoyment of life and liberty" (Box 6.1). Washington's statement was vague, but it was the most comprehensive one ever made about privileges and immunities. Because he was sitting as a circuit judge at the time, however, his comment had no precedential value. In fact, much of what he said had no bearing on the case's outcome anyway, it was mere *obiter dictum*, which meant that his statement expressed an opinion not directly essential to the outcome of the case.

Box 6.1   Justice Bushrod Washington on privileges and immunities, sitting as a trial judge in *Corfield* v. *Coryell* (1823), excerpt

Protection by the government; the enjoyment of life and liberty, with the right to acquire and possess property of every kind, and to pursue and obtain happiness and safety; subject nevertheless to such restraints as the government may justly prescribe for the general good of the whole. The right of a citizen of one state to pass through, or to reside in any other state, for purposes of trade, agriculture, professional pursuits, or otherwise; to claim the benefit of the writ of habeas corpus; to institute and maintain actions of any kind in the courts of the state; to take, hold and dispose of property, either real or personal; and an exemption from higher taxes or impositions than are paid by the other citizens of the state; may be mentioned as some of the particular privileges and immunities of citizens, which are clearly embraced by the general description of privileges deemed to be fundamental: to which may be added, the elective franchise, as regulated and established by the laws or constitution of the state in which it is to be exercised. These, and many others which might be mentioned, are, strictly speaking, privileges and immunities.

Corfield v. *Coryell* 1823 / U.S. Department
of Justice / Public domain

The privileges and immunities clause in Article IV protects US citizens as residents of one state who might travel to another state. The Fourteenth Amendment, on the other hand, prohibits the states from undermining the privileges and immunities of citizens of the United States. Missing is a third possibility: the infringement of the privileges and immunities by a citizen's own state. This possibility developed when the Butchers' Benevolent Association, a group of independent slaughterers, faced a threat from their own state of Louisiana in 1869. The men challenged a state law designed to stop pollution from flowing into the Mississippi River. The state determined that runoff generated by slaughterhouses in and around New Orleans caused the spread of cholera. The law forced the closings of all slaughterhouses in the city and the parishes, except one in New Orleans, the Crescent City Livestock Landing and Slaughterhouse Company. It had an exclusive franchise to operate a slaughterhouse for 25 years.

All butchers now had to discontinue individual slaughtering and haul their livestock to this company. The butchers sued Crescent City, claiming the monopoly violated the Thirteenth Amendment, which outlawed slavery and involuntary servitude, and all three provisions of the Fourteenth Amendment: it abridged their privileges and immunities as citizens of the United States, it seized their property without due process of law, and it denied them the equal protection of the laws.

In the 1873 *Slaughterhouse Cases*, Justice Samuel Miller, writing for a bare majority, held that the law was constitutional. First, with hardly a comment he dismissed the Thirteenth Amendment argument. The butchers were not slaves. The law merely exercised the state's police power to protect the citizens' health and welfare. Second, "privileges and immunities" never guaranteed a person's livelihood as a citizen of the United States. Miller noted that the fundamental privileges of a citizen included the right "to come to the seat of government to assert any claim he may have upon that government, to transact any business he may have with it, to seek its protection, to share its offices, to engage in administering its functions." Miller himself had overturned a Nevada law six years earlier in 1867 in *Crandall* v. *Nevada*, which required the payment of a $1 exit tax when anyone left the state by railroad, carriage, or any other conveyance. The butchers, however, had not traveled outside of Louisiana.

Acknowledging now a third possibility, Miller wrote, "It is a little remarkable, if this clause was intended as a protection to the citizen of a state against the legislative power of *his own state* [italics added], that the words 'citizen of the state' should be left out when it is so carefully used, and used in contradistinction to 'citizens of the United States' in the very sentence which precedes it. It is too clear for argument that the change in phraseology was adopted understandingly and with a purpose." State legislators, under their police power, could pass any law they thought best for their citizens. That was how he dismissed the privileges and immunities clause. With that, Miller summarily determined that the law also did not violate the due process or equal protection clauses. In effect, the decision relegated the privileges and immunities clause to judicial oblivion for over 125 years.

Four justices dissented. Astounded by how Miller undermined the clause, Stephen Field argued that if anything, the clause protected "the right to pursue lawful employment," precisely what the Louisiana law had denied to the butchers in New Orleans. Justice Joseph Bradley complained that the Court's decision narrowly construed the Constitution. While the Court did not have to develop "an authoritative declaration of some of the most important privileges and immunities of citizens of the United States," they were already "in the Constitution itself," in all the rights and liberties laid out in the document.

Women's Rights

If the Fourteenth Amendment offered little promise for white butchers, it also failed to support the efforts of women to achieve equality. Throughout the second half of the nineteenth century and into the twentieth, many states and the Court maintained the second-class role of women. This was true especially considering the rise of the doctrine of domesticity that emerged after 1850. Two years earlier, a group of women's rights activists met in convention at Seneca Falls, New York, to discuss women's equality and their subservient role in society. Led by Elizabeth Cady Stanton, Lucretia Coffin Mott, and Susan B. Anthony, they challenged men to understand that a new age had dawned. In Stanton's words, "there can be no true dignity or independence where there is subordination to the absolute will of another, no happiness without freedom." They also attacked slavery, alcohol abuse among men, and prostitution.

Twenty-five years later, Myra Bradwell applied for a license to practice in Illinois after reading the law in her husband's firm. ("Reading the law" is the way most lawyers in the eighteenth and nineteenth centuries were admitted to the bar. There were few law schools, thus they read the law as apprentices under the mentorship of a practicing attorney and, when he thought they were ready, they were admitted to the bar. Today, four states, California, Vermont, Washington, and Virginia, still permit people to read the law without having a law degree.) A state circuit court judge examined her and found her competent. Illinois, however, denied her application because she was a married woman who had no right to enter into a legal contract. The state supreme court upheld this ruling. The judges argued that "God designed the sexes to occupy different spheres of action." Upholding Illinois's decision in 1873, the same year as *The Slaughterhouse Cases*, eight justices, again led by Justice Miller, argued that the privileges and immunities clause of the Fourteenth Amendment did not include the right of a married woman to practice law.

More revealing than Miller's opinion was Justice Joseph Bradley's now-famous concurrence. Bradley expressed the doctrine of domesticity in the most succinct form. "Man is, or should be, woman's protector and defender. The natural and proper timidity and delicacy which belongs to the female sex evidently unfits it for many of the occupations of civil life … The paramount destiny and mission of woman are to fulfill the noble and benign offices of wife and mother." Women and men are different. Men are aggressive, competitive, and rational. Women are submissive, emotional, and domestic. Her duty is to nurture her husband and children's emotional needs and remain at home to care for the family. Only Chief Justice Salmon Chase dissented but without a written opinion. Bradwell, a women's rights activist in her own right, wrote bills that became law in Illinois giving women control over their earnings and property. She also supported the women's suffrage movement. In 1890, four years before her death, she was finally admitted to the Illinois bar.

Three years later, a decision under Chief Justice Morrison Waite for the first time involved the Fifteenth Amendment's voting rights guarantees. Some women hoped that the amendment enfranchised them, at least in federal elections. Those hopes were dashed when Susan B. Anthony was arrested after she voted in an 1872 federal election. For the next two years, Anthony gave the same speech in every postal district in the county where her trial was to take place: over 40 venues. In "Is It a Crime for a US Citizen to Vote?" she demanded that Congress "pass a law to require the States to protect women in their equal political rights." The court found her guilty, and she was fined $100, which she refused to pay. Three years later, the Supreme Court stepped in when another woman attempted to vote in Missouri. Writing for a unanimous Court, Waite ruled in *Minor* v. *Happersett* that women did not have the right to register and vote, because "the Constitution of the United States does not confer the right of suffrage on anyone."

Persecution of Newly Freed Slaves

In 1876, a case came before the Court regarding the Enforcement Act of 1870 that passed when Radical Republicans still controlled both houses of Congress. They were harshly orchestrating Reconstruction in the South, seeking to protect the newly freed Black slaves from angry white mobs. The law made it a federal crime for two or more people to conspire to deprive people of their civil rights. More pointedly, Congress intended it to stop "night riding," the nighttime attacks on Blacks by the Ku Klux Klan (KKK) and other white supremacist vigilante groups like the Knights of the White Camelia.

In *United States* v. *Reese*, the Court, with Waite writing for a seven to two majority, seriously limited the Enforcement Act. Officials in Lexington, Kentucky, refused to allow a Black man to register to vote. He claimed he could register because he could pay the $1.50 poll tax. The federal government stepped in after Hiram Reese and Mathew Foushee, two election officials, violated the act. A federal circuit court, however, held that the language of the Enforcement Act overstepped the authority of the Voting Rights Amendment. On appeal to the Supreme Court, Waite upheld the circuit court's ruling, practically repeating his words verbatim from *Minor*. The amendment "does not confer the right of suffrage upon any one." It only prevented "the States, or the United States, however, from giving preference ... to one citizen of the United States over another on account of race, color, or previous condition of servitude." While no section of the law stated that it protected prospective voters based on race or color, the law did not conform to the requirements of the Fifteenth Amendment. It therefore only applied to federal, not state and local, elections.

Congress passed two more Enforcement Acts, both in 1871. One provided federal supervision for congressional elections, and the other, also called the KKK Act, prohibited conspiracies against the United States by those in "disguise." The latter also barred any person from depriving another person of the equal protection of the laws under the Fourteenth Amendment. This provision denotes a major shift because it went beyond state action to include private acts. The law empowered the president to send federal troops to any state if he feared an insurrection against the United States. Under the authority of the law, President Grant deployed troops to South Carolina, Louisiana, and Georgia. When challenged 12 years later, the Supreme Court in *United*

States v. *Harris* overturned it. The states were now free to place as many barriers as they wished to block Black voting power: poll taxes, grandfather clauses, literacy tests, character references, and more.

During the same term that the Court decided *Reese*, it also dealt with the dreadful consequences of the Colfax massacre. Many southerners who continued to fume over Radical Republican Reconstruction policies took out their frustration and anger on Black citizens. On Easter Sunday 1873, in Colfax, Louisiana, a militia of white men attacked and killed dozens of Black people. The federal government indicted several white men, including William Cruikshank. The indictment claimed that he and his co-defendants deprived Blacks of several constitutional rights: the First Amendment right to assemble peacefully, the Second Amendment right to possess firearms, and the Fourteenth Amendment right to life and liberty. Found guilty, the men appealed and won a reversal in the Supreme Court. Citing Marshall's opinion in *Barron*, Chief Justice Waite noted for a unanimous bench in *United States* v. *Cruikshank* that the Bill of Rights "was not intended to limit the powers of the State governments in respect to their own citizens, but to operate upon the National government alone." The men went free, thus opening a century of harassment, murder, and mutilation of Blacks throughout the South by the KKK and other groups intent on undermining their newly won freedom.

The slave republic began with a renewed emphasis on the spread of the democratic spirit among ordinary white citizens during Andrew Jackson's presidency. The nation could not escape discussing and then fighting over the one issue that the constitutional convention in 1787 avoided: what to do about slave labor. The Civil War and Reconstruction amounted to the most tumultuous period in American history when the nation literally split apart and went to war over slavery, but also the economic divisions that separated the North from the South. The controversy over the tariff acts displays the financial stakes involved in sectional differences, coupled with arguments over nullification and slavery.

The power of the president significantly swelled largely due to the two outsized personalities of Andrew Jackson and Abraham Lincoln. Neither one feared taking on Congress when necessary or, in the case of Lincoln during the Civil War, seizing authority that was constitutionally questionable but required to save the Union. The Supreme Court ruled on many of their actions. During the Civil War, the Court upheld the president's actions as a matter of national survival. By the end of the war and beginning of Reconstruction, executive power vis-à-vis Congress had grown. It then entered a period of rapid decline as the legislative branch reasserted its primary responsibility to make all laws for the country. The contested 1876 election of the moderate Rutherford B. Hayes only added to the decline of the presidency until the end of the century.

Meantime, women and the newly freed Black slaves were left behind when the courts, including the US Supreme Court, consistently voted against expanding the equal protection clause of the Fourteenth Amendment to protect their rights. For women, the right to vote in elections would have to wait for the Nineteenth Amendment in 1920 and for progress involving African Americans, the civil rights movement of the 1950s and 1960s, a hundred years later.

Part 3
The Free Market Republic, 1877–1937

The slave republic closed with the end of Reconstruction in 1877. For the next 60 years, the United States experienced marked industrial and commercial growth that eventually led to economic collapse and the Great Depression of 1929. After the Civil War, Americans both benefited from and occasionally complained about the rise of the railroads, factory system, and many new corporations in the oil, steel, meat packing, and the textile, iron, and brass industries. When Congress passed economic regulations, the Court often struck them down as violations of substantive due process rights. Exceptions included laws like the Sherman Antitrust Act, enacted at the end of the century, which broke up monopolies in the oil and tobacco industries because they upset free-market forces and engaged in the restraint of trade.

At the beginning of the twentieth century, presidents gradually began to assume new leadership roles in policy development, wresting control from Congress. Theodore Roosevelt, who succeeded to the presidency after the 1901 assassination of William McKinley, viewed presidents as the "stewards" of the people, engaged in bringing world leadership to the United States and in solving social, environmental, and economic problems. Leading the country into World War I in 1917, Woodrow Wilson transformed the nation into a war-making machine and established what some historians have called a "war dictatorship." While the United States was at war and during its aftereffects, the Supreme

American Constitutional History: A Brief Introduction, Second Edition. Jack Fruchtman.
© 2022 John Wiley & Sons, Inc. Published 2022 by John Wiley & Sons, Inc.

Court dealt with groundbreaking First Amendment issues, siding with laws that restricted verbal and written commentary during a national emergency. In the meantime, the states ratified six new constitutional amendments.

Constitutional Amendments

After the 1870 ratification of the Fifteenth Amendment, no further additions to the Constitution took place until 1913 when the states ratified two amendments: the Sixteenth empowered Congress to impose a federal income tax on individuals and corporations while the Seventeenth permitted the people to elect US senators directly rather than indirectly by state legislators.

From the time of Alexander Hamilton's service as the first secretary of the treasury and for years afterward, federal income depended mainly on import duties and excise taxes. During the Civil War, Congress imposed a federal income tax, so it was not a novel idea when Congress attempted to tax Americans in 1894 by adding a federal income tax provision to the Wilson–Gorman Tariff Act. By the mid to late nineteenth century, with the rise of corporations, stocks, bonds, and other forms of income, politicians could readily imagine taxes that went beyond excise and import duties to include taxes on corporate and personal incomes. A year later, in *Pollock* v. *Farmers' Loan & Trust Co.*, the Supreme Court nullified the Income Tax Act, which, the Court ruled, was not uniform among the states, a requirement of Article I, Section 8, that "all duties, imposts, and excises shall be uniform throughout the United States." The Sixteenth Amendment overcame this flaw by clarifying that taxes could be levied "without apportionment among the several States." Its inclusion into the Constitution was groundbreaking. It quickly became the most significant source of federal revenue.

The Seventeenth Amendment moved the election of United States senators from state legislatures to the people. The original Constitution provided for the direct election of members of the House of Representatives, but not senators, because the Senate represented states, not people. Many reformers argued that the indirect election of senators violated the principles of democratic government. They contended that the

Senate had become the refuge of millionaires, corporate lawyers, and party bosses. The House successfully passed a direct election amendment five times between 1893 and 1902, but the Senate either ignored or defeated it. After 29 states established preferential primaries to influence state legislatures in their Senate choices, it became clear that national sentiment favored the change.

Other amendments followed. The national prohibition of the manufacture, sale, and distribution of alcoholic beverages began in 1918 after the states ratified the Eighteenth Amendment. By 1916, 19 states were dry, and within three years all were until 1933 when the Twenty-First Amendment nullified the Eighteenth, ending Prohibition.

In addition, women gained the right to vote in 1920. By 1916, 11 states permitted women to vote in state elections. With the US entry into World War I in 1917, women played even greater roles in industry and professional life with so many men in uniform. Eighteen months after the start of Prohibition, the Nineteenth Amendment extended voting rights to women, reflecting changes in the status of women that had now been ongoing for a hundred years.

Finally, in 1933, the states ratified the Twentieth Amendment, which reset the inauguration of the president to January 20. It also required Congress to meet at least once a year beginning on January 3, and it set forth what must occur should the president and vice president become disabled or otherwise unable to continue in office. It empowered Congress to provide for a president and vice president should their offices become vacant.

Congress made one other important step in judicial reform when the Judiciary Act of 1891 established the intermediate circuit courts of appeal. This legislation effectively ended the requirement that the justices had to "ride circuit" to hear appeals with federal district judges before they reached the Supreme Court. In addition, the act significantly decreased the Court's caseload. From 1874 to 1888, the Court's work increased so much that it heard 3470 appeals. Chief Justice Morrison Waite alone wrote 872 opinions. The new United States Circuit Courts of Appeal were divided into groups of states so that today, for example, the Fourth Circuit consists of Maryland, Virginia, West Virginia, and North and South Carolina. Thirty-four years later, the Judiciary Act of 1925 established discretionary review for the

Court, allowing it to choose which cases it wanted to hear. Instead of mandatory appeals, litigants submitted *certiorari* petitions to the Court to request a hearing. Soon, the justices developed the "rule of four," which means that at least four justices must agree to hear a case before scheduling it for oral argument and review by the full Court.

7

The Development of Substantive Due Process

The United States experienced phenomenal economic growth in the years following the Civil War. By 1900, it was the leading industrial nation in the world, producing more steel and iron than the combined efforts of Britain and Germany. From 1860 to 1900, the railroads grew from 30,000 to 300,000 miles of track while the population grew from 31 million people to 71 million. In 1860, just 16 percent of Americans lived in urban areas but by 1900 this had risen to nearly 40 percent as people began to move from the country to the cities. The number of states increased from 33 in 1860 to 45 by 1900.

Industrialists found sympathetic allies in the Republican Party, which typically supported high tariffs, manufacturing-friendly banking regulations, and subsidies. They believed in the common-law doctrine of vested rights that had been introduced into the Constitution by the Supreme Court in its first four decades. The doctrine held that government ought not to impose arbitrary regulations that infringed on certain fundamental rights like an owner's enjoyment of his private property. When the states and even the federal government began to place controls on the railroads and other industries, many lawyers turned to the due process clause of the Fifth and Fourteenth Amendments to defeat these efforts. For the most part, they were successful.

American Constitutional History: A Brief Introduction, Second Edition. Jack Fruchtman.
© 2022 John Wiley & Sons, Inc. Published 2022 by John Wiley & Sons, Inc.

Procedural Due Process

The phrase "due process of law" evolved over the years. Both the Fifth and Fourteenth Amendments provide for due process: the former binds the federal government as of 1791; the latter the states as of 1868. The basic meaning of due process is rooted in the Magna Carta of 1215 as "the law of the land." The Magna Carta reinforced baronial feudal rights and privileges when King John signed it after the Battle of Runnymede. However, it was decidedly not a statement of fundamental human rights but a major step toward English constitutionalism. For the first time the king officially acknowledged the rights and privileges of others. Due process of law, as it developed in the seventeenth and eighteenth centuries in the Anglo-American legal tradition, was understood as procedural due process, as the Magna Carta mostly specified. American constitutional theory holds that due process forbids the government from depriving any person of life, freedom, or property – and note that the amendments do not specify "citizens" or "free men," only "persons" – unless they first have had access to courts of law and all the essential safeguards that courts offer.

The government may not execute, imprison, or fine defendants, that is, deprive them of life, liberty, or property, until it provides them with certain guarantees, many of which are embodied in the Fourth, Fifth, Sixth, Seventh, and Eighth Amendments:

1. They must not be subjected to unreasonable searches and seizures (Fourth Amendment).
2. Law enforcement officers must have good reasons for the government to issue a warrant in advance of a search (Fourth Amendment).
3. They must have access to legal counsel (Sixth Amendment).
4. They must have a speedy and public trial by jury (for criminal cases, Article III and the Sixth Amendment; for civil cases, the Seventh Amendment).
5. They must not be subjected to double jeopardy in that they will not have to stand trial a second time after a court has acquitted them of a crime (Fifth Amendment).
6. They must be allowed to confront the witnesses against them (Sixth Amendment).
7. They must not be subjected to excessive bails or fines or "cruel and unusual" punishments (Eighth Amendment).

These protections underscore the importance of procedural due process: the government must guarantee to those accused of crimes certain legal remedies, procedures, and protections that are fair, equitable, and just: the principle of innocent until proven guilty. Although they were not originally binding on the state governments, the Supreme Court gradually incorporated most of them into the due process clause of the Fourteenth Amendment and applied them to the states. This is known as the doctrine of incorporation or the nationalization of the Bill of Rights.

Substantive Due Process

As the United States industrialized and developed into a world power, the idea of due process embodying legal procedures expanded in the second half of the nineteenth century. The Supreme Court viewed the denial of due process as a repudiation of certain substantive, not only procedural, rights. This was also embodied in the Magna Carta when it prohibited the government from depriving a man of "his freehold," his property.

Substantive due process, according to many late nineteenth-century justices, protects rights in the economic sphere. As Chief Justice Taney noted in his 1857 *Dred Scott* ruling, he could not allow a slave, Dred Scott, to go free just for passing from a slave state to a free territory: "An act of Congress which deprives a citizen of the United States of his liberty or property, merely because he came himself or brought his property into a particular Territory of the United States, and who had committed no offense against the laws, could hardly be dignified with the name of due process of law." That is, the law deprived Scott's owner of his property (Scott himself) without due process of law. It was, in part, the earlier vested rights principle wrapped in new cloth.

The Court created substantive due process rights to apply most of the rights in the first 10 amendments to the states. This means that every time the Court affirms a right or liberty under the due process clause that is unrelated to procedural due process, it uses substantive due process. The first time the Court applied a provision of the Bill of Rights to the states occurred in 1896 when it applied the Fifth Amendment's prohibition against government seizure of private property for public use without just compensation (the takings clause). *Missouri Pacific Railway Co. v. Nebraska* involved the taking of private property for the benefit of the railroad company. It upheld this position again the very next year in a similar case, *Chicago, Burlington, & Quincy Railroad* v. *Chicago*.

Meantime in line with Taney's thinking about ownership in slaves as a substantive property right, many nineteenth-century industrialists and corporate lawyers adopted the doctrine of laissez-faire or free market economics, which held that government regulation of the economy must be minimal to allow invisible market forces to lead inexorably to the nation's growing prosperity. Inspired by the economic thought of the Scottish eighteenth-century philosopher, Adam Smith, the theory asserts that government regulations depress the production of goods, lead to fewer profits for the owners of industry, and result in less work and income for wage earners. Smith described the free market economy as guided by an "invisible hand." Workers could expect to see their wages rise when the invisible hand of economic prosperity operated freely, as the laws of supply and demand automatically correct themselves. He incorporated this theory in the very title of his well-known 1776 work: the free market economy inevitably produces *The Wealth of Nations*.

Two other intellectual forces were also at work. The British social philosopher Herbert Spencer was developing a concept of societal evolution as Charles Darwin was working on his ideas of natural selection. In 1851, Spencer published *Social Statics* in Britain, and 14 years later it appeared in the United States. Spencer believed that as society developed, and as human beings became more civilized, increased freedom must be available to individuals as long as their freedom did not harm others. In this way, society-like lifeforms inevitably progressed. Meantime, in 1859, Charles Darwin presented his theory of evolution in *On the Origin of Species*. He argued that all creatures developed through a process of natural selection. Those best fitted to the environment or with the capacity to adapt to it survived to produce the next generation. The result was the evolution of a species to a higher lifeform.

Spencer's theories and Darwinian ideas came together at the end of the century in the writings of William Graham Sumner of Yale who argued that government needed to issue few economic rules and regulations for society to prosper. Poverty may occur, but only as a by-product of economic natural selection. The proponents of laissez-faire economics had two heroes in Darwin and Spencer in what became known as Social Darwinism. For industrialists and their supporters in the press and on Wall Street, government must avoid commercial and business regulation as much as possible. For those who supported this idea, a free market operated in the economic sphere in the same way as free government operated in the political: democracy and capitalism went hand in hand.

Congress, however, stepped in many times to regulate the economy in the late nineteenth century. In 1887, the Interstate Commerce Act regulated the railroads by curtailing the monopolistic activities of their owners who colluded on rate fixing. The act did not set specific rates for the shipment of goods and passage of people but required rates to be reasonable and just. One outcome was the creation of the first federal agency, the Interstate Commerce Commission, to oversee and enforce these regulations. Several years later, in 1903, Congress authorized the new Department of Commerce to stimulate economic growth and prosperity. It was the first new department in the federal government since the Department of Justice opened its doors in 1870. Twenty years later, Congress passed the Sherman Antitrust Act to prohibit businesses engaged in interstate commerce from forming monopolies. It also empowered federal authorities to prosecute corporations that formed monopolies or practiced restraint of trade or price fixing. In 1913, Congress created a new central banking system for the first time since President Jackson vetoed the extension of the Second Bank of the United States. The new institution was the Federal Reserve System.

Many members of the Supreme Court disputed whether the federal government or the states had the power to regulate industry. Chief Justice Waite generally accepted the 1787 Constitution's federalism, which in practice meant that states did most of the regulating. His ruling in favor of the Granger movement proponents in 1877, upholding the Illinois law that set maximum rates on grain elevator storage fees, illustrates this position. His successor, Chief Justice Melville Fuller, and Justice Stephen Field opposed most regulations. Both men had previously represented corporate interests and were sympathetic to industry arguments concerning the free market. Field vigorously dissented in the grain storage case, arguing that Waite's ruling was, to use contemporary language, a confiscatory, regulatory taking.

The Court gave additional authority to industry in 1886. Embedded in an otherwise uninteresting tax case, Chief Justice Waite remarked that corporations occupied the status of "legal persons." As such, they enjoyed the full protection of the Fourteenth Amendment's equal protection clause. In *Santa Clara County* v. *Southern Pacific Railroad*, Waite stated before oral argument that "we are all of the opinion" that the equal protection clause of the Fourteenth Amendment "applied to these corporations." John Marshall Harlan's opinion for the Court did not address this issue, but the Court's reporter, John Chandler Bancroft Davis, included the remark in his headnote. From that time, the justices assume that the Constitution includes the legal fiction that corporations and human beings possessed equal economic rights under the Fourteenth Amendment. Some commentators believe that Waite's words were mere dictum, that is, they expressed his view and set no constitutional precedent.

These arguments failed to persuade many progressive observers. They argued that the economy without government regulations would never benefit all social classes and that the wealthy always deployed strategies to maximize profits at the expense of workers. They believed that to ensure higher gains for themselves, rich employers compelled wage earners to endure long working hours with low pay in poor working conditions. By the 1880s, these progressive reformers believed that a free market economy inevitably led to the concentration of wealth and the exploitation of the working poor. They challenged free market doctrine, demanding maximum working hours, minimum wages, and more humane working conditions in the workplace. These advocates comprised the Progressive Movement.

Restraint of Trade in the Free Market Era

American constitutional development in this period reflected the tension between free marketers and progressive reformers. Each group aimed to control the economic growth and prosperity of the nation. Free marketers fought attempts to curb the power and concentration of industry by challenging maximum hour, minimum wage, and child labor laws. They argued, often successfully, that such laws infringed on the individual's constitutional right to engage in a free economy. They maintained the distinction between production and manufacturing of goods on the one hand, and their distribution and transportation on the other.

A Court majority in the waning years of the nineteenth century and first 37 years of the twentieth often agreed with them. In 1895, under the authority of the Sherman Antitrust Act, the United States challenged the merger of the American Sugar Refining Company with E.C. Knight and three other corporations, potentially creating a monopoly that would control over 98 percent of all sugar production in the country. In an opinion by Chief Justice Fuller, the Court held that the act did not apply to E.C. Knight because all of its production occurred in New Jersey and Pennsylvania. Fuller wrote in *United States v. E.C. Knight Co.* that the company's distribution of sugar throughout the nation was irrelevant. Its impact on "trade or commerce might be indirectly affected." His opinion, therefore, distinguished between the "direct" and "indirect" effects that an economic activity had on interstate commerce. If only indirect, Congress had no authority to regulate it. The sugar refining operations in these states bear "no direct relation to commerce between the states or with foreign nations. The object was manifestly private gain in the manufacture of the commodity, not through the control of interstate or foreign commerce." The facts proved only that "trade or commerce might be indirectly affected," which "was not enough to entitle complainants [the United States] to a decree."

Only Justice John Marshall Harlan dissented. He found the distinction between production and distribution nonsense. Echoing and liberally quoting Chief Justice John Marshall's expansive view of Congress's interstate commerce power, as he had laid it out in *Gibbons v. Ogden* in 1824, Harlan wrote that the Sherman Antitrust Act demanded congressional intervention and control over production as well as transportation and distribution. "To the general government has been committed the control of commercial intercourse among the states, to the end that it may be free at all times from any restraints except such as Congress may impose or permit for the benefit of the whole country." The Court did not overturn the Sherman Antitrust Act in this case but ruled only that it did not apply to its narrow definition of "interstate" commerce.

During the tenure of Chief Justice Edward White (1910–1921), the first sitting justice ever to become chief, the Court also heard two cases involving the Sherman Antitrust Act. In *Standard Oil Co. v. United States* (1911), the justices examined the largest oil conglomerate in the nation. Controlled by John D. Rockefeller, the company had gobbled up every small and medium-sized oil concern until it alone controlled the production of oil in the United States. The Supreme Court, in an opinion by Chief Justice White, sustained a federal district court's ruling that the company's size and control of oil production violated the

Sherman Antitrust Act as a restraint on trade. But his opinion was not at all sweeping. White added that the Court would demand the breakup of only those combinations that placed an "unreasonable" restraint on trade. The words "reasonable" or "unreasonable" did not appear anywhere in the act but were based on the common-law standard of reasonableness. He thus significantly amended the law through a judicial opinion. Justice John Marshall Harlan's concurrence noted that the Court amended the statute when only Congress had the responsibility to change it. In any event, because the Court found that Standard Oil's control of all oil production constituted an unreasonable restraint, the justices demanded the company's breakup. The same day, the Court decided that the American Tobacco Company also presented a monopoly in an unreasonable restraint of trade and ordered it too to sell off many of its subsidiaries.

Progressives argued the Court had emasculated the Sherman Antitrust Act while business leaders criticized the opinion insofar as it left them uncertain as what the standard of "reasonableness" meant.

Liberty of Contract

Meantime, many free market industrialists began to claim that laws benefiting workers, like those establishing minimum wages and maximum hours, interfered with the proper relationship between factory owners and their employees. They argued that all working people should be free to determine with business owners the number of hours they worked each day and what they earned for that work (most pay was by the day, not the hour). A person's "labor" was like a commodity that workers sold, and the factory owner bought. In other words, both should freely negotiate employment "contracts" into which wage earners entered with the owners of industry.

The theory of "the liberty of contract" attracted many justices in these years. Many like Fuller and Waite had earlier worked as corporate lawyers. In 1897, the Court unanimously held in an insurance case that the Fourteenth Amendment's due process clause protected a corporation owner's unenumerated right of liberty of contract. Justice Rufus Peckham, who wrote the opinion of the Court in *Allgeyer* v. *Louisiana*, had been a legal advisor and professional confidant to J. Pierpont Morgan, John D. Rockefeller, Cornelius Vanderbilt, and other successful nineteenth-century industrialists. He wrote that "the 'liberty' mentioned in [the Fourteenth] Amendment means not only the right of the citizen to be free from the mere physical restraint of his person, as by incarceration, but the term is deemed to embrace the right of the citizen to be free in the enjoyment of his faculties; to be free to use them in all lawful ways; to live and work where he will; to earn his livelihood or avocation, and for that purpose to enter into all contracts which may be proper, necessary, and essential to his carrying out to a successful conclusion the purposes above mentioned." Peckham literally wrote the right to a liberty of contract into the Constitution. Because the phrase does not appear there in actual words, he in effect "constitutionalized" it.

The key ruling came nine years later in 1905 in *Lochner* v. *New York* in another opinion by Peckham. The case began four years earlier, in the second week of April 1901, concerning Joseph Lochner's bakeshop in Utica, New York. At the end of the Civil War, the standard that many progressive social reformers and fledgling union organizers sought was the eight-hour day. In an unusual twist, Lochner's workers were hired to work by the hour rather than by the day. When Lochner allowed them to stay on the job, some at their request, for more than 10 hours a day that April morning in 1901, he found himself in trouble.

Six years earlier, in 1895, the New York State legislature had passed a law forbidding a bakeshop employer from requiring or permitting any employee from working more than 10 hours a day or 60 hours a week. The law also set forth various sanitation standards. As for the first of these, the part that Lochner violated, the law was in many respects a response to the eight-hour day crusade. Adherents of the Progressive Movement often cited bakeries as among the worst working environments. Unlike the factory system, bakeries were typically small in size and in terms of the number of men who worked in them, usually around four or five, under the supervision of a master or "boss" baker. These bakeries were highly labor intensive. The major piece of equipment was an oven. The rest of the business required storage space for flour and other ingredients, some utensils, and labor to mix, knead, and bake the dough.

In New York City, bakeries were often relegated to damp, smelly basements, which were underground cellars where the sewers of the tenements drained offal and other materials that the tenants disposed of or threw away. Because these often-leaky sewers were unvented, they smelled horribly from the foul odors emanating from the sewer drain. Some drains were simply encased in wood on top of which the bakers placed racks to store baked bread. If ventilation was poor, so was the lighting as the bakeries were underground, some with very low ceilings hardly measuring 6 feet high. The bakers hired to work in these establishments suffered not only under these conditions but also had to deal with flour constantly being inhaled into their lungs.

The cellars were hardly ever cleaned and, even worse, the bakers themselves rarely washed their hands before work. Wasting, or lung, diseases, especially tuberculosis, were common, causing them to have continuous coughing spells, to spit up blood, and to experience fatigue and have a general sense of malaise. It is not clear whether Lochner's small bakery in Upstate New York paralleled these New York City conditions: a photograph taken years later showed an airy, first-floor bakeshop, but there is no record of what his establishment looked like six years earlier. The baking industry, with new inventions and mechanisms, was rapidly changing in these years.

An essential principle underlying the Progressive Movement was that the government must intervene to solve social problems whenever and wherever they appeared. These included regulating the hours of operation and developing standards of cleanliness and sanitation. The Bakeshop Act of 1895 incorporated both provisions. Lochner was found guilty of violating the hours of operation restrictions. He had a choice: pay a $50 fine or go to jail for 50 days.

Lochner appealed his case to the appellate division of the New York Supreme Court. When he lost, he appealed to the New York Court of Appeals, the state's highest tribunal. That court agreed that his conviction was constitutional. He then appealed to the United States Supreme Court. In a five to four decision, he won, and the Court overturned the law.

Historians proclaim this the beginning of the "Lochner era" in American constitutional history. It lasted until 1937. Peckham wrote the majority opinion with spirited dissents by Oliver Wendell Holmes Jr. and John Marshall Harlan (Box 7.1). According to Peckham, the Fourteenth Amendment's due process clause protected private property – Lochner's interest in his business was to be as profitable as possible. The New York "statute necessarily interfered with the right of contract between the employer and employees concerning the number of hours in which the latter may labor in the bakery of the employer." While he appeared to position the owner of the business and his workers as equal partners, in the very next sentence Peckham made clear that he really addressed only the right of the businessman to earn a profit under the liberty component of the Fourteenth Amendment's due process clause. A state may not "deprive any person [now, including corporations] of life, liberty or property, without due process of law." Thus, "the general right to make a contract in relation to his business is part of the liberty of the individual protected by the Fourteenth Amendment of the Federal Constitution."

Box 7.1 *Lochner v. New York* (1905), excerpt

It is manifest to us that the limitation of the hours of labor as provided for in this section of the statute under which the indictment was found, and the plaintiff in error convicted, has no such direct relation to, and no such substantial effect upon, the health of the employee, as to justify us in regarding the section as really a health law. It seems to us that the real object and purpose were simply to regulate the hours of labor between the master and his employees (all being men, sui juris), in a private business, not dangerous in any degree to morals, or in any real and substantial degree to the health of the employees. Under such circumstances the freedom of master and employee to contract with each other in relation to their employment, and in defining the same, cannot be prohibited or interfered with, without violating the Federal Constitution.

Justice Rufus Peckham
Lochner v. *New York* 1905 / U.S. Department
of Justice / Public domain

Peckham's opinion angered Holmes who was certain that Peckham had merely expressed his personal business views. "This case is decided upon an economic theory [laissez-faire economics] which a large part of the country does not entertain." He then quickly added that the Social Darwinian cause of the free market theorists did not extend to constitutional protections. "The Fourteenth Amendment does not enact Mr. Herbert Spencer's Social Statics," he proclaimed, because "a constitution is not supposed to embody a particular economic theory, whether of paternalism and the organic relation of the citizen to the state or of," and here he was explicit, "*laissez faire* … A reasonable man might think [the New York statute] a proper measure on the score of health." In other words, the state's police power, its authority to act on behalf of the safety, health, welfare, and morals of the people, extended to the regulation of a contract between employer and employees. The Tenth Amendment conferred this power on the states, which was precisely what New York attempted to achieve.

Regulating Industry

Progressive leaders in Congress continued the battle to regulate the economy in addition to those in state legislatures. For most of the period between 1905 and 1937, the Court overturned several state and federal laws that intervened in the economy or interfered with a worker and employer to enter into contracts freely with one another. A major exception occurred in 1908 when the Court upheld an Oregon law that limited the working hours for women to 10 hours a day. Curt Muller, the owner of a laundry, who was convicted under the law, appealed to the Supreme Court.

An Oregon organization, the National Consumers League agreed that women were weaker than men and thus supported the state's efforts. A member of the group, Josephine Goldmark, recruited her brother-in-law, Louis D. Brandeis, a Boston lawyer and progressive leader, to argue a test case of the law. Brandeis wanted to show the reasonableness of the law based on factual evidence. Accordingly, in his written brief in *Muller* v. *Oregon*, which Goldmark participated in preparing, he gathered 30 reports that demonstrated the negative impact of long working hours on women. His 113-page argument, now known as a "Brandeis brief," contained only two pages of legal arguments while the rest included sociological data and expert opinion. He successfully used this approach in several other cases involving wage and hour laws. Woodrow Wilson nominated Brandeis to the Supreme Court in 1916.

However, *Muller* was an exception. The same year that Brandeis joined the Court, Congress passed the Federal Child Labor Act, prohibiting the shipment in interstate commerce of goods made by children under the age of 14 or by children between the ages of 14 and 16 who worked more than eight hours a day or six days per week. Roland Dagenhart, the father of two young boys, one under 14 and the other between 14 and 16, challenged the law. He wanted his sons to work in a local North Carolina cotton mill. Justice William Day, who had spent 25 years as a corporate lawyer in Canton, Ohio, agreed with Dagenhart along with four other justices. Congress had unconstitutionally overstepped its commerce power in forbidding the interstate flow of ordinary commodities produced by child labor. It was true that Congress had earlier forbidden the passage through interstate commerce of certain commodities that had a harmful result or possessed an evil character: shipments of lottery tickets, women for purposes of prostitution, and food and drugs that may be tainted or rotten. The Court had upheld these laws. Now, Day wrote, the textiles the Dagenhart boys produced in a cotton mill were not inherently harmful or evil. Their production was therefore purely a matter of state regulation. When Congress passed the Child Labor Act, it invaded "the control of a matter purely local in its character, and over which no authority has been delegated to Congress in conferring the power to regulate commerce among the states."

As he had in *Lochner*, Holmes again angrily dissented. Basing his views on an expansive vision of Congress's power to control interstate commerce and the economy, he argued that its power was "unqualified." "It would not be argued today that the power to regulate does not include the power to prohibit. Regulations mean the prohibition of something, and when interstate commerce is the matter to be regulated, I cannot doubt that the regulation may prohibit any part of such commerce that Congress sees fit to forbid."

The Court continued to overturn commercial regulations for many years. In 1923, the justices, again in a five to four decision, overturned a Washington, DC, law that set a minimum wage for women. Based on *Lochner*, the majority held that the law interfered with employer/employee liberty of contract under the due process clause of the Fifth Amendment. Justice George Sutherland, writing for the Court in *Adkins v. Children's Hospital*, ruled that the law was merely "price-fixing," and a woman has the same capability to negotiate her wages as a man. Dissenting along with Holmes, Chief Justice William Howard Taft (1921–1930) argued that *Muller* controlled this case as a matter of a woman's health and welfare. He claimed *Muller* had overruled *Lochner* without explicitly saying so, or "*sub silentio*," as he put it.

That year, the Court also overturned an industrial labor court in Kansas that settled labor disputes (*Wolf Packing Co. v. Court of Industrial Relations*). The trend of negating state and federal regulatory laws continued into the years of the Great Depression of 1929 and the attempts by Congress and President Franklin D. Roosevelt to stimulate the economy. The core of the majority in *Adkins* remained on the Court in 1936 to strike down several laws, including a New York minimum wage law as an interference with the liberty of contract. Economic rights, as protected by the Supreme Court, generally fell into a secondary position versus individual and civil rights until the late twentieth century.

The Great Depression

With the nation in the midst of economic chaos after 1929, Roosevelt decisively defeated incumbent Herbert Hoover in the 1932 election by 472 to 59 electoral votes, that is, by over 7 million popular votes (57.5 percent). In his inaugural address, Roosevelt promised to get the country moving again with these inspiring words: "the only thing we have to fear is fear itself – nameless, unreasoning, unjustified terror which paralyzes needed efforts to convert retreat into advance. In every dark hour of our national life a leadership of frankness and vigor has met with that understanding and support of the people themselves which is essential to victory. I am convinced that you will again give that support to leadership in these critical days."

FDR announced his plan, the New Deal, promising activist federal programs to put people back to work and to safeguard their savings by regulating the banks and protecting their investments. This meant the creation of programs to employ millions of people, a social security safety network, and the regulation of industry, all by the federal government. In other words, the United States would provide these services and controls. "I am prepared under my constitutional duty to recommend the measures that a stricken nation in the midst of a stricken world may require. These measures, or such other measures as the Congress may build out of its experience and wisdom, I shall seek, within my constitutional authority, to bring to speedy adoption," a view that put him at odds with a bare five-member majority of Supreme Court justices.

Led by what the press at the time called "the four horsemen" – the name alluded to the Four Horsemen of the Apocalypse who forecast the doom of mankind – the Court for the first two years of the New Deal, with few exceptions, overturned congressional program after congressional program often by a bare five, sometimes six-vote majority. This dismayed and angered Roosevelt. The four horsemen were Justices James McReynolds, Pierce Butler, George Sutherland, and Willis Van Devanter. They often attracted the votes of Justice Owen Roberts and/or Chief Justice Charles Evans Hughes (1930–1941), who had previously served as an associate justice from 1910 to 1916. Hughes had resigned to run as the Republican nominee for president against Woodrow Wilson but lost. Five justices thus undermined Roosevelt's recovery program that swiftly moved through the Democratic-controlled Congress. On the Court, the five were opposed by the "Three Musketeers": Louis Brandeis, Benjamin Cardozo, and Harlan Fiske Stone.

The upshot was that between 1935 and 1937 the Court whipsawed many major New Deal laws, including both the National Recovery and the National Recovery Industrial Acts, which created a national planning and public works program; the Bituminous Coal Conservation Act, which regulated employment practices in the coal industry; the Railroad Retirement Act; and the Agriculture Adjustment Act, a farm subsidies measure, and a New York minimum wage law for women. Roosevelt's call for everyone to work together to emerge from the Depression could not withstand the force of an arch-conservative Court majority. The president was not only frustrated, he was furious. Despite his call to refrain from fear, he was frightened that major pieces of the New Deal yet to come could well be endangered. These included the National Labor Relations Act, which created a procedure for collective bargaining between labor and management, the Social Security Act, and the Public Utility Holding Company Act. The standoff between Roosevelt and the Court came to a head in 1937 at a moment that marked the beginning of the social welfare state.

8

Civil Rights After Reconstruction

During the free market republic, the federal government both restricted and extended individual rights, depending on the specific laws in dispute. Ten years after the 1873 *Slaughterhouse Cases*, the Supreme Court overwhelmingly overturned a federal law, the Civil Rights Act of 1875, which required equality in places of public accommodation. It was one of the last acts of the Radical Republicans. Under the act, owners or operators of schools, churches, taverns, hotels, restaurants, cemeteries, and other such establishments could not deny to anyone "the full enjoyment thereof" based on race or religion. If they did, they faced criminal charges in federal court.

Equality and African Americans

In the *Civil Rights Cases*, by an eight to one vote, the Court held that the Thirteenth or Fourteenth Amendment did not focus on private discrimination (Box 8.1). The Thirteenth outlawed slavery and nothing more, while the Fourteenth protected individuals against discrimination involving state, not private, action. The Court made clear that equality under the law never extended to social equality, but only to legal equality. Black and white people could equally enter into contracts, make purchases, and go to court, but the Fourteenth Amendment did not mean that social discrimination and personal prejudice against Blacks were illegal.

American Constitutional History: A Brief Introduction, Second Edition. Jack Fruchtman.
© 2022 John Wiley & Sons, Inc. Published 2022 by John Wiley & Sons, Inc.

Box 8.1 *The Civil Rights Cases* (1883), excerpts:
Justice Joseph Bradley and Justice John Marshall Harlan

Can the act of a mere individual, the owner of the inn, the public conveyance, or place of amusement, refusing the accommodation, be justly regarded as imposing any badge of slavery or servitude upon the applicant, or only as inflicting an ordinary civil injury, properly cognizable by the laws of the state, and presumably subject to redress by those laws until the contrary appears?

After giving to these questions all the consideration which their importance demands, we are forced to the conclusion that such an act of refusal has nothing to do with slavery or involuntary servitude, and that if it is violative of any right of the party, his redress is to be sought under the laws of the state; or, if those laws are adverse to his rights and do not protect him, his remedy will be found in the corrective legislation which congress has adopted, or may adopt, for counteracting the effect of state laws, or state action, prohibited by the fourteenth amendment. It would be running the slavery argument into the ground to make it apply to every act of discrimination which a person may see fit to make as to the guests he will entertain, or as to the people he will take into his coach or cab or car, or admit to his concert or theater, or deal with in other matters of intercourse or business. ...

Mere discriminations on account of race or color were not regarded as badges of slavery.

Justice Joseph Bradley

I am of opinion that such discrimination is a badge of servitude, the imposition of which congress may prevent under its power, through appropriate legislation, to enforce the thirteenth amendment; and consequently, without reference to its enlarged power under the fourteenth amendment, the act of March 1, 1875, is not, in my judgment, repugnant to the constitution.

Justice John Marshall Harlan
The Civil Rights Cases 1883 / U.S. Department
of Justice / Public domain

The Court's decision led to a vigorous, blistering dissent from John Marshall Harlan, a former Kentucky slave owner, but a supporter of the Union during the Civil War and a Lincoln Republican. Social discrimination was by its very nature "a badge of slavery and servitude," he wrote. After Congress successfully protected the legal equality of the newly freedmen, it could of course also protect social equality.

Harlan affirmed that "no state nor the officers of any state, nor any corporation or individual wielding power under state authority for the public benefit or the public convenience can, consistently either with the freedom established by the fundamental law, or with that equality of civil rights which belongs to every citizen, discriminate against freemen or citizens, in their civil rights, because of their race." In other words, all accommodations open to white people must also be accessible to Black people. These were not merely social, but legal, rights.

The Court's invalidation of the Civil Rights Act of 1875 stimulated legislators in many states to pass laws making it legally impermissible for Black people to associate in public with white. These laws, collectively known as Jim Crow laws, required separate accommodations for Black and white persons. This development emphasized the ongoing position the Court took in the *Civil Rights Cases* in distinguishing legal from social equality. In 1880, for example, the Court dealt with whether a Black man indicted for murder in West Virginia could move his case from state to federal court in light of West Virginia's ban on Black people from serving on juries. In *Strauder* v. *West Virginia*, the Court dealt again with legal, not social equality. In an opinion by Justice William Strong for six other justices, the Court ruled that the case could be moved because of the denial of legal rights to Black people: "the very fact that colored people are singled out and expressly denied by statute all right to participate in the administration of the law, as jurors, because of their color, though they are citizens, and may be in other respects fully qualified, is practically a brand upon them, affixed by the law, an assertion of their inferiority, and a stimulant to that race prejudice which is an impediment to securing to individual of that race that equal justice which the law aims to secure to all others." The same year, in *Ex parte Virginia*, the Waite Court held that a state judge could not legally bar Blacks from serving on juries. Legal rights simply did not encompass social rights, including the right to integrate public accommodations like railway cars.

Political leaders in several southern states talked openly about the obvious relationship between segregated railway cars and schools.

Their argument was that if Congress could provide separate schools for Black and white children in Washington, DC, it was legitimate for states to segregate the races whenever and wherever the encounter of white and Black citizens was "objectionable." State leaders thought that under their police power segregated facilities reasonably maintained the peace and safety of the community. Although most of these facilities were not precisely equal in terms of quality, white southern leaders were convinced that equality only meant that the same kind of facilities had to exist for Blacks.

The larger question was whether state could prohibit racial integration or even promote racial discrimination. Florida became the first state to implement such a law in 1888 when it required Black and white people to sit in different railway passenger cars. Several states in the Deep South followed suit, including Louisiana. In that state, several, mainly Creole, citizens joined together after the passage of a law in 1890 requiring the races to be segregated on passenger trains. Creoles, who had been living in the state for generations, were French speakers of mixed blood often called mulattoes. Calling themselves the Citizens' Committee to Test the Constitutionality of the Separate Car Law, they claimed the law violated the Fourteenth Amendment's guarantee of equal protection.

A member of the committee was Homer Plessy, whose last name was probably French in origin. A shoemaker who was one-eighth Black – he had one Black great-grandparent – he lived in an integrated neighborhood in New Orleans. On June 7, 1892, he was arrested for sitting in a first-class railcar reserved for whites only. Plessy was not the first man to challenge the law. A few months earlier, Daniel Desdunes, who was also one-eighth Black, had ridden in a first-class car from New Orleans to an out-of-state destination. In his case, the judge, John Ferguson, ruled that the law did not apply insofar as out-of-state travel fell under federal government's jurisdiction through its interstate commerce power. Plessy's ticket was different. It took him from New Orleans to Covington, both in Louisiana.

While Plessy could easily "pass" for white, that did not matter to the white citizens of Louisiana. Once they learned of people's racial background, the slightest link to a Black heritage damned them. In setting up the case to challenge the law, the citizens' group involved the East Louisiana Railway Company itself. Companies typically did not like Jim Crow laws. They cost money that ate into their profits. The railroad companies had to add another car even if only one Black passenger purchased a ticket for a train. Moreover, if the white cars were full, white passengers could not simply ride with Black passengers as the segregation laws prohibited that too. A white man discovered riding in a car reserved for Blacks faced the same criminal penalties as did Plessy. In any case, the conductor was most likely either waiting for Plessy or, once Plessy announced his racial background, the conductor called the police.

After his arrest, Plessy appeared before John Ferguson, the same judge who presided over the Desdunes case. Before going to trial, Plessy asked the Louisiana Supreme Court to stop the judge from trying him, because the law was unconstitutional based on three constitutional provisions: the prohibition of slavery in the Thirteenth Amendment and the privileges and immunities and equal protection clauses of the Fourteenth. Discrimination, his lawyers argued, was a form of slavery, which the Thirteenth forbade. Plessy claimed the right to ride in whatever car he wished under the privileges and immunities clause. He also contended that denying him that right violated the Thirteenth Amendment's prohibition of slavery. Besides, separate cars violated the equal protection clause on its face. Plessy's chief counsel, Albion Winegar Tourgée, a former Union officer, novelist, and abolitionist who fought against lynching and segregation, argued that while justice was blind, her daughter, the law, ought to be "color-blind." Justice Harlan later used this metaphor in his historic dissent.

When the Louisiana Supreme Court refused to grant the writ, Plessy appealed to the Supreme Court on a writ of error, which the Chief Justice of the Louisiana Supreme Court allowed. *Plessy* v. *Ferguson* (1896) was the first time that a challenged Jim Crow law successfully reached the Supreme Court. Plessy lost in a seven to one decision. Like the doctrine of the liberty of contract, the Court now "constitutionalized" Jim Crow or "separate but equal" laws. The Court literally wrote the separate but equal doctrine into the document. It held that these laws did not contravene the equal protection clause of the Fourteenth Amendment.

Justice Henry Brown wrote the opinion of the Court (one justice did not participate after he failed to hear the oral arguments). Brown came from a wealthy New England family and had graduated from Yale and undertaken legal studies at Yale and Harvard. Like many of his colleagues on the Court, he was a Social Darwinist who aimed to protect property rights under the Fifth and Fourteenth Amendments. It was no surprise that he supported Peckham's majority opinion in *Lochner* with a concurrence. His ruling reinforced the idea that the goal of the Fourteenth Amendment was only designed to protect legal equality.

"It could not have been intended to abolish distinctions based upon color, or to enforce social, as distinguished from political, equality, or a commingling of the two races upon terms unsatisfactory to either. Laws permitting, and even requiring, their separation, in places where they are liable to be brought into contact, do not necessarily imply the inferiority of either race to the other, and have been generally, if not universally, recognized as within the competency of the state legislatures in the exercise of their police power." State legislatures have broad authority under police power to protect the public peace and good order. If they decide that the achievement of this goal required the segregation of the races, so be it. With this decision, the Court successfully restored control of race relations to the states by codifying the principle of separate but equal.

As he had in the *Civil Rights Cases*, only John Marshall Harlan provided a lone, impassioned dissent. He imagined the logical outcome of states forcing the separation of the races in public accommodations: if states may require Blacks to sit separately from whites in railway passenger cars, they could do just about anything, including making them walk on specific sides of the streets. His response was that such a requirement was unreasonable, even absurd. While the white race may be dominant in America, we "have no caste here" and, echoing Tourgée, he went on, "Our constitution is color-blind, and neither knows nor tolerates classes among citizens. In respect of civil rights, all citizens are equal before the Law." Jim Crow laws produce "race hate" because they "proceed on the ground that colored citizens are so inferior and degraded that they cannot be allowed to sit in public coaches occupied by white citizens." They are hostile to both "the spirit and letter" of the Constitution (Box 8.2).

Box 8.2 *Plessy* v. *Ferguson* (1896), excerpts: Justice Henry Brown and Justice John Marshall Harlan

The object of the [Fourteenth] Amendment was undoubtedly to enforce the absolute equality of the two races before the law, but, in the nature of things, it could not have been intended to abolish distinctions based upon color, or to enforce social, as distinguished from political, equality, or a commingling of the two races upon terms unsatisfactory to either. Laws permitting, and even requiring, their separation, in places where they are liable to be brought into contact, do not necessarily imply the inferiority of either race to the other, and have been generally, if not universally, recognized as within the competency of the state legislatures in the exercise of their police power. The most common instance of this is connected with the establishment of separate schools for white and colored children, which have been held to be a valid exercise of the legislative power even by courts of states where the political rights of the colored race have been longest and most earnestly enforced. ...

In this connection, it is also suggested by the learned counsel for the plaintiff in error that the same argument that will justify the state legislature in requiring railways to provide separate accommodations for the two races will also authorize them to require separate cars to be provided for people whose hair is of a certain color, or who are aliens, or who belong to certain nationalities, or to enact laws requiring colored people to walk upon one side of the street, and white people upon the other, or requiring white men's houses to be painted white, and colored men's black, or their vehicles or business signs to be of different colors, upon the theory that one side of the street is as good as the other, or that a house or vehicle of one color is as good as one of another color. The reply to all this is that every exercise of the police power must be reasonable, and extend only to such laws as are enacted in good faith for the promotion of the public good, and not for the annoyance or oppression of a particular class.

Justice Henry Brown

It was said in argument that the statute of Louisiana does not discriminate against either race, but prescribes a rule applicable alike to white and colored citizens. But this argument does not meet the difficulty. Every one knows that the statute in question had its origin in the purpose, not so much to exclude white persons from railroad cars occupied by blacks, as to exclude colored people from coaches occupied by or assigned to white persons. Railroad corporations of Louisiana did not make discrimination among whites in the matter of accommodation for travelers. The thing to accomplish was, under the guise of giving equal accommodation for whites and blacks, to compel the latter to keep to themselves while traveling in railroad passenger coaches.

No one would be so wanting in candor as to assert the contrary. The fundamental objection, therefore, to the statute, is that it interferes with the personal freedom of citizens. "Personal liberty," it has been well said, "consists in the power of locomotion, of changing situation, or removing one's person to whatsoever places one's own inclination may direct, without imprisonment or restraint, unless by due course of law" [citing William Blackstone's *Commentaries*]. If a white man and a black man choose to occupy the same public conveyance on a public highway, it is their right to do so; and no government, proceeding alone on grounds of race, can prevent it without infringing the personal liberty of each.

It is one thing for railroad carriers to furnish, or to be required by law to furnish, equal accommodations for all whom they are under a legal duty to carry. It is quite another thing for government to forbid citizens of the white and black races from traveling in the same public conveyance, and to punish officers of railroad companies for permitting persons of the two races to occupy the same passenger coach. If a state can prescribe, as a rule of civil conduct, that whites and blacks shall not travel as passengers in the same railroad coach, why may it not so regulate the use of the streets of its cities and towns as to compel white citizens to keep on one side of a street, and black citizens to keep on the other? Why may it not, upon like grounds, punish whites and blacks who ride together in street cars or in open vehicles on a public road or street? Why may it not require sheriffs to assign whites to one side of a court room, and blacks to the other? And why may it not also prohibit the commingling of the two races in the galleries of legislatives halls or in public assemblages convened for the consideration of the political questions of the day? Further, if this statute of Louisiana is consistent with the personal liberty of citizens, why may not the state require the separation in railroad coaches of native and naturalized citizens of the United States, or of Protestants and Roman Catholics?

Justice John Marshall Harlan
Plessy v. *Ferguson* 1896 / U.S. Department
of Justice / Public domain

The *Plessy* decision sparked the imagination of many, some of whom organized the National Association of the Advancement of Colored People in 1908, known later by its initials as the NAACP. Its goal was to overrule *Plessy*, especially after it established its Legal and Education Defense Fund. Separate but equal cases made little progress until the 1954 landmark school desegregation decision in *Brown* v. *Board of Education.*

Parents and Educational Rights

Two important cases during the tenure of Chief Justice Taft, the only chief to have previously served as president of the United States, concerned individual rights stemming from laws that undercut parental control of their children's education. A good deal of anti-German sentiment developed in the United States during World War I. Some jurisdictions prohibited the playing of German music, such as compositions by Mozart, Beethoven, and Brahms, and some prohibited German- or Austrian-born musicians, like the violinist Fritz Kreisler, from performing in public.

In 1919, the Nebraska state legislature prohibited the teaching of all foreign languages in schools until children reached eighth grade. The legislature's rationale was that students developed into patriotic Americans only if they learned their subjects in the English language. Police in the small town of Hampton charged, Robert Meyer, a teacher, with reading from the Bible in German to a 10-year-old boy. After his conviction, Meyer appealed to the Supreme Court, which in 1923 overturned his conviction and the law by a vote of seven to two. Writing for the Court in *Meyer* v. *Nebraska*, James McReynolds held that the police powers of the government did not cover the prohibition of teaching a foreign language. The law had nothing to do with health, security, welfare, or morals: "It is well known that proficiency in a foreign language seldom comes to one not instructed at an early age, and experience shows that this is not injurious to the health, morals or understanding of the ordinary child."

Two years later, McReynolds ruled on a case involving the right of parents to decide whether their children should attend a public or private school. In 1922, the Oregon state legislature passed the Compulsory Education Act, requiring students between the ages of 8 and 16 to attend public school. Like *Meyer*, the goal was to ensure youngsters develop into good Americans with a common culture and common values. When a local parochial school corporation, the Society of Sisters of the Holy Names of Jesus and Mary, challenged the law, the Court, in *Pierce* v. *Society of Sisters*, unanimously ruled that it was unconstitutional. McReynolds held that the precedent in *Meyer* opinion was controlling. He made it "entirely plain that the Act of 1922 unreasonably interferes with the liberty of parents and guardians to direct the upbringing and education of children under their control."

These two cases, *Meyer* and *Pierce*, set the stage for the Court throughout the twentieth century to rule broadly on issues of individual rights, such as the right to marry, have children, or not to have children. Just a few days after the Court decided *Pierce*, it began once again to extend various provisions of the Bill of Rights to the states on a case-by-case basis. It had already applied the takings clause of the Fifth Amendment to the states in 1896 and 1897, but now through the process of incorporation, the Court applied more provisions to the states through the due process clause of the Fourteenth Amendment. These are addressed in the next chapter, which focuses on executive power during the free market republic.

The Right to Be Let Alone

Finally, the Court considered an important Fourth Amendment search and seizure case in 1928 in *Olmstead* v. *United States*. During Prohibition, which lasted from 1918 until 1933, federal agents placed a warrantless wiretap on Roy Olmstead's telephone after suspecting him of violating the National Prohibition Act by illegally importing and selling liquor. After prosecutors introduced evidence at his trial from wiretapped conversations, he was convicted and appealed to the US Court of Appeals for the Ninth Circuit, which upheld his conviction. His argument before the Supreme Court stated that the evidence that the agents obtained violated the Fourth Amendment prohibition against unreasonable and warrantless searches and seizures and the Fifth Amendment prohibition of self-incrimination. With a bare five to four majority, Chief Justice Taft held that as the wiretap was outside of Olmstead's home on a telephone pole, federal agents had not trespassed onto his property. A warrant was therefore unnecessary. Because they acted reasonably, the agents did not violate Olmstead's Fourth Amendment rights.

In dissent, Justice Louis D. Brandeis responded that the framers of the Constitution understood that the Fourth Amendment above all protected a person's privacy, "the most comprehensive of rights and the right most valued by civilized men." But his was the minority view: the trespass theory in terms of searches and seizures remained the law for the next four decades until 1967.

9

The Re-emergence of Executive Power

Executive power declined during the Radical Reconstruction era, but enjoyed a re-emergence in the free market republic, especially after the turn of the century. The period began with a powerful Congress dominating the president and ended with a powerful president leading Congress and the American people. At least one nineteenth-century commentator thought that presidents after Abraham Lincoln failed to exercise requisite leadership.

Leadership and the Presidency

In 1885, a young Johns Hopkins University political science graduate student wrote that the political events in the 20 years after the Civil War demonstrated the rise of Congress as the predominant force in American government while the presidency wilted. Its author, Woodrow Wilson, transformed his Hopkins doctoral dissertation into a book, *Congressional Government: A Study in American Politics*, even before he submitted it to his doctoral committee. With its publication, he hoped to stimulate a renewal of presidential power. "Whereas Congress at first overshadowed neither president nor federal judiciary," he wrote, "it now on occasion rules both with easy mastery and with a high hand." Soon, he became a professor of politics at Princeton University and later its president.

American Constitutional History: A Brief Introduction, Second Edition. Jack Fruchtman.
© 2022 John Wiley & Sons, Inc. Published 2022 by John Wiley & Sons, Inc.

Wilson argued "congressional rule" was based on the corrupt standing-committee system in the House, something a strong president could overcome. Congressional committees acted with no accountability to the electorate. If a strong president did not emerge, perhaps a cabinet system founded on the British model was the best alternative. Wilson later revised his assessment in light of how the United States finally assumed world power status after the 1898 Spanish–American War, which was followed by the strong presidency of Theodore Roosevelt. In his 1908 book, *Constitutional Government in the United States*, Wilson expressed delight at the changes that had taken place under Teddy Roosevelt who greatly enhanced presidential power in the years of his presidency, 1901–1909. He thought of himself as a steward of the people, a president who could do anything and everything to protect the public interest if the Constitution or the law did not forbid such action.

Known as a "trust buster," as president, Roosevelt effectively broke up the railroad trust in the Northwest Pacific under the Sherman Antitrust Act. He advocated controls over the food and drug industry and was instrumental in Congress's passage of the Pure Food and Drug Act in 1906. The law prohibited the interstate shipment of food, drugs, medicine, and alcoholic beverages that were "adulterated or misbranded or poisonous or deleterious." Moreover, Roosevelt brought the United States onto the world stage with an aggressive foreign policy. He proclaimed a corollary to the Monroe Doctrine in 1905 that prohibited the establishment of a foreign military base anywhere in the Caribbean. The following year, he won the Nobel Peace Prize for negotiating a truce between Russia and Japan to end the Russo-Japanese War of 1904–1905, often called the first great war of the twentieth century. Roosevelt also created commissions to deal with striking workers, most notably those in the 1902 United Mine Workers strike. Having promised to bring to all Americans what he called a "Square Deal," he helped the miners gain increased pay while working fewer hours. Wilson viewed all of this from his Princeton quarters. Two years later, he won the gubernatorial election in New Jersey, and then, just two years after that, he was ready to take his ideas to the White House as the 28th president of the United States.

America and World War I

America's entry into World War I in 1917 continued the sustained growth of presidential power. The war raised new questions involving the relationship between the president and Congress as well as wartime necessity in relationship to the First Amendment. As an example of the first, Congress passed several laws that delegated its authority to the president. Perhaps under peacetime conditions these laws would never have arisen or, at the very least, the Supreme Court might well have found them unconstitutional delegations of power. The Court, however, never reviewed them. One such law, the Lever Food Control Act, ensured food production and distribution in America. Congress drafted it in such broad terms that it virtually allowed the president to do what he thought was necessary to fulfill its wartime provisions. These included his authority to seize factories and mines and even fix prices. Moreover, the government, for the first time since the Civil War, reinstated the military draft, leaving it to the president to raise an army and navy sufficiently large and well trained to prosecute the war. In addition, the president possessed the authority to seize privately owned ships and other common carriers should, in his judgment alone, military forces need them for the war effort. Although Wilson now possessed more power than most previous presidents, perhaps even Lincoln, he did not personally exercise it. He delegated it to new administrative agencies and bureaus, such as the Office of Food Administration and the War Industries Board.

Most important, for purposes of the government's relationship to the individual, Congress passed the Espionage Act of 1917 and its 1918 amendment, known as the Sedition Act, mostly relating to speech and expression during wartime. They vastly increased the prosecutorial power of the president. The United States experienced an earlier limitation on speech and expression under the common-law principle of seditious libel. That principle prohibited any criticism of the government or any public official, even when the criticism was true. In colonial America, printers, not writers, were most liable for prosecution and imprisonment under the principle. A major turning point came in 1735 with the prosecution of printer John Peter Zenger in New York. Accused of printing materials in his paper that criticized the royal governor, Zenger was prosecuted for seditious libel or, more specifically, for printing "many things tending to raise factions and tumults among the people of this province, inflaming their minds with contempt for his majesty's government." At trial, however, the court for the first time acquitted a person for printing information that was true. But that was in colonial New York and not under the Constitution. Despite the ratification of the First Amendment in 1791, the common law continued to promote prosecutions of licentiousness and seditious libel in the United States.

Although the First Amendment guarantees that "Congress shall make no law … abridging the freedom of speech, or of the press," as previously noted, in 1798 Congress passed the Sedition Act, which made it a crime for "any false, scandalous writing against the government of the United States." The act expired in 1801, but the Supreme Court did not rule that federal prosecutions under the common-law principle of seditious libel were unconstitutional until 1812 (*United States* v. *Hudson*).

One hundred twenty years later, the 1917 Espionage Act became the legal vehicle for prosecutions against speech and press in the twentieth and twenty-first centuries (Box 9.1). The act had its origins in the fear expressed by President Wilson of disloyal Americans as the country drew closer to war. He expressed this fear in a Flag Day speech in 1916 and soon the attorney general crafted the legislation. Wilson's fear of disloyalty stood in stark contrast to the sentiment he had expressed in *Constitutional Government in the United States* when he served as president of Princeton. In that work, he wrote that Americans were so accustomed "to free, outspoken argument for change, to an unrestrained criticism of men and measures carried almost to the point of license, that to us it seems a normal, harmless part of the familiar processes of popular government … Speech is not the only vent opinion needs; it needs also the satisfactions of action." The Espionage Act directly contradicted these views. It enforced criminal sanctions on anyone who made or conveyed "false reports or false statements with the intent to interfere with the operations or success of the military or naval forces of the United States or to promote the success of its enemies." In addition, those charged may face prosecution if they "willfully cause or attempt to cause insubordination, disloyalty, mutiny, or refusal of duty, in the military or naval forces of the United States."

Another provision permitted the government to prohibit the movement through the US Postal Service of certain journals, papers, and other printed material. Some issues of the *New York Times* and the *Saturday Evening Post* suffered confiscation as did *The Masses*, a left-wing journal critical of America's military policies. Finally, the act held that people may be charged if they "willfully obstruct the recruiting or

Box 9.1 The Espionage Act of 1917 and Sedition Act of 1918, excerpts

The Espionage Act of 1917 authorized the prosecution of anyone who, "when the United States is at war, shall willfully make or convey false reports or false statements with intent to interfere with the operation or success of the military or naval forces of the United States or to promote the success of its enemies and whoever when the United States is at war, shall willfully cause or attempt to cause insubordination, disloyalty, mutiny, or refusal of duty, in the military or naval forces of the United States, or shall willfully obstruct the recruiting or enlistment service of the United States, to the injury of the service or of the United States." Punishment consisted of "a fine of not more than $10,000 or imprisonment for not more than twenty years or both."

The 1918 amendment to the act is known as the Sedition Act. It authorized criminal prosecutions of those who were accused of the following:

"To make or convey false reports, or false statements, or say or do anything except by way of bona fide and not disloyal advice to an investor ... with intent to obstruct the sale by the United States of bonds ... or the making of loans by or to the United States, or whoever, when the United States is at war.

"To cause ... or incite ... insubordination, disloyalty, mutiny, or refusal of duty, in the military or naval forces of the United States.

"To utter, print, write, or publish any disloyal, profane, scurrilous, or abusive language about the form of government of the United States, or the Constitution of the United States, or the military or naval forces of the United States, or the flag ... or the uniform of the Army or Navy of the United States, or any language intended to bring the form of government ... or the Constitution ... or the military or naval forces ... or the flag ... of the United States into contempt, scorn, contumely, or disrepute.

"To willfully display the flag of a foreign enemy.

"To urge, incite, or advocate any curtailment of production in this country of any thing or things ... necessary or essential to the prosecution of the war."

Sedition Act of 1918 / U.S. Department of Justice / Public domain enlistment services of the United States, to the injury of the service of the United States."

Events throughout 1917 in Imperial Russia, while an ally of Britain, France, and later the United States, complicated the relationship and upset the allied war effort. In late winter of 1917, due to the impact of the war on an already shaky economy and political system, the Russian Revolution erupted, leading to the fall of the imperial government in March. While Tsar Nicholas II may have taken steps to liberalize the government and economy while personally commanding the war front, he turned domestic affairs over to his reactionary empress and her incompetent and possibly mad advisor, the monk Rasputin. Seven months later, the provisional government collapsed just as it was supposedly drawing up a democratic constitution for Russia. The Bolsheviks (or Communists) under Vladimir Lenin seized power. The Soviet Union was born, and with it the first Red Scare in America and Europe (the second occurred after World War II). Many Americans were astounded by the success of a small group of dedicated Marxists, calling themselves Bolsheviks, who espoused an ideology based on world revolution. They now controlled the largest nation in the world.

A few months later, the new Soviet government signed a separate peace with Germany and Austria–Hungary, releasing German troops to move to the Western Front to fight the allies. For many Americans, especially Wilson and other policymakers, the separate peace was a betrayal of the cause, a stab in the back by communists whom they now thought could never be trusted. Under these conditions, the Espionage Act had an impact when American socialists and communists criticized the government or obstructed military recruitment. Even worse, during the war, revolutionary activity, though sporadic, erupted in America. Americans feared a communist conspiracy was prevalent throughout the nation and would try to overthrow the US government.

In fact, there were instances of violence. One night in June 1919, a bomb exploded outside A. Mitchell Palmer's house, along with those of seven other important officials. Palmer, the new attorney general of the United States, ordered raids on radical groups that led to the arrests and deportations of over 3000 people, most of whom were members of the American Communist Party or the Communist Labor Party. These included Emma Goldman and Alexander ("Sasha") Berkman, two well-known radical leaders. In the aftermath of the Palmer Raids, no one was ever charged or tried for undertaking the bombings on that June night. They did, however, give salience to the

Espionage Act. At the same time, they stimulated the growth of a new organization, the National Civil Liberties Bureau of the American Union against Militarism, which advised World War I draft resisters. The agency was run by the progressive reformer and civil libertarian, Roger Nash Baldwin. In 1920, he changed the name to the American Civil Liberties Union. For over a century, the organization has defended free speech and free press rights and, later, included efforts to desegregate public schools and places of public accommodation like restaurants, bars, hotels, and theaters.

Legally and constitutionally, the Espionage Act raised an ironic question: how could the authorities enforce it in light of the First Amendment? A good deal depended on the "intentions" of the speaker or writer. The old English common-law principle regarding expression was based on "the rule of proximate causation," that is, the relationship between spoken or written words and subsequent illegal actions. The first key case before the Supreme Court involved Charles T. Schenck, the secretary of the Socialist Party of America, who printed, distributed, and mailed to draft-eligible men information that advocated opposition to US involvement in the war. The leaflets argued that the war had nothing to do with working men. It was a war between great capitalist and imperialist powers. Working men were expendable commodities for the men who owned industries, or, in Marxist terms, the owners of the means of production. The benefits of the war would never affect those who worked in the factories or on the farms. The leaflets urged working men to resist the draft.

Schenck was convicted of violating the Espionage Act. On appeal, a unanimous Supreme Court in March 1919, in an opinion by Justice Oliver Wendell Holmes Jr., upheld the act and sustained Schenck's conviction. Holmes had already had a distinguished legal career long before he joined the Court in 1902 when he was 60 years old. Not only had he served on the Massachusetts Supreme Judicial Court, the highest court in that state, but he had an earlier distinguished career as a professor of law at Harvard from where he had graduated in 1861, just as the Civil War broke out. He had joined the Twentieth Massachusetts Volunteer Division as a lieutenant and saw action in the major battles of Ball's Bluff, the Peninsula Campaign, and Antietam. Wounded three times, he nearly died from two of his wounds.

In 1919, writing for the Court in *Schenck* v. *United States*, Holmes dismissed Schenck's argument that claimed conscription was akin to slavery. "Conscription," the leaflet proclaimed, "was despotism in its worst form and a monstrous wrong against humanity in the interest of Wall Street's chosen few." It also asserted that draft-eligible young men had the right and even duty to oppose the draft. Holmes wrote that Schenck would not have printed and distributed the leaflet unless he intended to disrupt the military services and war effort. In other words, Holmes focused on Schenck's intentions, the common-law rule of proximate causation. Circumstances were important, said Holmes, who laid out one of the most memorable images in constitutional history. "The most stringent protection of free speech would not protect a man in falsely shouting fire in a theatre and causing a panic." He now set forth for the first time "the clear and present danger test": a court must decide whether the words used by a defendant were "used in such circumstances and are of such a nature as to create a clear and present danger that they will bring about the substantive evils that Congress has a right to prevent."

However, Holmes confounded clear and present danger by linking it to "bad tendency," an outgrowth of the common-law principle of proximity and degree. Words uttered in peacetime may be constitutionally prohibited during wartime emergencies. So, "the character of every act depends upon the circumstances in which it is done." The law may forbid certain words uttered during wartime when they "are such a hindrance to its effort that their utterance will not be endured so long as men fight." Because the Espionage Age prohibited actual obstruction of the draft and even conspiracies to obstruct, the First Amendment did not protect Schenck and his leaflet. "If the act, (speaking or circulating a paper,) its *tendency* and the *intent* with which it is done are the same, we perceive no ground for saying that success alone warrants making the act a crime" (emphasis added). Thus, Holmes crafted in a single opinion both the clear and present danger and the bad tendency tests and constitutionalized them, as earlier justices had constitutionalized the liberty of contract and separate but equal doctrines. Clear and present danger and bad tendency were vague in terms of application. The image of falsely shouting fire in a crowded theatre hardly helped clarify either one of them.

The Court had no evidence that Schenck's leaflet had fired up anyone at an induction station. Few people even saw it. In any event, during the war the authorities arrested more than 2000 citizens under the Espionage Act, and of these 1055 were convicted. One victim of the Espionage Act was Eugene V. Debs, the Socialist leader and a five-time presidential candidate. In a speech in Canton, Ohio, he declared, "You need to know that you are fit for something better than slavery and cannon fodder." Holmes, again writing for unanimous Court, decided Debs's case one week after *Schenck* and again focused on the speaker's intentions. In *In re Debs*, he said, "If the manifest intent of the more general utterances was to encourage those present to obstruct the recruiting service ... the immunity of the general theme [socialism] may not be enough to protect the speech." The First Amendment failed to protect Debs, and his conviction was upheld. The jury, Holmes determined, had properly found that Debs's words "had as their natural tendency and reasonably probable effect to obstruct the recruiting service," again echoing the common-law principle of proximity and degree. Originally sentenced to 10 years, Debs eventually spent 2.5 years in federal prison. While there, in 1920, he again ran for president and received more than 900,000 votes.

Not all lawyers and judges agreed with Holmes' common-law assessment of speech during wartime. Some jurists argued that Debs said nothing that would have interfered with America's effort to raise an army through the draft. One critical voice was that of Ernst Freund, a University of Chicago law professor who argued in *The New Republic* magazine that "to know what you may do and what you may not do, and how far you may go in criticism, is the first condition of political liberty." Freund detested Holmes' use of the bad tendency test with its muddiness and uncertainty. "Justice Holmes would make us believe that the relation of the speech to obstruction is like that of the shout of Fire! in a crowded theater to the resulting panic," but that was, he argued, "manifestly inappropriate." The problem is that if we cannot accept even the expression of opinions with which we disagree, we will not have free institutions.

Along these same lines, Judge Learned Hand of the United States District Court for New York heard a case two years earlier. The journal, *The Masses*, had sued the government when the US Postal Service refused to allow it through the mail. The government concluded that the journal's articles encouraged America's enemies and hampered the war effort. When the editor, Max Eastman, asked which specific articles led to the postal ban, the government identified four articles and four political cartoons. One article contained a poem about radical writers Emma Goldman and Sasha Berkman while another piece mentioned that they had been arrested for their actions. Others included letters from conscientious objectors and an editorial concerning the importance of individualism in wartime. The political cartoons displayed the evil of war. One made it appear that businessmen were running the war effort, depicting a group of industrialists reviewing war plans while members of Congress looked on, saying, "When do we come in?"

Judge Hand acknowledged that the words and ideas these pieces conveyed were fiery and an incitement, but "if one stops short of urging upon others that it is their duty or their interest to resist the law, it seems to me one should not be held to have attempted to cause its violation. If that be not the test, I can see no escape from the conclusion that under this section every political agitation which can be shown to be apt to create a seditious temper is illegal. I am confident that by such language Congress had no such revolutionary purpose in view." On appeal, the United States Court of Appeals for the Second Circuit reversed Hand's decision and the Supreme Court, with Holmes writing, agreed.

Holmes was clearly unsettled by all the criticism of his opinions in *Schenck* and *Debs*, both of which were decided in March 1919. He spent the summer rethinking his position. He even considered writing a response to Freund's criticism, but decided not to. He read a *Harvard Law Review* article written by Zechariah Chafee Jr., a Harvard law professor, who argued that, in a democracy, more speech was better than less speech, even in wartime. Chafee attacked the Espionage Act, saying that the judges had interpreted it "so broadly as to make practically all opposition to the war criminal." Without free speech, all the other operations of government would suffer, even when a person's speech opposed the government. "The pacifists and Socialists are wrong now," he proclaimed, "but they may be right the next time. The only way to find out whether a war is unjust is to let people say so." At the same time, Judge Hand, the author of *The Masses* decision in federal district court, corresponded with Holmes over the summer about his interpretation of the First Amendment in wartime. By the fall, Holmes had changed his position.

Once the revolution in the Soviet Union degenerated into a brutal civil war, many allies began to intervene, including Japan, Britain, France, and even the United States. The US made two armed incursions into the Soviet Union. First, it was particularly concerned with war materiel in the northern Russian cities of Archangel and Murmansk after the separate peace that the Soviets made with Germany. It did not want the weapons to fall into either German or Soviet hands, so American troops went after them. Second, the US government knew that a contingent of

Czech soldiers, who had fought for Austria–Hungary, were being held prisoner in the Far East but wanted to join the allied war effort. The Americans sent troops to bring them to the West. During these interventions, the allies often fought against the Red Army on the side of its opponents, the White movement. The Soviet coastline was even blockaded for a while.

Many radicals in the United States believed that, with American troops intervening in Russia, the United States intended to bring down the new Soviet government. Jacob Abrams and four of his comrades were among those who protested American military actions. Born in Russia, he and his socialist friends in New York City threw pamphlets out of their windows, attacking the intervention. They also called for a general strike at factories that produced military equipment. Their pamphlets had little if any impact. Still, federal authorities charged them with violating the Sedition Act of 1918, the amendment to the Espionage Act, which made it a crime to "willfully utter, print, write, or publish any disloyal, profane, scurrilous, or abusive language about the form of the Government of the United States" or to "willfully urge, incite, or advocate any curtailment of the production" of materiel "necessary or essential to the prosecution of the war." The wording echoed the Sedition Act of 1798, making it a federal crime to criticize the government's policies or its leaders.

Tried and convicted in federal district court, Abrams and four others were sentenced to 15–20 years imprisonment. When they appealed to the Supreme Court, Justice John Clarke upheld their convictions along with six other justices in November 1919, eight months after *Schenck*. In *Abrams* v. *United States*, Clarke ruled that while their pamphlets addressed local workers about American intervention in Soviet Russia it was really intended to disrupt the war effort against Germany. "Even if their primary purpose and intent was to aid the cause of the Russian Revolution, the plan of action which they adopted necessarily involved, before it could be realized, defeat of the war program of the United States."

In his remarkable turnaround, Holmes, along with Brandeis, now dissented. Holmes argued that the words of the Sedition Act must be viewed "in a strict and accurate sense." This meant that it would be impossible to imply intent in the appellants' words to undermine America's war effort against Germany. "I do not see how anyone can find the intent required by the statute in any of the defendants' words." Consequently, the First Amendment protected the appellants' pamphlets. In what has become one of the most quoted and well-known statements in free speech cases, Holmes proclaimed that "when men have realized that time has upset many fighting faiths, they may come to believe even more than they believe the very foundations of their own conduct that the ultimate good desired is better reached by free trade in ideas – that the best test of truth is the power of the thought to get itself accepted in the competition of the market, and that truth is the only ground upon which their wishes safely can be carried out." All that happened here were "expressions of opinion and exhortations."

Criminal Anarchy and Criminal Syndicalism in the 1920s

Prosecutions of those dissenting from the policies of the United States and favoring the new Soviet model continued throughout the 1920s. Holmes and Brandeis continued to hold an expansive view of the First Amendment but, under most circumstances, they were in the minority. The Red Scare continued throughout the decade and into the next.

In 1925, in a historic dissent, Holmes addressed the conviction of socialist Benjamin Gitlow who had been convicted of violating the New York Criminal Anarchy Act of 1902. Many states had passed such legislation after an anarchist assassinated President William McKinley shortly after his second inauguration. The law prohibited advocacy of "criminal anarchy," the doctrine that "organized governments should be overthrown by force or violence, or by the assassination of the executive head of or any of the executive officials of government, or by any unlawful means." Gitlow published a pamphlet, *Left-Wing Manifesto*, which was narrowly distributed and rarely read. Following standard communist ideology, it promoted the view of inevitable revolution leading to the establishment of a socialist state. No unlawful action followed its publication. He received a sentence of 5–10 years in prison, the maximum allowed under the law. His appeal to the Supreme Court was upheld, again with only Holmes and Brandeis dissenting.

In *Gitlow* v. *New York*, Justice Edward Sanford ruled for the Court that Gitlow's language was not the mere "expression of philosophical abstraction" but encompassed "the language of incitement." The State of New York, under its police power – to maintain order and protect the people's safety – confirmed the validity of the statute. The state could not measure the impact of speech "in the nice balance of a jeweler's scale." Using overwrought language, he wrote that a "single revolutionary spark may kindle a fire that, smoldering for a time, may burst into a sweeping and destructive conflagration." New York's action was neither unreasonable nor arbitrary, two important elements in laws under a state's police power. If speech, "its natural tendency and probable effect," may bring about "the substantive evil which the legislative body might prevent," the state has a right to forbid it, because it presents "a clear and present danger." The Court obviously used language straight from *Schenck*, decided six years earlier.

Holmes, joined by Brandeis, again objected as he had in *Abrams*. He wrote that "that there was no present danger of an attempt to over-throw the government by force on the part of the admittedly small minority who shared the defendant's views." Slightly twisting Sanford's word, "incitement," and using his metaphor of "conflagration," Holmes argued that yes, the manifesto included harsh words, and the Court majority was right to describe them as constituting "an incite-ment." But "every idea is an incitement," wrote Holmes, "Eloquence may set fire to reason." In responding to the majority even more directly, Holmes said that the pamphlets "had no chance of starting a conflagration." Wrongly arrested, convicted, and sentenced, the appel-lants should be released because the law was vague and unconstitu-tional. The indictments rested only on the mere "publication [of the pamphlet] and nothing more."

Sanford's majority opinion included the dictum (a passage in a legal opinion unrelated to the case's outcome) that the speech and press clauses of the First Amendment applied to the states through the lib-erty component of the Fourteenth Amendment's due process clause. Until this time, most commentators assumed, with but one notable exception, that all the provisions of the Bill of Rights applied only against intrusion by the federal government and not the states. As we have seen, in 1896 and 1897, the Court ruled that the Fifth Amendment's takings clause applied to the states through the due process clause: states could not seize land for a public use without just compensation to benefit the expansion of the railroads. In 1925, the Court again raised the idea of "incorporation," that is, whether any of the other provisions of the first eight amendments applied to the states through the Fourteenth Amendment's due process clause. That said, Sanford's dictum was just that (the formal legal term is *obiter dictum*). Its inclusion in the opinion had no direct bearing on the final decision to uphold Gitlow's conviction. Some legal scholars have long contended that, because Gitlow lost his case, the dictum was unrelated to the application of the First Amendment to the states.

A more appropriate case, decided six years later, occurred when public officials forcibly shut down a newspaper when its editor violated a Minnesota anti-defamatory act in *Near v. Minnesota*. Chief Justice Charles Evans Hughes constitutionalized by writing into the Constitution the common-law doctrine that forbids prior restraints of expression. The government could not prosecute publishers, printers, editors, and writers for publishing material prior to its appearance in print. He also made clear that the First Amendment guarantee of freedom of speech and the press applied to Minnesota and the other states of the Union by the doctrine of incorporation.

Left-wing agitation continued throughout the 1920s and into the 1930s. At the same time, the Court continued to deal with the convictions of those found guilty of violating state anti-sedition, anti-anarchy, and anti-communist laws. One of those was Anita Whitney, a niece of Justice Stephen Field, the conservative justice who had served on the Court from 1867 to 1897. Whitney attended a rally in Northern California and was subsequently convicted of violating the 1919 California Criminal Syndicalism law. It prohibited attendance at meetings of organizations that promoted "advocating, teaching or aiding and abetting the commission of crime, sabotage … or unlawful acts of force and violence or unlawful methods of terrorism as a means of accomplishing a change in industrial ownership or control, or effecting any political change." Originally aimed at preventing gatherings of Industrial Workers of the World (IWW, or "Wobblies" as they were known), it was sufficiently broad to include the Communist Labor Party of California, which the state claimed was engaged in criminal syndicalism.

No one disputed whether Whitney, the daughter of a wealthy Oakland lawyer and state senator and a leader in the women's reform movement, was present at one of their meetings in Alameda County in November 1919 during the height of the Red Scare. Her presence automatically associated her with the party's goals. She therefore violated the California law because she was guilty by association. With Sanford again writing, the Court upheld her conviction and sentence of 1–14 years in prison.

Holmes and Brandeis this time joined in a concurrence that Brandeis prepared. Whitney should have argued, he wrote, that her attendance at the meeting was not for criminal syndicalism purposes and that she posed no "clear and present danger" to the state of California. She was an evolutionary socialist who believed that the progress from capitalism to socialism to communism was part of natural economic forces. She attended the meeting to make the point that revolutionary activity was unnecessary to achieve progressive ends. Capitalist countries would achieve socialism through voting, not fighting. However, she declined to make the argument that she posed no clear and present danger. Instead, she focused only on the claim that her attendance was perfectly legal under the First Amendment's right of freedom of assembly.

Brandeis contended that the court had convicted her based only on her guilt by association, and not on anything she did or said. For Brandeis and Holmes, no "clear and present danger of serious evil" existed when the California meeting took place. "She claimed below that the statute as applied to her violated the federal Constitution; but she did not claim that it was void because there was no clear and present danger of serious evil." Testimony at trial demonstrated that there was a conspiracy afoot, which would be "furthered by the activity of the society of which Miss Whitney was a member." On that count alone, her conviction should stand. Still, Brandeis wrote in a remarkable defense of free speech that "even advocacy of violence, however reprehensible morally, is not a justification for denying free speech where the advocacy falls short of incitement and there is nothing to indicate that the advocacy would be immediately acted on."

In arguing that the Court was correct in upholding Whitney's conviction, Brandeis also devoted a portion of his opinion to a discussion of the substantive meaning of liberty under the due process clause of the Fourteenth Amendment. "It is settled that the due process clause of the Fourteenth Amendment applies to matters of substantive law as well as to matters of procedure. Thus, all fundamental rights comprised within the term liberty are protected by the federal Constitution from invasion by the states." The protection of free speech and "the right to teach and the right of assembly" were "fundamental rights" that must not "be denied or abridged." The men "who won our independence believed that the final end of the state was to make men free to develop their faculties, and that in its government the deliberative forces should prevail over the arbitrary. They valued liberty both as an end and as a means. They believed liberty to be the secret of happiness and courage to be the secret of liberty."

Like Holmes, Brandeis believed that more speech was better than less speech if people were to achieve anything close to the truth. "Without free speech and assembly discussion would be futile; that with them, discussion affords ordinarily adequate protection against the dissemination of noxious doctrine; that the greatest menace to freedom is an inert people; that public discussion is a political duty; and that this should be a fundamental principle of the American government." Governor Clement Young pardoned Whitney on June 20, 1927.

Cases like these continued into the 1930s, especially as communist fear among Americans crept across the land. Holmes died in 1932 and Brandeis seven years later so it was left to a later generation of justices to review attacks on individual free expression and to check, whenever possible, the growing authority of the executive branch over matters of sedition and loyalty.

The free market republic began with the rise of industry and railroads and concluded with the Great Depression. It began with an emphasis on individualism, especially for the businessman and industrialist, but that was soon challenged by those who felt deeply about the exploitation of wage earners, the working poor, and those who were silenced by fear and oppression in the workplace. Particularly disadvantaged were first the newly freed slaves, who believed that the Fourteenth Amendment would go a long way to cure many of the racist features of society. *The Civil Rights Cases* and *Plessy* v. *Ferguson* thwarted that hope when it became clear that social equality was different from political and legal equality. Freely entering into contracts was one thing; forcing an owner of a business to open his doors to all people was quite another.

Meantime, the federal government increasingly relied on executive leadership, especially in wartime. Although World War I began in Europe in August 1914, the United States, despite its theoretical neutrality, always assumed an alignment with Britain and France. It was only a matter of time before the United States entered the war, and, when that occurred in April 1917, Congress delegated a great deal of its authority to the president.

Civil liberties and the rights of the individual suffered during the war years and into the period of the New Deal beginning in 1933. After the assassination of President McKinley, many states had anti-leftist legislation on their books and those states without it added anti-criminal syndicalism acts in 1919, in many ways echoing the federal Espionage and Sedition Acts. Limitations on free speech and press and guilt by association became the order of the day during the first Red Scare in American history. Many people, including well-known politicians like Eugene Debs, were convicted and sentenced to long prison terms simply for expressing their beliefs and opinions about public policy issues.

Part 4
The Welfare State Republic, 1937–1995

In contrast to the free market republic, federal spending in the welfare state republic vastly increased. Congress justified its authority to create new social programs under its interstate commerce power. The commerce clause also provided the rationale for congressional civil rights laws that ensured equal employment opportunities, desegregation of public schools, and racial integration of places of public accommodation. As the federal budget grew, so did the national debt. The period also witnessed the expansion of presidential power, especially after the recovery from the Great Depression of 1929 and World War II. Moreover, several regional wars followed, including a long, hard war in Vietnam along with military interventions in Latin America and the Middle East. Most importantly, the United States entered into a long and costly Cold War with the Soviet Union, pitting Communism against the West's liberal democracies. At the end of the period, the Soviet Union collapsed along with the fall of Communism throughout Eastern Europe. The United States became the unchallenged superpower of the world but soon faced threats of international terrorism and economic competition with the rise of new industrial powers like India and China.

The welfare state republic included the advent of new judicial doctrines. Judges typically investigated whether laws reasonably achieved legitimate goals. In the mid-twentieth century, the justices recognized

American Constitutional History: A Brief Introduction, Second Edition. Jack Fruchtman.
© 2022 John Wiley & Sons, Inc. Published 2022 by John Wiley & Sons, Inc.

a new test to deal with cases involving fundamental rights like free speech and equal protection. They called the test "strict scrutiny." In the 1970s, they developed "intermediate" or "heightened" scrutiny when deciding cases of discrimination against women. In addition, toward the end of the twentieth century, a rigorous debate developed over constitutional interpretation. It pitted proponents of an evolving or "living" constitution against advocates of "originalism." The living constitution doctrine demands that judges interpret the document as times change. Its rival, originalism, emerged during the Reagan administration when Attorney General Edwin Meese III in 1985 called for "a jurisprudence of original intentions." He suggested that the constitutionality of a law or executive action should be based only on the original intentions of those who wrote its provisions. Soon, the doctrine's adherents sought to uncover the original understanding or meaning of the Constitution's provisions at the time they were written. The doctrine was not new: Thomas Jefferson argued in 1823 that we must "carry ourselves back to the time when the Constitution was adopted, recollect the spirit manifested in the debates and, instead of trying what meaning may be squeezed out of the text or invented against it, conform to the probable one in which it was passed." And Chief Justice Taney used it in his infamous *Dred Scott* opinion in 1857.

Constitutional Amendments

The states ratified seven constitutional amendments, the most since the ratification of the Bill of Rights in 1791. In 1951, after Franklin Roosevelt's election to an unprecedented fourth presidential term, the Twenty-Second Amendment limited presidents to two terms. After several years of complaints from residents of the District of Columbia, the Twenty-Third Amendment allowed them to vote in presidential elections. Because the District is not a state and has no congressional representatives, Congress decided that the number of Electors would be based on the size of the District's population, which in 2021 stood at 712,000.

Three years later, the Twenty-Fourth Amendment prohibited poll and other taxes as prerequisites to voting in federal elections. Then, following President John F. Kennedy's assassination in 1963, the

Twenty-Fifth Amendment defined presidential succession in the event of the death or disability of a president and vice president. In 1971, Congress, in the Twenty-Sixth Amendment, lowered the voting age to 18 for all federal elections.

Finally, the states ratified the Twenty-Seventh Amendment in 1992. It was among the first 12 submitted to the states by the first Congress. Drafted by James Madison, it lay dormant until a student at the University of Texas, Austin, rediscovered it and fought hard for ratification. It provides that members of Congress may raise their own salaries only if the increase takes effect in the next, not the current, session.

10

Advocates and Enemies of Social Welfare

The most significant aspect of the welfare state republic was the increase in federal intervention in the economy. Beginning with the "first 100 days" of his presidency, Franklin Delano Roosevelt (FDR) submitted several programs to Congress to stimulate the nation's emergence from the Great Depression. Known collectively as the New Deal, these programs included money and banking regulations, laws setting minimum wages and maximum hours, public works, housing development, social security for retirees, conservation of natural resources, and farm subsidies. Many conservatives challenged these programs as an unconstitutional federal interference in the free market. On the Supreme Court, the "four horsemen" – Justices Sutherland, McReynolds, Van Devanter, and Butler – composed the core opposition when these programs were challenged. In 1935, the four horsemen attracted the vote of either Chief Justice Charles Evans Hughes (1930–1941) or Justice Owen Roberts to overturn all or part of six of eight major new programs, such as pension programs, wage and hour laws, and price controls. Left in doubt was the constitutionality of the National Labor Relations or Wagner Act and the Social Security Act.

Roosevelt's re-election in November 1936 outpaced his first performance. He defeated Alfred Landon by an astounding 523 electoral votes to 8. Fearing that the Court would overturn his remaining New Deal programs, 54 days after his second inauguration on January 20, 1937, he announced a plan to increase the number of justices to 15 for

American Constitutional History: A Brief Introduction, Second Edition. Jack Fruchtman.
© 2022 John Wiley & Sons, Inc. Published 2022 by John Wiley & Sons, Inc.

each justice over the age of 70 or with 10 years of service (Box 10.1). He designed his "court packing" plan, a term used only by his critics, to ensure the continuation of his economic recovery programs. Chief Justice Hughes and other justices openly opposed the plan, and Congress never acted on it. Hughes and Roberts, however, reconsidered their positions. On March 29, 1933, Roberts abandoned the four horsemen and voted with Brandeis, Cardozo, Stone, and Hughes to uphold Washington State's minimum wage law for women and minors in *West Coast Hotel Company* v. *Parrish*, overruling the 1923 *Adkins* decision.

Two weeks later, Hughes wrote his historic opinion affirming the constitutionality of the National Labor Relations Act, which created a federal agency to oversee collective bargaining between labor and management. It set forth "cooling-off" periods to forestall unfair labor practices and workers' strikes. The Court, for the moment, returned to John Marshall's 1824 expansive view of interstate commerce that encompassed buying, selling, and transportation of goods as well as their manufacture and production. In *National Labor Relations Board* v. *Jones & Laughlin Steel Corporation*, Hughes ruled that the company was a huge manufacturing outfit subject to the commerce clause, because its products entered into a stream of commerce, and labor strife could well affect the national economy. Congress possessed "the power to control" the company's activities, which had "a substantial relation to interstate commerce." This phrase became the standard for future commerce clause cases. After the company, Jones & Laughlin, declined to recognize the right of its employees to organize, the workers threatened to strike. Hughes ruled that men in the labor force have a constitutional right to organize as a union "to select representatives of their own choosing for collective bargaining or other mutual protection without restraint or coercion by their employer." Only the four horsemen dissented.

Box 10.1   President Franklin Delano Roosevelt, Ninth Fireside Chat, March 9, 1937, excerpts

The Court in addition to the proper use of its judicial functions has improperly set itself up as a third house of the Congress – a super-legislature, as one of the justices has called it – reading into the Constitution words and implications which are not there, and which were never intended to be there.

> We have, therefore, reached the point as a nation where we must take action to save the Constitution from the Court and the Court from itself. We must find a way to take an appeal from the Supreme Court to the Constitution itself. We want a Supreme Court which will do justice under the Constitution and not over it. In our courts we want a government of laws and not of men.

Two months later, in *Steward Machine Company* v. *Davis*, a bare majority upheld the constitutionality of the Social Security Act involving unemployment compensation and old age insurance for retirees. The issue invoked the tax and spending clause power of Congress "to lay and collect taxes" and "to provide … for the General Welfare of the United States." A payroll tax was imposed on employees, which employers collected and turned over to the government to fund the program. Again, the four horsemen dissented. A companion case, *Helvering* v. *Davis*, upheld old age insurance on the same grounds. It enjoyed a lopsided seven to two majority.

The Court Changes

Van Devanter resigned immediately after the Court decided *Steward Machine*, and soon the other three horsemen either retired or died. Within five years, Roosevelt named nine new justices, a number placing him second only to George Washington's eleven. In place of the four horsemen, there were now strong New Deal supporters: Alabama Senator Hugo Black, Solicitor General Stanley Reed, Harvard law professor Felix Frankfurter, and William O. Douglas, who was to serve for a record-setting 36 years, 7 months. In 1940, the Senate confirmed Frank Murphy, Roosevelt's attorney general. Associate Justice Harlan Fiske Stone succeeded Hughes as chief in 1941 and served until his death in 1946. Although a Republican, he was a progressive justice since his appointment in 1925. Robert Jackson, also one of FDR's attorneys general, took Stone's vacated seat. Finally, DC circuit court judge Wiley Rutledge, another pro-Roosevelt Democrat, joined his New Deal colleagues two years later.

In 1941 and 1942, the Court reiterated Congress's power to regulate the national economy. In *United States* v. *Darby Lumber Co.*, the issue was whether the owner of a small lumberyard was subject to the Fair Labor Standards Act (FLSA), a law that established federal minimum wages and maximum hours. Congress set the wage at $0.20 an hour and required employers to maintain wage and hour records. When Fred Darby declined to do either, a federal grand jury indicted him. Writing for a unanimous Court, Chief Justice Stone upheld the indictment and overruled *Hammer* v. *Dagenhart* (1918) and other decisions that prohibited the federal government from interfering in local production and manufacturing.

In a second major decision, the Court reviewed the Agriculture Adjustment Act, which set standards for wheat production. The owner of a small dairy farm in Ohio planted more than twice the number of acres of wheat and harvested more bushels than the Department of Agriculture allotted him. A trial court fined him $117.11, which he refused to pay, claiming he grew the wheat solely for home consumption. In *Wickard* v. *Filburn*, Robert Jackson wrote for a unanimous Court that even if the wheat Roscoe Filburn grew never entered interstate commerce, that fact was "not enough to remove him from the scope of federal regulation." Jackson adopted Hughes's standard from *Jones & Laughlin* that when the activity had "a substantial relation to interstate commerce," Congress could regulate it through its interstate commerce power. In effect, he ruled that Filburn's wheat harvest in the aggregate had a substantial effect on interstate commerce: his wheat may have been reserved for his own household, but his production was covered by the law, because "his contribution, taken together with that of many others similarly situated, is far from trivial."

Wickard was the last landmark commerce clause case the Court dealt with, and its principles guided Congress until Ronald Reagan's presidency in 1981 and William Rehnquist's chief justiceship (1986–2005). Congress and the president continued to intervene in the economy when, for example, President Lyndon B. Johnson proposed his "Great Society" programs designed to reduce poverty and racial injustice. Congress created two new major entitlement programs, Medicare (1964) and Medicaid (1965): medical and health care for the elderly and the poor, respectively. In addition, Congress created several programs to reduce poverty in Johnson's so-called War on Poverty. The great society programs continued to grow under Johnson's successor, Richard M. Nixon, and then Gerald Ford after Nixon resigned in 1974.

Nixon nominated William H. Rehnquist to be an associate justice in 1972, and he joined the Court with Nixon nominees Harry Blackmun (1970) and Lewis Powell (1972). Three years later, when Gerald Ford chose John Paul Stevens to succeed William O. Douglas, Republican justices held a majority on the Court for the first time since Roosevelt's first term. One of Rehnquist's goals was to reduce Congress's expansive interstate commerce power. In 1976, he persuaded four justices to join him to limit Congress's interstate commerce power in *National League of Cities* v. *Usery*. This case focused on the constitutionality of the 1974 amendments to the FLSA that required federal wage and hour standards to apply to state employees. Rehnquist held that the states should decide whether they would set their own minimum wage and maximum hour laws or abide by the federal standard. It marked the first time in four decades that the Court used the Tenth Amendment to overturn a law. Harry Blackmun reluctantly joined Rehnquist's majority with a concurring opinion. Nearly a decade later, however, in *Garcia* v. *San Antonio Metropolitan Transit Authority*, the Court heard a case that raised the same question. In 1985, Blackmun changed his mind and with a bare majority he overruled *National League of Cities*: "We perceive nothing in the overtime and minimum-wage provisions of the FLSA, as applied to SAMTA, that is destructive of state sovereignty or violative of any constitutional provision."

By the 1980s, the nation grew more conservative, launching a major challenge to big government. The Court reflected this change when a conservative majority articulated the ideas of the presidents who nominated them. In 1981, Reagan nominated the first woman to the Court, Sandra Day O'Connor. Five years later after Chief Justice Warren Burger (1969–1986) retired, Rehnquist became only the third associate justice in history to become chief justice. Antonin Scalia, who styled himself as an originalist, took Rehnquist's vacated seat. Two years later, Reagan nominated Anthony Kennedy to succeed Lewis Powell. Like Scalia, Kennedy was conservative but, like Rehnquist, he was no originalist. In 1991, President George H.W. Bush nominated Clarence Thomas to succeed Thurgood Marshall. Thomas, like Scalia, was an originalist (Box 10.2).

Box 10.2　Originalism (Justice Antonin Scalia) vs. The Living Constitution (Justice William Brennan), excerpts

I am one of a small number of judges, small number of anybody – judges, professors, lawyers – who are known as originalists. Our manner of interpreting the Constitution is to begin with the text, and to give that text the meaning that it bore when it was adopted by the people. I'm not a "strict constructionist," despite the introduction. I don't like the term "strict construction." I do not think the Constitution, or any text should be interpreted either strictly or sloppily; it should be interpreted reasonably. Many of my interpretations do not deserve the description "strict." I do believe, however, that you give the text the meaning it had when it was adopted.

> Justice Antonin Scalia, excerpt from an address
> at the Woodrow Wilson Center for Scholars,
> Washington, DC, March 14, 2005

We current justices read the Constitution in the only way that we can: as twentieth-century Americans. We look to the history of the time of framing and the intervening history of interpretation. But the ultimate questions must be what do the words of the text mean in our time? For the genius of the Constitution rests not in any static meaning it might have had in a world that is dead and gone, but in the adaptability of its great principles to cope with current problems and current needs.

> Justice William Brennan, excerpt from
> an address at Georgetown University, 1985

New Social Welfare Programs

Presidents Ronald Reagan, George H.W. Bush, and George W. Bush all promoted conservative causes, and yet it was not a wholesale conservative victory. Social Security, Medicare, and Medicaid continued to grow throughout the period as did the size of the federal budget and government. The first President Bush nominated David Souter in 1990 to succeed William Brennan. Conservatives thought that Souter would join the Rehnquist, O'Connor, and Scalia camp to provide a reliable conservative core. Liberals hoped he would turn out to be a closet progressive. Known as the "stealth candidate," he turned out to be independent. After his election to the presidency in 1992, Bill Clinton nominated two justices in 1993 and 1994, respectively: Ruth Bader Ginsburg, the second woman on the Court, succeeded Byron White; and Stephen Breyer took Harry Blackmun's seat. They became two moderately liberal justices. After 1994, the Court comprised the same group of justices to serve together for 11 years, one of the longest periods in the institution's history.

President Clinton attempted to reform national health care as an added social welfare entitlement along with social security, Medicare, and Medicaid. The effort failed. George W. Bush, who succeeded Clinton in 2001, successfully worked with Congress to implement a prescription drug plan for seniors as part of Medicare. Shortly thereafter, with a conservative majority on the Court, beginning in 1995, the Court made clear that Congress's interstate commerce power was no longer "plenary," "unlimited," and "complete," as Marshall had written in 1824, unless the government could prove that its actions had "a substantial relationship to interstate commerce," the standard set out in 1937 in the *National Labor Relations Board* case. Chief Justice Rehnquist persuaded four justices – O'Connor, Scalia, Kennedy, and Thomas – to join him. David Souter notably voted with the dissenters.

11

The Growth of Civil Liberties

During the welfare state republic, the federal government expanded citizens' rights and liberties. This expansion required the Court to incorporate most of the remaining provisions of the first eight amendments into the due process clause of the Fourteenth Amendment and apply them to the states. These included specific and implied rights of criminal suspects, the separation of church and state, and the right to privacy.

Free Expression

The post World War II era experienced a replay of the Red Scare of the 1920s. Although the Soviet Union was an ally of the United States and Britain during the war, the relationship dissolved into the Cold War, which lasted for 53 years: from the fall of Poland and Czechoslovakia to communism in 1948 until the dissolution of the Soviet Union in 1991. Many members of Congress feared that the threat of communism to American democracy posed the greatest threat to the United States. In 1940, even before America's entry into World War II, Congress passed the Alien Registration or Smith Act, the first peacetime sedition law since the Alien and Sedition Acts of 1798. It made it illegal for anyone to teach or advocate the overthrow of the US government through force or violence.

American Constitutional History: A Brief Introduction, Second Edition. Jack Fruchtman.
© 2022 John Wiley & Sons, Inc. Published 2022 by John Wiley & Sons, Inc.

During his 1948 run for re-election, President Harry Truman, who as vice president became president after FDR's death in 1945, needed to appear strong on communism. Attorney General Tom Clark asked J. Edgar Hoover, director of the Federal Bureau of Investigation (FBI), to round up dozens of New York communists on suspicion of being Soviet spies. Some were engaged in espionage, others were not. Among those arrested were Eugene Dennis and 10 comrades. A federal district court convicted them of violating the Smith Act when they were caught teaching themselves communism, chiefly from four books by Karl Marx, Vladimir Lenin, and Joseph Stalin, and a history of the Soviet Communist Party. Judge Learned Hand, who in 1919 had helped persuade Holmes to change his mind about clear and present danger, rejected their appeal when it reached the United States Court of Appeals for the Second Circuit. Hand upheld their convictions and created a new judicial formula based on Holmes's clear and present danger test. Courts must consider "whether the gravity of the 'evil,' discounted by its improbability, justifies such invasion of free speech as is necessary to avoid the danger." He determined that the gravity of the evil was indeed very great.

When the case reached the Supreme Court in 1950, the justices, voting six to two, adopted the Hand formula. Justice Tom Clark, Truman's former attorney general, recused himself, because he had led the original roundup of the men. In *Dennis* v. *United States*, Chief Justice Fred Vinson (1946–1953), who succeeded Stone, wrote that the appellants had organized themselves into a political party designed to overthrow the government of the United States: "speech of this sort ranks low." Words "cannot mean that before the Government may act, it must wait until the *putsch* [revolt] is about to be executed, the plans have been laid and the signal is awaited." Congress must protect the nation, because the men involved in this case comprised "a conspiracy which creates the danger."

The Court dealt with other communist-oriented speech cases in the 1950s and early 1960s. The justices in *Yates* v. *United States* overturned the convictions of second-tier communists in 1957 but declined to overturn the Smith Act. Joining the Court in 1955, John Marshall Harlan, grandson of the first John Marshall Harlan, abandoned clear and present danger and instead promoted a balancing test. He thought the Court should weigh the restrictions on an individual's speech against the need for a secure society. This view led him to uphold the conviction of Lloyd Barenblatt, a college instructor in Michigan, two years later for advocating communism. The balance of liberty against security favored the government. In 1961, the Court sustained the Internal Security of 1950 or McCarran Act, requiring members of the Communist Party to register their names with the US attorney general. The Court ended most cases involving clear and present danger in *Brandenburg* v. *Ohio* in 1969. Clarence Brandenburg, a member of the Ku Klux Klan, was convicted under the Ohio Syndicalism Act of 1919 for "advocating ... the duty, necessity, or propriety of crime, sabotage, violence, or unlawful methods of terrorism as a means of accomplishing industrial or political reform." In a *per curiam* or unsigned opinion, the Court overturned the law, because "the statute's bald definition of the crime in terms of mere advocacy [was] not distinguished from incitement to imminent lawless action." It was, in short, vague.

The Vietnam War brought several free speech cases involving opponents of the American military effort in Southeast Asia. Many of these involved symbolic speech when an individual expressed a political opinion by undertaking an action without the use of words. The first case focused on the destruction of a Selective Service registration certificate (a draft card) to protest the war effort. Article I, Section 8, of the Constitution grants Congress the power "to raise and support armies" and "to provide and maintain a navy" but does not specify how the government may achieve these ends. One way is by a military draft or conscription, forcing young men into the service of the United States. The Selective Service under the Universal Military Training and Service Act, which became law in 1965, required all young American men at age 18 to register with their local draft boards and to carry their card with them at all times. Moreover, the law forbade them from destroying the card.

In 1966, David Paul O'Brien and others burned their draft cards while standing on the South Boston courthouse steps right in front of FBI agents. Convicted of violating the Selective Service Act, O'Brien claimed that his First Amendment right of free speech trumped the government's requirement that draft-age men carry the card. With Chief Justice Earl Warren (1953–1969) writing for a seven to one majority, the Court ruled that the draft law was generally applicable and not directed at abolishing O'Brien's speech. The chief set out the so-called *O'Brien* test, based on four prongs. First, the government must constitutionally have authority to pass the law in question. Second, the law must further a valid and legitimate governmental purpose. Third, the law must be unrelated to the suppression of speech, and, finally, if there is a restriction on speech, it must only be incidental. Warren found that the Selective Service Act satisfied all of these prongs and upheld O'Brien's conviction.

A year later, another symbolic speech case came to the Court, involving secondary school students, John and Mary Beth Tinker. To show their opposition to the war, they decided to wear black armbands to school. When administrators learned of their plans, they banned armbands with the penalty of suspension for any student who disobeyed. John and Mary Beth wore their armbands to school and were suspended. When their case reached the Court as *Tinker* v. *Des Moines Independent Community School District*, they won by a seven to two vote. Justice Abe Fortas, who wrote the opinion of the Court, famously ruled that "it can hardly be argued that either students or teachers shed their constitutional rights to freedom of speech or expression at the schoolhouse gate."

Gregory Johnson also protested his country's policies, specifically those carried out during Ronald Reagan's first administration. In 1984 in Texas, Johnson burned an American flag outside the Republican National Convention meeting in Dallas. He was convicted for violating a state law that made it crime to desecrate a "venerable" object like the American flag. The Supreme Court overturned his conviction in *Texas* v. *Johnson* in 1989 by a vote of five to four. Justice William Brennan rejected the Texas argument that the flag held special and even hallowed significance: "If there is a bedrock principle underlying the First Amendment, it is that the Government may not prohibit the expression of an idea simply because society finds the idea itself offensive or disagreeable."

During the welfare state republic, for the first time, the Court tried to determine whether the First Amendment protected expressions of pornography and obscenity. The Court ruled that, like fighting words, obscenity and pornography failed to rise to First Amendment protection. Marvin Miller was convicted of violating a California obscenity law when he mailed unsolicited material that included images of men and women engaged in sexual acts. In 1973, ruling five to four, the justices upheld the act and Miller's conviction on the grounds that "obscene material is unprotected by the First Amendment." Chief Justice Warren Burger laid out what became known as the *Miller* test with three prongs. The conduct at issue "must be specifically defined by the applicable state law as written or authoritatively construed. A state offense must also be limited to works which, taken as a whole, appeal to the prurient interest in sex, which portray sexual conduct in a patently offensive way, and which, taken as a whole, do not have serious literary, artistic, political, or scientific value." Many justices, law professors, and commentators hoped that the *Miller* test provided the basis for the Court to decide all future cases involving obscenity and pornography. However, the Court soon ignored it. In the 1990s, Congress attempted to pass laws to stop children from accessing pornography on the Internet or to eliminate web pages that display images of child pornography. These laws faced constitutional challenges, and when they reached the Court, the justices hardly gave lip service to *Miller*.

Free Press

If the Court devoted time to reviewing several questions concerning free speech, it also handled several cases involving a free press. Two major press cases in the era were the *New York Times Company* v. *Sullivan* in 1964, and *New York Times* v. *United States* in 1971.

The first case began after an advertisement appeared in the *New York Times* with inaccuracies involving police misconduct in Montgomery, Alabama, following a civil rights demonstration. Although the ad named no public officials, L.B. Sullivan, a city commissioner, claimed that anyone who read it would have thought he was responsible for the alleged police brutality. As a commissioner, he was specifically charged with overseeing the police department. He sued the *Times* for libel, claiming the ad contained misstatements of the facts, which it did. The trial court awarded Sullivan $500,000 in damages. By the time the case reached the Supreme Court, lower courts had resolved several other libel actions against the *Times* and several other news organizations amounting to approximately $300 million in awards.

The Supreme Court, in an opinion by William Brennan, unanimously overturned the award and held that "a public official" may not recover "damages for a defamatory falsehood relating to his official conduct unless he proves that the statement was made with actual malice – that is, with knowledge that it was false or with reckless disregard of whether it was false or not." In other words, the burden of proof to demonstrate that the information appearing in print was false fell on the plaintiff. He must prove that whoever wrote the statement knew at the time it was false and that it was printed with reckless disregard for the truth.

Seven years later, in 1971, the Court dealt with a national security/free press issue at the height of the Vietnam War. While working for a military-oriented think tank, Daniel Ellsberg leaked to the *New York Times* copies of a 47-volume study, *A History of US Decision-Making Process on Vietnam Policy* later known as the Pentagon Papers. The history revealed that the United States had made several major military and intelligence mistakes in the longest war in its history to date and the government had lied to the American people about many facets of the war. The study supposedly included information classified as "top secret," a designation that means that if enemies of the United States discover the information, the nation may well be placed "in grave danger." The Nixon administration's position was that the publication of the documents violated national security and thus endangered the nation and the war effort in Southeast Asia. As the Court of Appeals for the Second Circuit was enjoining (stopping) the *Times* from publishing, Ellsberg sent copies to the *Washington Post*, which began to print them. As the *Post* continued to publish, the Nixon administration again asked a DC district court to stop the *Post* from printing, which it did. But when the DC Circuit Court of Appeals dismissed the government's suit and allowed the *Post* to continue to publish, the *Times* filed an expedited appeal to the Supreme Court. By that time, the Pentagon Papers had appeared in the *Boston Globe* and in several papers owned by the Knight Ridder chain (today owned by McClatchy) in Miami, Philadelphia, and elsewhere.

The six to three decision came with a *per curiam* opinion with nine signed opinions, ten in all. The majority emphasized that press freedom prohibited prior restraints in light of the 1931 *Near* decision. The government may not constitutionally prohibit a newspaper from publishing a story in advance but could punish it after publication if the material released violated a law. In this way, the government avoided censoring the press. Most commentators agree that Potter Stewart's concurring opinion voiced the Court's essential ruling: perhaps the government was correct about some of the documents endangering national security, but, he wrote, "I cannot say that disclosure of any of them surely result in direct, immediate, irreparable damage to our nation or its people." The government thus failed to carry the burden of proof to persuade the Court that such damage would occur. Later that year, the *Times* won the Pulitzer Prize for publishing the Papers.

Religious Establishments

Constitutional developments also arose concerning religious establishments under the First Amendment. The phrasing of the religion clauses, like many in the Constitution, is vague and inconclusive: "Congress shall make no law respecting an establishment of religion, or prohibiting the free exercise thereof." At the time of the debate over the religion clauses in 1789, no one defined "establishing a religion" or set limits on laws "respecting free exercise." One misunderstood analogy is that establishment demands the separation of church and state because a "wall" must divide them. While the Constitution does not contain that phrase, it was in use from at least the seventeenth century. After Massachusetts officials expelled Roger Williams, whose religious views were far too liberal for his Puritan colleagues, he founded the colony of Rhode Island based on the separation of church and state. He was among the first to use the "wall of separation" metaphor. As president, in 1802 Thomas Jefferson used the wall of separation metaphor in a famous letter to the Danbury Baptist Association in Connecticut. Religion was a private matter between the individual and his God, he observed. The intention underlying the religion clauses was to build "a wall of separation between Church and State."

The Court wrote the phrase into the First Amendment in 1947 in *Everson* v. *Board of Education of Ewing Township* when the justices, voting five to four, constitutionalized the wall of separation metaphor and applied the establishment clause to the states. *Everson* asked whether public officials in a New Jersey town, as a matter of public safety, could provide free school transportation to all children regardless of whether they attended public or private, including parochial, schools. The plan directly reimbursed the parents, not the schools, to ensure that all children arrived safely by bus. Challenged as a violation of the establishment clause because the program included parochial schoolchildren, the Court ruled that the plan was constitutional: the funds subsidized parents, not churches, and the transportation benefited children, known in the law as the child welfare or benefit theory.

Writing for the Court, Hugo Black incorporated the establishment clause and applied it to the states through the Fourteenth Amendment. He then set forth the principle that "neither a state nor the Federal government can set up a church" nor could it levy a "tax in any amount, large or small ... to support any religious activities or institutions." If there were any doubt about his intentions, he cited the letter that

Jefferson wrote in 1802 to the Danbury Baptist Church: "in the words of Jefferson, the clause against establishment of religion by law was intended to erect 'a wall of separation between Church and State'" (Box 11.1). New Jersey's plan subsidized parents' transportation fees for their children. The law was a general child welfare enactment designed to protect children going to and from school. It did not subsidize religious institutions. The wall of separation between church and state embodied in the First Amendment "must be kept high and impregnable. We could not approve the slightest breach. New Jersey has not breached it here."

Several cases related to school-sponsored prayer and Bible readings in public schools followed, beginning in the early 1960s. The lead action, *Engel* v. *Vitale*, in 1962, asked whether a prayer prepared by the New York State Board of Regents for students to recite each day violated the establishment clause. In a six to one decision, with two justices not voting (one was going off the Court, one coming on), the Court invalidated the prayer in an opinion again prepared by Hugo Black. The following year, in a set of cases, the Court ruled that Bible readings and the recitation of the Lord's Prayer in public schools also violated the establishment clause. In 1985, in *Wallace* v. *Jaffree*, the Court reviewed whether an Alabama law requiring a moment of silence rather than state-sponsored prayer in public schools satisfied the requirements of the establishment clause. With a six to three majority, John Paul Stevens ruled that the legislative record demonstrated that the sponsor of the original bill specifically argued that a moment of silence was the first effort to return prayer to the public schools. Moments of silence when designed as a precursor to prayer's return violated the First Amendment. William Rehnquist's dissent maintained that government must "accommodate" religion in the public sphere.

Box 11.1 *Everson* v. *Board of Education of Ewing Township* (1947), excerpts

The "establishment of religion" clause of the First Amendment means at least this: Neither a state nor the Federal Government can set up a church. Neither can pass laws which aid one religion, aid all religions, or prefer one religion over another. Neither can force nor influence a person to go to or to remain away from church against his will or force him to profess a belief or disbelief in any religion. No person can be punished for entertaining or professing religious beliefs or disbeliefs, for church attendance or non-attendance. No tax in any amount, large or small, can be levied to support any religious activities or institutions, whatever they may be called, or whatever from they may adopt to teach or practice religion. Neither a state nor the Federal Government can, openly or secretly, participate in the affairs of any religious organizations or groups and vice versa. In the words of Jefferson, the clause against establishment of religion by law was intended to erect "a wall of separation between Church and State." ... The First Amendment has erected a wall between church and state. That wall must be kept high and impregnable. We could not approve the slightest breach. New Jersey has not breached it here.

Everson v. *Board of Education* 1947 /
U.S. Department of Justice / Public domain

By this time, the Court had developed four main tests to interpret the establishment clause in terms of prayer in public schools: separation of church and state (Hugo Black); government neutrality in regard to religion (John Paul Stevens); prohibition of an endorsement of religion (Sandra Day O'Connor); and accommodation of religion (William Rehnquist). Seven years later, in *Lee* v. *Weisman*, the Court developed a fifth test based on whether coercion was involved. The case involved the constitutionality of a prayer a rabbi recited at the end of a graduation ceremony in a public school. With a bare five to four majority, Anthony Kennedy wrote that the students attending the ceremony were a captive audience because their commencement was so momentous that they would want to attend. Listening to the prayer, no matter how non-denominational it was, forced the students to pay attention to it. "The state-imposed character of an invocation and benediction by clergy selected by the school combine to make the prayer a state-sanctioned religious exercise in which the student was left with no alternative but to submit." Kennedy's test measured the coercion.

Different from prayer cases were those that focused on state financial aid to parochial schools, sometimes referred to by the term, parochiaid.

When the first major case reached the Court in 1971, the justices thought that they could draw a bright line between what was and was not a constitutional violation of public funding of parochial education. Three cases, heard together, raised the issue, with *Lemon* v. *Kurtzman* giving it its name, the *Lemon* test. All involved state funding of a portion of the costs of the secular subjects and teachers' salaries in parochial schools in two states: Rhode Island and Pennsylvania. In a unanimous opinion, Chief Justice Warren Burger drew on precedent to develop a three-pronged test that many justices were confident set forth an interpretive blueprint for future parochiaid cases. The *Lemon* test states that "first, the statute must have a secular legislative purpose; second, its principal or primary effect must be one that neither advances nor inhibits religion; finally, the statute must not foster 'an excessive government entanglement with religion.'" As long as the purpose of a law is to promote secular not religious practices, the financial program was constitutional. Having laid out the *Lemon* test with its three parts, Burger then found that the Pennsylvania and Rhode Island programs violated the establishment clause.

Subsequent cases demonstrated that the Court ignored the *Lemon* test after Burger announced it. The justices chose instead to use more specific gauges to determine whether a religious practice violated the First Amendment. In his dissent in the 1992 *Weisman* decision, Scalia voiced his frustration with the Court's development of made-up tests: entanglement, neutrality, accommodationist, coercion, endorsement. "Our religion-clause jurisprudence has become bedeviled (so to speak) by reliance on formulaic abstractions that are not derived from, but positively conflict with, our long-accepted constitutional traditions." The battle over how to determine where the line lay between church and state has continued into the twenty-first century where it still resists a final resolution.

Criminal Suspects and Capital Punishment

In addition to these developments, the Court focused on individual rights regarding the Fourth, Fifth, Sixth, and Eighth Amendments. The Fourth Amendment relates to searches and seizures: how people have the right to be secure in their homes, papers, offices, and effects from warrantless searches and seizures. The Fifth is an omnibus amendment with several provisions, including the prohibitions against double jeopardy and self-incrimination, the right of suspects to obtain witnesses in their favor, and due process rights. The Sixth, also with many provisions, requires a trial by jury in all criminal cases, the right of suspects to know the charges against them, and to have the assistance of legal counsel.

The welfare state republic continued the Court's path to expand incorporation doctrine. In 1937, the Court heard a case involving the Fifth Amendment's double jeopardy clause, which holds that no person shall "be subject for the same offence to be twice put in jeopardy of life or limb." Tried for first-degree murder, Frank Palko was initially sentenced to life imprisonment. After the prosecution won the right to a second trial, Palko was convicted of first-degree murder and sentenced to death. He appealed. Writing for an eight to one majority, Benjamin Cardozo ruled that some rights were more fundamental to a democratic order than others. Double jeopardy, a right to a trial by jury, and an indictment by a grand jury were not among those essential to a democratic order: "they are not of the very essence of a scheme of ordered liberty." A year later, Frank Palko was executed. Three decades later, the Court overruled *Palko* in *Benton* v. *Maryland* and applied the prohibition of double jeopardy to the states.

Some justices argued that when members of Congress added the due process clause to the Fourteenth Amendment, they intended to incorporate all the provisions and apply them all at once to the states, known as total incorporation. John Marshall Harlan argued this position in an 1884 dissent in *Hurtado* v. *California* when the state failed to provide for an indictment by a grand jury, even in murder cases. He repeated his position 24 years later in a dissent in *Twining* v. *New Jersey*. There, the Court held that the prosecution may comment negatively on a defendant's failure to testify on his own behalf without violating the Fifth Amendment's prohibition against self-incrimination. In 1947, Hugo Black, like Harlan, defended total incorporation in a dissent in *Adamson* v. *California*. Once again, the prosecution commented on a defendant's failure to testify. Black, an originalist or textualist as he preferred to call himself, thought that *Twining* should be reversed: "the original purpose of the Fourteenth Amendment [was] to extend to all the people of the nation the complete protection of the Bill of Rights." Black's dissent so incensed Justice Frankfurter that he recruited one of his former students, Professor Charles Fairman, to answer Black in a *Stanford Law Review* article. Fairman argued that the framers of the amendment never originally thought they were applying all the provisions of the Bill of Rights to the states.

In the 1960s, under Chief Justice Warren, the Court incorporated several criminal suspect rights and applied them to the states. In *Mapp* v. *Ohio* in 1961, the Court applied the exclusionary rule to the states. This judge-made rule excludes evidence from a trial when law enforcement officers violate the Fourth Amendment's protections on searches and seizures. Two years later, the Court guaranteed the Sixth Amendment's right to counsel for all state trials involving a felony, no matter how petty, in *Gideon* v. *Wainwright*. In 1966, the Court in *Miranda* v. *Arizona* required police at the state level to read aloud a suspect's basic rights before interrogating them. And in *Terry* v. *Ohio* in 1968, the Court held that a police officer with 35 years' experience could undertake a warrantless pat down of a suspect who appeared as if he were about to rob a store. Known thereafter as "Terry stops," they involve a police officer's reasonable suspicion that a crime is about to take place, resulting in stopping, questioning, and frisking of suspects. Afterwards, the Court has often allowed police searches based on "reasonable" suspicion.

Meantime, the Court also determined the limits of capital punishment in America. The Eighth Amendment prohibits the government from inflicting "cruel and unusual punishments" on all persons. For originalists like Scalia and Thomas, these words meant that that the government has the authority to impose the death penalty on a defendant found guilty of committing a capital crime. On the other hand, proponents of the living constitution like Arthur Goldberg, William Brennan, and Thurgood Marshall argued that the death penalty was no longer necessary: it denigrated the principles of American democracy and demeaned human integrity. Others opposed the death penalty in light of studies that displayed the high number of error rates in capital trials. One study showed that as many as 60 percent of those found guilty of a capital crime facing execution may not have committed the crime. Because of the rise of "innocence projects" in many states where undergraduate and law students have reopened investigations into these matters, courts exonerated several hundred people serving time on death row.

The contemporary challenge to capital punishment came in 1972 in *Furman* v. *Georgia*. In a five to four split decision, the Court overturned a murder conviction. The justices prepared 10 opinions: one *per curiam*, five concurring, and four dissenting. The *per curiam* opinion merely declared that "the Court holds that the imposition and carrying out of the death penalty ... constitute[s] cruel and unusual punishment in violation of the Eighth and Fourteenth Amendments." Potter Stewart's concurrence set the precedent when he held that when the government implemented the death penalty in an arbitrary manner, it was cruel and unusual. "These death sentences are cruel and unusual in the same way that being struck by lightning is cruel and unusual." The Eighth Amendment "cannot tolerate the infliction of a sentence of death under legal systems that permit this unique penalty to be so wantonly and so freakishly imposed."

After *Furman*, many state officials rewrote their death penalty laws to provide safeguards to overcome the penalty's arbitrary character. By 1975, 37 states reimposed capital punishment. The laws typically included a list of death-eligible crimes; two-part trials with the first part focused on the guilt phase, the second on sentencing; a list of aggravating and mitigating circumstances; and automatic review by the state's highest court. In 1976, the first challenge reached the Court in *Gregg* v. *Georgia*. By a vote of seven to two, the Court reinstated the penalty. The same year, in *Coker* v. *Georgia*, the Court held, by a different seven to two lineup, that a state could not constitutionally impose the death penalty for rape alone.

In 1987, the Court in a five to four decision in *McCleskey* v. *Kemp* rejected the idea that race motivated death penalty convictions. Warren McCleskey, an African American, was sentenced to death for killing a white police officer. Basing his appeal on a study in Georgia undertaken by Columbia University law professor David Baldus, McCleskey argued that prosecutors sought the death penalty 70 percent of the time when a Black man was charged with killing a white man but only 32 percent when a white man killed a white victim. Justice Powell rejected his argument: "For this claim to prevail, McCleskey would have to prove that the Georgia Legislature enacted or maintained the death penalty statute *because of* an anticipated racially discriminatory effect" on African Americans. Four years later, McCleskey raised a second question. He argued that police forced him to make incriminating statements without the assistance of counsel. The Court, by a vote of six to three, rejected this appeal in *McCleskey* v. *Zant*. Justice Kennedy narrowed the road to how prisoners condemned to death may use the writ of habeas corpus to appeal their penalty to a federal court. A prisoner must raise all issues at the same time and not serially over time. Otherwise, he said, they abuse the writ. McCleskey was executed six months later.

By 2021, capital punishment was still legal in 24 states.

Privacy

In 1965, the Court discovered a new unenumerated right in the Constitution: privacy, with far-reaching effects. The words "private," "privacy," or any synonym alluding to it, appear nowhere in the Constitution. The issue was not whether Americans enjoy privacy, but whether the document protects it as a guaranteed right.

In 1890 in an article in the new *Harvard Law Review*, Louis D. Brandeis and his law partner, Samuel D. Warren, two young lawyers, published "The Right to Privacy." There, they argued that liberty included "the right to be let alone ... Of the desirability – indeed of the necessity – of some such protection, there can, it is believed, be no doubt." Twenty-six years later, Brandeis, a nominee of President Wilson, joined the Court, after a distinguished career in the law and legal education. In 1928, he voiced his views about privacy, which had not changed since his 1890 article. In *Olmstead* v. *United States*, Brandeis dissented with a strong defense of the right to privacy using the same words he and Warren had used. Agents of the FBI placed a wiretap on Roy Olmstead's home telephone line to gather information about his illegal activity in violation of the National Prohibition Act. The Court upheld his conviction with the argument that no "trespass" had taken place because the wire was placed on a telephone line outside of Olmstead's house. As no entry had taken place, a search warrant was unnecessary. Brandeis disagreed. While the framers of the Constitution and Bill of Rights had no hint of wiretaps on a telephone, they surely would not have approved of this violation of the Fourth Amendment. "They sought to protect Americans in their beliefs, their thoughts, their emotions and their sensations. They conferred, as against the government, the right to be let alone – the most comprehensive of rights and the right most valued by civilized men."

Four decades later, the Court wrote the right to privacy into the Constitution, in every respect adopting the Brandeis view. In 1965, the Court ruled seven to two that the implied right to privacy lay hidden in the "penumbras" or hints or shadows of the First, Third, Fourth, Fifth, and Ninth Amendments. This right prohibited Connecticut from outlawing the dissemination of information about and the use of con-traceptives. In *Griswold* v. *Connecticut*, Justice William O. Douglas reviewed a Connecticut law that prohibited the dissemination of information about and the use of contraceptives to everyone, including married couples. Although Douglas wrote for the Court, the justices who followed typically ignored Douglas' reliance on so-called penumbras. Instead, the justices adopted John Marshall Harlan's less expansive view, which he outlined in his concurrence: the liberty component of the due process clause of the Fourteenth Amendment embodies a substantive right to be left alone. While the Court in *Griswold* was careful to focus on marital privacy, seven years later, in *Eisenstadt* v. *Baird*, the Court extended the right to single women to use contraception.

Two years after *Griswold*, the Court overruled *Olmstead* by a seven to one vote in *Katz v. United States*. Agents of the FBI placed an electronic listening device, obtained without a warrant, outside of a telephone booth to record conversations between Charles Katz in Los Angeles and his bookies in Boston and Miami. When the prosecutor used the recordings at trial, Katz was convicted of illegal bookmaking. The Supreme Court, in an opinion by Potter Stewart, ruled that the Fourth Amendment protected "people not places." When Katz closed the door of the phone booth, even if a casual observer could see in, he had a right to keep out "the uninvited ear." Stewart thus overturned the trespass theory that the Court set out in *Olmstead*. However, he declined to write into the Constitution a general right to privacy within the bounds of the Fourth Amendment. That task was, once again, left to John Marshall Harlan whose concurrence set the standard that the Court used in future Fourth Amendment cases. Katz, in his attempt to make a telephone call that he did not want anyone to overhear, possessed "a constitutionally protected reasonable expectation of privacy." Two important principles determined the bounds of this expectation. First, Katz had to demonstrate that he had a subjective "expectation of privacy," something he had shown by closing the door. Second, his expectation had to match what society as a whole might recognize as "reasonable." Whenever a privacy issue came before the Court, the justices turned to Harlan. Now it was the "reasonable expectation of privacy" standard, not Stewart's protection of "people not places" test.

The Court expanded privacy rights in the 1970s, especially in the landmark case of *Roe* v. *Wade* in 1973 to determine that the several provisions of the Bill of Rights protected a woman's right to an abortion under certain conditions. Building on Harlan's concurrence in *Griswold*, the Court now addressed whether the liberty component of the Fourteenth Amendment's due process clause was sufficiently expansive to cover abortion rights. With only two dissenters, Harry Blackmun, writing for the Court, overturned the Texas law that prohibited abortion unless it was necessary to save the life of the woman. He determined that under the due process clause, a woman had a limited protected right to an abortion. The state possessed "an important and legitimate interest" in the preservation of fetal life, but the life and health of the mother were also paramount. He declined to be drawn into a debate of when in a pregnancy human life begins. "When those trained in the respective disciplines of medicine, philosophy, and theology are unable to arrive any consensus, the judiciary, at this point in the development of man's knowledge, is not in a position to speculate as to the answer."

Blackmun acknowledged that medical science could determine the "viability" of a fetus: the moment at which it could survive outside of the womb either with or without artificial support, such as oxygen and an incubator. He thus neatly divided pregnancy into three stages. The "trimester" approach meant that as the fetus developed in the womb, the state's interest in its life and survival increased. From his research and as former legal counsel to the Mayo Clinic in Minnesota, Blackmun determined that viability occurred around seven months (or 28 weeks), although he acknowledged it may occur earlier as medical science advanced. He thus used the trimester system to determine the limits of a woman's abortion right.

During the pregnancy's first trimester, approximately the first 13 of 39 weeks of a pregnancy, a woman may choose an abortion in consultation with her physician without government interference. During the second trimester, the pregnancy moved into "a compelling point" when the state may regulate, but not prohibit it: "until the end of the first trimester mortality in abortion may be less than mortality in normal childbirth." At the point of viability, the state's interest in the life and preservation of fetal life takes precedence. In the third trimester, the state may outright ban abortion "unless it is necessary to preserve the life or health of the mother."

Almost two dozen cases involving abortion rights followed, most of which concerned various state restrictions in the second and third trimesters. They also included the government's refusal to grant public funding to poor women who could not afford abortions. The Court heard a major case in 1992, almost 20 years after *Roe*, which concerned several Pennsylvania restrictions. The issue reviewed in *Planned Parenthood of Southeastern Pennsylvania* v. *Casey* included five major restrictions: doctors had to inform a woman about fetal development; a woman had to wait 24 hours after giving her informed consent; a wife had to notify her spouse of her desire to have an abortion; minors had to gain their parents' consent or ask a judge to approve the procedure; and abortion clinics had to abide by certain reporting requirements. Writing for a plurality of three, Sandra Day O'Connor wrote into the Constitution her principle of "undue burden," which she first espoused in a dissent in 1983 in *Akron* v. *Akron Center for Reproductive Health*. The Court would uphold restrictions unless they placed "a substantial obstacle" that created "an undue burden" on a woman seeking an abortion.

O'Connor's opinion, which attracted David Souter and Anthony Kennedy's votes, upheld all the restrictions except for the spousal notification. She made clear that the Court continued to retain "the essential holding" of the *Roe* decision and thus maintained the long tradition of looking to precedent or *stare decisis*. O'Connor also noted, however, that because medical science had advanced since *Roe*, it made no sense to speak of a pregnancy divided into trimesters. A woman retained her right to an abortion before viability. After viability, the state had an interest "in protecting the health of the woman and the life of the fetus that may become a child." Viability at the time the Court decided *Roe* was around 28 weeks, but it had fallen to 24 weeks because of the advances in medical technology. She mused that it may be "even slightly earlier in pregnancy, as it may if fetal respiratory capacity can somehow be enhanced in the future."

12

The Civil Rights Movement

In 1909, the National Association for the Advancement of Colored People (NAACP) was founded to end racial segregation and the lynching of Blacks. Education became its main focus after 1935 when its new legal director, Charles Houston, who had served as dean of the Howard University School of Law, hired his former student, Thurgood Marshall, to litigate segregation cases. In 1940, Marshall became chief counsel of the NAACP. In the early 1950s, the organization persuaded the Supreme Court that segregated graduate and professional schools violated the equal protection clause but did not order integration. Many cases involved nonexistent or unequal facilities in the states for minority students. Schools had to upgrade their facilities or create them if they did not exist. Once Marshall realized that the focus on graduate and professional education was misguided in attacking segregation, he decided to concentrate on elementary and secondary schools.

School Desegregation

The civil rights movement began with the Supreme Court's 1954 ruling in *Brown* v. *Board of Education of Topeka, Kansas* desegregating public schools. Based on the sociological studies undertaken by Harvard researcher Kenneth B. Clark, Chief Justice Earl Warren

American Constitutional History: A Brief Introduction, Second Edition. Jack Fruchtman.
© 2022 John Wiley & Sons, Inc. Published 2022 by John Wiley & Sons, Inc.

concluded that "in the field of public education the doctrine of 'separate but equal' has no place. Separate educational facilities are inherently unequal" and violated the equal protection clause. *De jure* segregation, that is, segregation by law, was now constitutionally prohibited (Box 12.1).

Box 12.1   *Brown* v. *Board of Education of Topeka, Kansas* (1954), excerpt

We conclude that in the field of public education the doctrine of "separate but equal" has no place. Separate educational facilities are inherently unequal. Therefore, we hold that the plaintiffs and others similarly situated for whom the actions have been brought are, by reason of the segregation complained of, deprived of the equal protection of the laws guaranteed by the Fourteenth Amendment. This disposition makes unnecessary any discussion whether such segregation also violates the due process clause of the Fourteenth Amendment.

Brown v. *Board of Education of Topeka* 1954 /
U.S. Department of Justice / Public domain

On the same day, the Court decided *Brown*, it also unanimously overturned a Washington, DC, law that mandated separate public schools for Black and white children. In *Bolling* v. *Sharpe*, the Court could not cite the equal protection clause, because the Fourteenth Amendment addresses only the states. Washington, DC, is a federal city, not a state. Warren created a new constitutional doctrine: reverse incorporation. He ruled that the city violated the due process clause of the Fifth Amendment, which he incorporated into the equal protection clause and applied it to the federal government. No public schools in the United States could now legally segregate their students based on race.

One year later, the Court released a short enforcement decree. In *Brown* v. *Board of Education II*, Warren, again for a unanimous Court, wrote that desegregation efforts in public schools must begin "with all deliberate speed." Not all states complied with the order, and in many locations parents and residents resorted to violence. In 1956, 19 US senators and 77 House members signed the Southern Manifesto, which attacked the justices' "naked judicial power" for their ruling and claimed the decision destroyed "the amicable relations between the white and Negro races."

In 1955–1956, the civil rights movement gained momentum during the bus boycott in Montgomery, Alabama. Protesters denounced segregated seating in the public transit system: white people in the front, Blacks in the back. The Reverend Dr. Martin Luther King Jr. emerged as the iconic leader of the civil rights movement and then its martyr with his assassination in 1968. The boycott was a logical consequence of *Brown*. The *Brown* decision, the bus boycott, and other actions during the civil rights movement caused a violent backlash by those who resisted these efforts. Violence and rioting broke out in Little Rock, Arkansas, when the city began to desegregate the high school. In 1957, to restore peace and order, Governor Orval Faubus called out the National Guard to prevent Black children from entering Central High School. President Dwight D.Eisenhower federalized the Guard and ordered it to accompany minority children safely to school.

The local school board, led by William Cooper, asked a federal judge to delay integration for two and a half years to allow time for the violence to subside. John Aaron, one of the children seeking to attend school, objected. In one of the more unusual moments in Supreme Court history, all nine justices not only joined but signed the opinion in *Cooper* v. *Aaron*, which made clear that Article VI of the Constitution, establishing the supremacy of the Constitution, laws, and treaties of the United States, was only the beginning of federal power. Writing for the nine, Justice William Brennan established the Court's judicial supremacy in matters of constitutional interpretation: "the federal judiciary is supreme in the exposition of the laws of the Constitution," a principle that has gained the respect of "the Country as a permanent and indispensable feature of our constitutional system."

While the Court thus made clear that schools must desegregate, resistance to integration prevailed, mainly in the South where little to no school desegregation occurred. Under the threat of federal court action by the US Department of Justice, some municipalities and counties began to establish racial balancing by transporting students on buses between school districts. Many white parents and residents resented the effort to send their children across towns and cities to achieve integration. In some locations, outright protests led to violence, not only in the South, but also in northern cities like Boston, Massachusetts.

The first challenge to busing occurred in 1971 when a school desegregation plan in Charlotte-Mecklenburg County in North Carolina, approved by a federal court, reached the Court. James Swann and others challenged the busing order. For the first time, the justices ruled that such plans satisfied the equal protection clause and the Court's precedents. The unanimous decision in *Swann* v. *Charlotte-Mecklenburg Board of Education* is particularly noteworthy because the Nixon administration opposed busing to achieve integrated schools. Chief Justice Warren Burger, a Nixon nominee, wrote the opinion of the Court after a flurry of draft opinions and memoranda.

The Court's personnel dramatically changed with the addition of Antonin Scalia in 1986, Anthony Kennedy in 1988, and Clarence Thomas in 1990. By 1992, in *Freeman* v. *Pitts*, the Court unanimously called a halt to court orders mandating integration. Kennedy decried "heroic measures" to force schools to integrate, especially because no constitutional violation occurred when segregated schools resulted from where people chose to live (*de facto* segregation) rather than from law or government action (*de jure* segregation). Three years later, in 1995, *Missouri* v. *Jenkins* signaled the end of integration enforcement by federal courts when the Court ruled five to four that the schools in Kansas City were segregated due to choices individuals made about their place of residence.

Civil and Voting Rights

Meantime, after the assassination of President John F. Kennedy on November 22, 1963, his successor, President Lyndon B. Johnson, determined to guarantee equal access to public accommodations and voting rights. In 1964 and 1965, respectively, Congress passed two major laws, the Civil Rights Act, which stimulated the longest debate to date in congressional history, and the Voting Rights Act. Title II of the Civil Rights Act of 1964 also banned discrimination in employment. Congress claimed it possessed the authority to do so under its commerce power.

Two southern business owners challenged the act by suing Nicholas Katzenbach, the US attorney general, in two cases: *Heart of Atlanta Motel* v. *United States* and *Katzenbach* v. *McClung*. In the first, Moreton Rolleston Jr., the owner of the motel, declined to allow African Americans to rent rooms. In the second, James "Ollie" McClung refused to serve Blacks in his restaurant. Rolleston advertised in national magazines and Ollie's Barbeque offered to serve interstate white travelers. Writing for a unanimous Court, Justice Tom Clark ruled that the law was "carefully limited to enterprises having a direct and substantial relation to the interstate flow of goods and people." Places of public accommodation could no longer pick and choose which interstate guests it allowed into their establishments without government intervention.

The following year, Congress passed the Voting Rights Act under its Fifteenth Amendment authority, barring racial discrimination in voting by the imposition of various tests or devices, such as "good character" tests, literacy tests, property qualifications, and other means. It also permitted the Department of Justice to identify which states (mainly in the South), municipalities, and counties had low voter registration and turnout. South Carolina challenged the law on two grounds: an interference with the state's right to control elections under the Tenth Amendment and a violation of the equal treatment of the states. By a vote of eight to one in *South Carolina* v. *Katzenbach* the Court upheld the act. Chief Justice Warren ruled that Fifteenth Amendment authorized Congress to have "full remedial powers" to prevent racial discrimination in voting "by appropriate legislation." The act was therefore "a legitimate response" to the "insidious and pervasive" barriers that some states had erected to deny African Americans from registering and voting.

During this same period, the issue of apportioning or dividing state legislative and congressional districts came before the Court. In 1962, the Court voted six to two to rule that the judiciary possessed the authority to determine whether states divided their legislative districts into unequal sizes by population. Writing for the Court in *Baker* v. *Carr*, Justice William Brennan held that based on the equal protection clause of the Fourteenth Amendment, courts could intervene when states failed to reapportion their districts after the census was taken every 10 years. Tennessee had failed to do so for over 60 years and the result was that rural districts smaller in population had more representatives in the legislature than urban areas. For Brennan, this situation did not pose a political question that only the executive and legislative branches could handle; his decision overruled one from 1946, *Colegrove* v. *Green*, in which Justice Felix Frankfurter stated that it was a political question. Now, some 16 years later, Frankfurter was incensed in his dissent. Brennan's decision, he wrote, revealed "a sorry confession of judicial impotence in place of a frank acknowledgement that there is not under our Constitution a judicial remedy for every political mischief, for every undesirable exercise of legislative power. The Framers carefully and with deliberate forethought refused so to enthrone the judiciary. Appeal must be to an informed, civically militant electorate."

Three years later, in *Reynolds* v. *Sims*, the Court established the principle of "one person, one vote" (originally one man, one vote). Chief Justice Earl Warren declared for seven other justices that districts "based on population ... as nearly as practicable." He noted that it was "a practicable impossibility to arrange legislative districts so that each one has an identical number of residents, or citizens, or voters. Mathematical exactness or precision is hardly a workable constitutional requirement." His opinion left open an essential question: did the Court mean equal in population or in the number of eligible voters? In its 2015–2016 term, the Court answered that question in *Evenwel* v. *Abbott*: population.

Strict Scrutiny and Affirmative Action in Higher Education

A new phenomenon, affirmative action, emerged in the 1960s. Initially aimed at increasing opportunities for racial and ethnic minorities in education, public contracts, and employment, affirmative action later encompassed discrimination against women. Presidents John F. Kennedy and Lyndon B. Johnson issued executive orders stating that the federal government promoted affirmative action programs to overcome the effects of past discrimination and to increase diversity, especially in higher education and the workplace.

In 1978, the Court made its first major affirmative action decision in *Regents of the University of California* v. *Bakke*. The case involved the medical school admissions policy at the University of California, Davis. Officials set aside 16 of 100 places in its special admissions program for disadvantaged minority students whose grades or medical school board scores were lower than the required minimum. The school denied admission to Allen Bakke, a white applicant, both times he applied. Bakke claimed that the special admissions program excluded him because of his race in violation of the equal protection clause, a provision of the California Constitution, and Title VI of the Civil Rights Act of 1964, which provided that no person shall on the ground of race or color be excluded from participating in any program receiving federal funds. In a decision that mustered a staggering split vote of one to four to four, Lewis Powell held that the strict scrutiny test must be used when the Court evaluated the constitutionality of affirmative action programs.

The Court adopted the judge-made strict scrutiny test to deal with issues involving fundamental rights and equal protection. The test has its roots in a footnote that Justice Harlan Fiske Stone added to *United States v. Carolene Products* in 1938. Stone wrote that when the justices dealt with economic regulations they should use the rational basis test. When the issue focused on fundamental rights like free speech and equal protection, however, they should impose a more rigorous judicial scrutiny.

The distinction between the rational basis and strict scrutiny involves the level of inquiry the Court makes in ruling on a case (Box 12.2). It also asks which party bears the burden of proof. Throughout most of its history, the Court used the rational basis test in its cases, especially those involving the economy. Here, the burden of proof fell on the plaintiffs, namely the party challenging a law or action. Plaintiffs must persuade the Court that the government had no legitimate interest in enacting the law and that a reasonable person would agree with that conclusion. The outcome usually resulted in the Court upholding the challenged law or action because it was reasonable.

On the other hand, the strict scrutiny test arose when plaintiffs challenged a law infringing on a fundamental right or discriminating based on race or some other "suspect" category like religion or national origin. Here the government, not the plaintiffs, bears the burden of proof to show that it has a compelling, not merely a legitimate, interest to pass the law or undertake an action. The government must demonstrate that even if its interest or goal is compelling, the law or action achieves that interest in the most narrowly tailored way and with the least restrictive means. Although the Supreme Court often used these tests, it was not always consistent in applying them. They appear nowhere in the Constitution. The justices themselves invented them.

Box 12.2 Three judicial tests

To determine whether classifications on the basis of race or gender or other immutable human characteristics or qualities are legitimate or illegitimate, the Supreme Court began in the 1930s to develop basic judicial tests to help them review legislation under the First Amendment (like political speech or religious liberty) and the Fourteenth Amendment's equal protection clause. At first, there were two tests: the rational basis test, which the Court used in the vast majority of its cases, including those that involve non-Fourteenth Amendment and fundamental rights cases; and then later the Court began to use the strict scrutiny test when it considered laws affecting fundamental rights and "suspect categories," such as race. In the 1970s, the Court added a third or intermediate tier, known as heightened or intermediate scrutiny. The Court used this test when the challenged law discriminates against quasi-suspect categories, such as gender, or in First Amendment cases involving commercial speech.

Rational basis test

The Court applies the rational basis test to the vast majority of the cases it hears. The outcome usually results in the Court upholding the challenged law. Here, the burden of proof falls on the plaintiffs, that is, on those challenging the law. They must prove that: (1) the government has no legitimate interest in enacting the law; (2) because it is neither a reasonable nor plausible public policy. Many, but not all, of the Court's decisions using the rational basis test have focused on economic regulations.

Strict scrutiny test

The second test, which the Court applies to cases involving fundamental rights and suspect categories, is of more recent vintage. Its first suggestion appeared buried in a footnote in the 1938 case of *United States* v. *Carolene Products Co.* If people challenge a law on the grounds that it compromises a fundamental right like free speech or discriminates on the basis of race, they do not bear the burden to prove that they are right. The Court regards race as a "suspect" classification or category. According to the Court's strict scrutiny test, the burden of proof lies on the government to show that it had (1) a compelling interest to pass the law. Moreover, the government must also demonstrate that even if its interest is compelling, (2) it has achieved that interest through the most narrowly tailored and with the least restrictive means so that only minimal harm is possible.

Intermediate or heightened scrutiny test

Finally, the Court developed the heightened scrutiny test for nonracial classifications, such as gender, and in First Amendment cases involving commercial speech. Here, the burden is still placed on the government, but the standards are far lower than the requirements of the strict scrutiny test. The government need only show that (1) it has an important interest in enacting the law. It then must demonstrate that (2) the law achieves that interest in a way that is substantially related to the achievement of its objective, and the law or regulation is not more extensive than necessary to reach the interest.

Burden of proof	*Government interest*	*Legal standard*
Rational basis test (the Court usually upholds legislation when using this test)		
On plaintiff	A legitimate government interest	Reasonable person standard
Strict scrutiny (the Court uses this test in cases involving suspect classifications and fundamental rights. Legislation is rarely upheld)		
On government	A compelling government interest	The law is narrowly tailored to reach that interest with the least restrictive means
Intermediate scrutiny (the Court uses this test in matters involving gender discrimination and commercial speech)		
On government	An important governmental interest	The law is substantially related to achieve that objective and not more extensive than necessary

When reviewing the set aside of 16 of 100 students admitted to UC Davis Medical School, Powell agreed with the lower court that the program was unconstitutional, because it amounted to a numerical quota. It was not narrowly tailored according to requirements of the strict scrutiny test. He did, however, endorse an admissions program known as the "Harvard Plan" where admissions officers used race and ethnicity as one factor among many, and not by "the assignment of a fixed number of places to a minority group." Affirmative action programs may satisfy the equal protection clause if they do not present a quota system.

Two groups of justices differed over basic premises. One group of four, led by William Brennan, agreed with Powell that the Fourteenth Amendment could accommodate affirmative action programs but added that the Davis program was constitutional. A separate group of four held that the Davis program was unconstitutional as a violation of the equal protection clause and Title VI of the Civil Rights Act of 1964. This group, led by John Paul Stevens, made no judgment about the constitutionality of affirmative action programs.

Affirmative Action in Government Contracts

The Court also declined to approve numerical quotas or set asides that specified a clear number of minority hires, promotions, or public contracts and subcontracts. In 1989 and again in 1995, the Court confronted how affirmative action affected government-issued contracts in two cases: *City of Richmond* v. *J.A. Croson* and *Adarand Constructors Inc.* v. *Peña*. In the first, the Court overturned a Richmond, Virginia, affirmative action program requiring all contractors undertaking city work to award at least 30 percent of its subcontracts to minority-owned businesses, also known as Minority Business Enterprises (MBEs). In identifying racial minorities as a group, it triggered the strict scrutiny test, because race was a "suspect" category. Writing for a six to three majority, Sandra Day O'Connor ruled that the program was neither narrowly tailored to achieve the city's interest in increasing the number of MBEs in winning subcontracts nor the least restrictive means. It set forth a numerical quota, which the Court had outlawed in *Bakke*. "The city does not even know," she wrote, "how many MBEs in the relevant market are qualified to undertake prime or sub-contracting work in public construction projects." Instead, the city had argued that because racial discrimination was a nationwide problem in the construction business, it acted to overcome that discrimination at the local level.

Dissenting, Thurgood Marshall argued that strict scrutiny, when applied to racial minorities, should really be "relaxed" scrutiny. "My view has long been that race-conscious classifications designed to further remedial goals 'must serve important government objectives and must be substantially related to achievement of those objectives' in order to withstand constitutional scrutiny." He thought that racial classifications were impermissible when government action had long excluded African Americans. By including people, affirmative action legitimately helped African Americans and other distressed minorities enter the mainstream of American life.

If *Croson* established strict scrutiny for states, counties, and municipalities, in 1995, *Adarand* did so for the US government. Thereafter, state, local, and the federal governments had to provide hard evidence of past discrimination and then make a series of factual findings based on that evidence.

Women's Rights and Affirmative Action

In the 1970s, the Court added a third tier to its review, known as heightened or intermediate scrutiny. Echoing Marshall's dissent in *Croson*, a bare majority concluded that the strict scrutiny test was inappropriate for categories that were not suspect. These "quasi-suspect" categories included discrimination based on sex and commercial speech. While the government still bore the burden of proof, the standards were lower than those for strict scrutiny: the government must show that it had an important, not a compelling, interest to enact a law or undertaking an action. In addition, the government must demonstrate that the law or action achieved that interest in a way that was substantially related to the achievement of its objective and the law or regulation was not more extensive than necessary.

The contemporary women's rights movement coincided with the latter half of the civil rights movement. During the decade of the 1970s, women made progress on two fronts. First, they gained reproductive rights to determine when and whether they would have children. Second, the establishment of sex equality began in earnest in 1972 with the drive to add an Equal Rights Amendment to the Constitution. It stated that "equality of rights under the law shall not be denied or abridged by the United States or any state on account of sex." It failed to achieve ratification. Several Supreme Court cases decided in the 1970s, however, pushed women's rights forward. Many cases were associated with Ruth Bader Ginsburg, later associate justice of the Court, who was the founder and head of the Women's Rights Project of the American Civil Liberties Union.

In his 1873 concurrence in the case involving a woman who was denied a law license in Illinois, Justice Joseph Bradley articulated the "doctrine of domesticity," arguing that the law of nature and the

Creator distinguished men from women. Afterwards, the Court upheld laws that prohibited women from tending bar and serving on juries. The twentieth century saw some social and cultural change regarding women's rights. After achieving the right to vote in 1920, thousands of women worked in factories doing "men's work" during World War II. The iconic poster of Rosie the Riveter depicted a young woman flexing her muscles while wearing blue work clothes and making war materiel and munitions. Following the war, with few exceptions, women returned to their traditional roles as wives and mothers. In some respects, the doctrine of domesticity that Bradley outlined returned. Florida, for example, made jury service mandatory for men, but optional for women.

A century after Bradley's statement, Ruth Bader Ginsburg assisted the lead lawyer in a case from Idaho that challenged a law that favored men over women in administering the estate of a deceased person. She won the first of five cases. Writing for a unanimous Court in *Reed* v. *Reed*, Chief Justice Burger overturned the law, ruling that sex discrimination embedded in the Idaho law demonstrated "the very kind of arbitrary legislative choice forbidden by the equal protection clause." Two years later, Ginsburg served as lead counsel in a landmark sex discrimination case, *Frontiero* v. *Richardson*. Air Force Lieutenant Sharron Frontiero sued Secretary of Defense Elliot Richardson after the department barred married female officers from receiving the same benefits as married male officers: these include larger living quarters, monetary supplements, and medical benefits. The department had always presumed that the husband of a married woman officer held a job that provided these benefits, and she did not need them. Frontiero's husband was a student with no benefits.

A plurality of four justices, led by William Brennan, failed to assemble a majority to declare that sex, like race, was a suspect class subject to the strict scrutiny test. Lewis Powell concurred but refused to raise sex to a suspect category because he thought the Equal Rights Amendment was headed toward ratification. By 1973, 35 states had approved it, and only three more were needed. Those three states never materialized. By the beginning of the 1980s, with the election of Ronald Reagan as president, the nation witnessed a conservative retrenchment. Several state legislatures that had ratified the amendment rescinded their earlier ratification vote, and it was never adopted though attempts have been made to revive it well into the twenty-first century.

In 1976, the Court resolved the standard by which it would scrutinize sex discrimination cases, known as heightened or intermediate scrutiny. The issue was an Oklahoma law concerning the purchase of low alcohol, or 3.2 percent, beer. Young women could buy it at 18, but young men had to wait until they were 21. The rationale was that young men were more likely than young women to have automobile accidents while driving under the influence of alcohol. In *Craig* v. *Boren*, Justice Brennan noted that "to withstand constitutional challenge," this case had to "establish that classifications by gender must serve important governmental objectives and must be substantially related to achievement of those interests."

Perhaps one of the major twentieth-century sex discrimination cases began when many single-sex colleges and universities in the 1960s and 1970s changed their policies and started to admit students of both sexes. An institution that investigated coeducation was the Virginia Military Institute (VMI). This public institution has a rigorous military training program required of all its students. Its leaders concluded that women were physically and mentally incapable of enduring the adversarial or "adversative" part of the program with its harsh physical and mental requirements. They declined to admit them. Some young women claimed they could perform on a level equal to men and filed suit. Because the discrimination entailed a potential violation of Title IX of the Civil Rights Act, the United States intervened.

In 1996, the Court, in an opinion by Justice Ruth Bader Ginsburg, ruled seven to one that VMI could not discriminate against women applicants. In *United States* v. *Virginia*, she used heightened scrutiny to determine that the state had no important governmental interest to exclude women from VMI. She ordered Virginia to integrate VMI by accepting female applicants: the school had offered no "exceedingly persuasive justification" for excluding women. In the sole dissent, Justice Antonin Scalia attacked the Court's invention of so-called tests. Rational basis, strict scrutiny, and heightened scrutiny, he declared, were "no more scientific than their names suggest." They were nothing more than an "element of randomness" when it was "largely up to us which test will be applied in each case." Justice Thomas recused himself because his son was a VMI student at the time.

13

Expanding Presidential Power

Early in the welfare state republic, the power of the president grew as a response to rapidly changing social and economic conditions and to the rise of totalitarian governments in Europe and Asia threatening Western democracies. The United States fought several wars and military conflicts, some declared, most not. These included World War II, the Korean War, the War in Vietnam as well as several American military interventions into the Middle East and Latin America. Most presidencies from the 1930s to the 1990s experienced war and military conflict. World War II began in Europe when German troops invaded Poland on September 1, 1939. Britain and France declared war on Germany after having guaranteed Polish independence. Although sympathetic to the allied cause, the United States remained neutral. With the fall of France in June 1940, the threat to American national security intensified in light of relentless military advances by Nazi Germany and its Italian fascist ally in Europe and an expanding imperial Japan in the Far East in China and Korea.

In early 1941, the United States sent war materiel to its British ally in a program authorized by the Lend-Lease Act of 1941. The measure empowered the president to sell, transfer, lend, or lease all materials that he thought necessary to ensure the security and defense of the United States. After Germany attacked the Soviet Union in June that year, the United States extended lend-lease to the Russians. In all, President Franklin Roosevelt signed agreements with 15 nations in aid that reached

American Constitutional History: A Brief Introduction, Second Edition. Jack Fruchtman.
© 2022 John Wiley & Sons, Inc. Published 2022 by John Wiley & Sons, Inc.

nearly $51 billion. His decisions mirrored ones made by Abraham Lincoln in the Civil War and Woodrow Wilson in World War I.

The United States entered the war in December 1941 after a Japanese aerial attack destroyed the US Pacific fleet in Pearl Harbor, Hawaii. Although the president asked Congress for a declaration of war, the United States was already at war, fighting the ambitious and expanding Japanese Empire. Within days, Germany declared war on the United States. Americans fought on two fronts, creating the necessity to mobilize nearly 15 million men and to transform hundreds of industries onto a wartime footing, costing over $300 billion. Factories and warehouses, ships and aircraft were drawn into the war effort. Americans faced rationing of gasoline and consumables. For the first time, women joined the workforce or military auxiliaries as the men were mobilized to the frontlines. Soon, minority and working-class laborers serving in the armed forces or supplying needed employment to the war industries sought many legal and economic rights, creating the groundswell of many battles that extended well beyond the end of the conflict.

Roosevelt was prepared to use his power to run the war effort or persuade Congress to provide it to him. As early as 1936, he unilaterally made decisions he thought were necessary to protect US interests. He signed several executive agreements guaranteeing that the United States would support its European allies and ensure neutral zones throughout the Western hemisphere. He took independent steps that ordinarily would have required congressional agreement, such as the transfer of some 50 destroyers to the British fleet, the termination of several agreements with the Japanese Empire, the use of convoys to protect lend-lease materials bound for Britain, and an actual shooting war with German submarines. After the Japanese attack on Pearl Harbor, the president used unprecedented executive power.

Presidential Power and Japanese Internments

At the time, many people immediately questioned the loyalty of Japanese descendants living primarily on the West Coast of the United States. One fear was that the attack in Hawaii inspired acts of sabotage and espionage among the Japanese Americans or Japanese immigrants living in the United States. Two months after Pearl Harbor, Roosevelt signed an executive order dividing the nation into military "zones." He authorized military commanders to prescribe exclusion zones and impose curfews on Japanese Americans. A month later, Congress affirmed the order with legislation. Soon General John L. DeWitt, the military commander of the West Coast of the United States, proclaimed the entire area as military zone. In March 1942, Congress created the War Relocation Authority to intern all Japanese Americans in "relocation" camps throughout the United States – upward of 120,000 Japanese Americans. They spent the rest of the war in various parts of the country. They lost their homes, their jobs, their businesses, and a large chunk of their lives.

An early challenge to the government's policy occurred in 1943 when the Court dealt with the legality of the curfew. Gordon Hirabayashi disobeyed DeWitt's order to remain indoors from 8:00 p.m. until 6:00 a.m. DeWitt first demanded that all Japanese Americans remain within the area he commanded but then ordered them to remain outside of it. In short, they could neither leave nor stay. They were to report to assembly centers where the American troops sent them relocation or internment camps. Hirabayashi, a senior at the University of Washington, disobeyed both the curfew and the relocation order. He believed they diluted his rights as an American citizen. Besides, he wanted to visit his girlfriend. Arrested and convicted on both counts, he appealed to the Supreme Court, which in *Hirabayashi* v. *United States* (1943) upheld his conviction and the curfew. In order to wage war successfully, Justice Harlan Fiske Stone wrote for a unanimous Court, the president possessed the authority to order the curfew. The justices declined to review the relocation order, only the curfew.

The decision left open whether, in a time of war, the federal government had the constitutional authority to intern American citizens and immigrants. In 1944, the Court answered affirmatively in *Korematsu* v. *United States*, decided six to three (Box 13.1). After Fred Korematsu was convicted for refusing to report to an assembly center to be transported to an internment camp, Justice Hugo Black ruled that "we are unable to conclude that it was beyond the war power of Congress and the Executive to exclude those of Japanese ancestry from the West Coast war area at the time they did." Congress must defer to the decisions by the president and the military in wartime. "Hardships are part of war, and war is an aggregation of hardships," he famously wrote. The temporary transfer of these people was reasonable after military authorities claimed to have discovered evidence of disloyalty among the Japanese. It was not a matter of racial discrimination. If it were, the Court should apply "the most rigid scrutiny." However, this was not the case.

Box 13.1 *Korematsu* v. *United States* (1944), Justices Hugo Black, Frank Murphy, and Robert Jackson, excerpts

We uphold the exclusion order as of the time it was made and when the petitioner violated it. In doing so, we are not unmindful of the hardships imposed by it upon a large group of American citizens. But hardships are part of war, and war is an aggregation of hardships. All citizens alike, both in and out of uniform, feel the impact of war in greater or lesser measure. Citizenship has its responsibilities as well as its privileges, and in time of war the burden is always heavier. Compulsory exclusion of large groups of citizens from their homes, except under circumstances of direst emergency and peril, is inconsistent with our basic governmental institutions. But when under conditions of modern warfare our shores are threatened by hostile forces, the power to protect must be commensurate with the threatened danger. ...

Korematsu was not excluded from the Military Area because of hostility to him or his race. He was excluded because we are at war with the Japanese Empire, because the properly constituted military authorities feared an invasion of our West Coast and felt constrained to take proper security measures, because they decided that the military urgency of the situation demanded that all citizens of Japanese ancestry be segregated from the West Coast temporarily, and finally, because Congress, reposing its confidence in this time of war in our military leaders – as inevitably it must – determined that they should have the power to do just this. There was evidence of disloyalty on the part of some, the military authorities considered that the need for action was great, and time was short. We cannot – by availing ourselves of the calm perspective of hindsight – now say that at that time these actions were unjustified.

Justice Hugo Black

I dissent ... from this legalization of racism. Racial discrimination in any form and in any degree has no justifiable part whatever in our democratic way of life. It is unattractive in any setting but it is utterly revolting among a free people who have embraced the principles set forth in the Constitution of the United States. All residents of this nation are kin in some way by blood or culture to a foreign land. ... They must accordingly be treated at all times as the heirs of the American experiment and as entitled to all the rights and freedoms guaranteed by the Constitution.

Justice Frank Murphy

Korematsu was born on our soil, of parents born in Japan. The Constitution makes him a citizen of the United States by nativity and a citizen of California by residence. No claim is made that he is not loyal to this country. There is no suggestion that apart from the matter involved here he is not law-abiding and well disposed. Korematsu, however, has been convicted of an act not commonly a crime. It consists merely of being present in the state whereof he is a citizen, near the place where he was born, and where all his life he has lived. ...

Had Korematsu been one of four – the others being, say, a German alien enemy, an Italian alien enemy, and a citizen of American-born ancestors, convicted of treason but out on parole – only Korematsu's presence would have violated the order. The difference between their innocence and his crime would result, not from anything he did, said, or thought, different than they, but only in that he was born of different racial stock.

Justice Robert Jackson

As Box 13.1 shows, the government's behavior appalled several justices. Robert Jackson complained that no evidence existed of disloyalty among the Japanese Americans and that only on DeWitt's "unsworn, self-serving statement, untested by cross-examination" led to the internments. Owen Roberts claimed this was a classic case of a denial of due process of law, "a case of convicting a citizen as a punishment for not submitting to imprisonment in a concentration camp, based on his ancestry, and solely because of his ancestry, without evidence or inquiry concerning his loyalty and good disposition toward the United States." Frank Murphy complained that the exclusion order "falls into the ugly abyss of racism." On the same day, however, the Court released one (and the only one) Japanese American, Mitsuye Endo, on a writ of habeas corpus. She proved she was loyal. William O. Douglas's decision seemed almost like an afterthought: a small bone thrown to critics of the internment program that Roosevelt had started with a mere executive order.

Military Tribunals

If the internment of thousands of people during the war expanded the power of the president so too did the military tribunals of enemy combatants that the president created during and after the war. The most important of these involved eight German saboteurs sent from their homeland to conduct operations of espionage and sabotage on American soil. After secretly landing in Florida and Long Island and burying their uniforms, they were arrested and taken to Washington for trial. FDR knew that a civilian court would acquit them: the only crime they had committed was illegally entering the country. Prisoners tried by military tribunals do not enjoy the same due process rights as defendants in civilian courts. The rules of evidence and counsel are very different. In a tribunal, prisoners may not see all the evidence because of national security interests nor do they have direct access to witnesses who might testify in their favor.

The president thought that a military tribunal was appropriate for these "illegal enemy belligerents" when they illegitimately slipped into the country without military uniforms. Their secret trial began on July 8, 1942, six days after Roosevelt signed the order creating the tribunal. Found guilty and sentenced to death, they appealed to the Supreme Court in *Ex parte Quirin* to challenge the government's right to try them by military tribunal. They argued they should have faced trial in the civilian courts, the standard established in 1866 in *Ex parte Milligan*. The justices heard arguments on July 29 and 30, 1942, and in a unanimous *per curiam* (or unsigned) opinion affirmed their conviction and sentence. Three months later, Chief Justice Harlan Fiske Stone published the full opinion for the Court. By that time, six of the men had been executed. Roosevelt reduced the seventh prisoner's sentence to 30 years' imprisonment while the eighth received a life term. This case, its rapidity, and outcome, along with *Korematsu*, demonstrated the increased power of the presidency during wartime.

After the war, the government conducted several more military tribunals, ultimately leading to the execution of over 900 Japanese officers and soldiers and the imprisonment of some 3000 others. In two well-known cases, the Supreme Court heard appeals from military tribunals: one led to the execution of a Japanese officer and the other to the incarceration of several German enemy combatants. The first case, decided in 1946, focused on General Tomoyuki Yamashita, found guilty by a military tribunal for failing to prevent his men from committing atrocities on civilians and American prisoners of war. The Court declined to hear his appeal, and he was hanged. In the second, another tribunal convicted 21 German soldiers captured in China for violating the laws of war. Sent to the Far East by the German command to support the Japanese war effort, they continued to fight after Germany surrendered. They asked the justices to determine whether prisoners tried outside of the United States's sovereign territory possessed the same due process rights as American citizens. *Johnson* v. *Eisentrager*, decided in 1950, answered the question in the negative. The Court ruled that nonresident aliens possessed no rights to appeal a decision of a military tribunal to a federal court. This decision would have an impact in the twenty-first century after the September 11, 2001, terrorist attacks in the United States.

Vietnam and Its Aftermath

Wars and military interventions after World War II increased executive authority. Congress did not declare war in either the Korean or Vietnam conflicts. Korea was officially a "police" action undertaken through the United Nations Charter after North Korean troops invaded the South in June 1950. The war in Vietnam involved no congressional declaration of war. In its history, Congress formally declared war just five times: the War of 1812; the Mexican-American War (1846–1848); the Spanish–American War of 1898; World War I; and World War II. Presidents Lyndon B. Johnson and Richard M. Nixon argued that their authorization to send combat troops rather than military advisors to Vietnam was rooted in the 1964 Gulf of Tonkin Resolution after North Vietnamese soldiers allegedly launched a surprise attack on American gunboats in a Vietnam waterway. Congress accepted President Johnson's version of the attack and empowered him "to take all necessary measures to repel any armed attack against the forces of the United States and to prevent further aggression." Johnson sent over half a million men to Vietnam in a conflict that lasted until 1975, leaving over 58,000 American troops dead and thousands injured and maimed, physically and mentally.

In minor military interventions, American presidents intervened without formal congressional war declarations. These included Lebanon in 1958, the Dominican Republic in 1965, Lebanon again and Grenada in 1983, Panama in 1989, Iraq in 1991, and Somalia in 1992–1993. The trend continued into the twenty-first century. Some incursions involved congressional "authorizations for the use of force" that "authorized" presidents to protect US interests. Congress left to them the decision as to the nature and size of forces and the length of time of combat.

With the end of the war in Vietnam, the power of the presidency momentarily began to wane. For the first time, the nation witnessed the resignation of a president and vice president. Vice President Spiro Agnew resigned in 1973 after a criminal investigation by the Department of Justice revealed his participation in widespread corruption when he served as governor of Maryland. A year later, President Nixon resigned in disgrace as a result of an event known as the Watergate scandal. In an effort to ensure Nixon's re-election in 1972, members of his campaign committee hired several men to break into the National Democratic Headquarters located in the Watergate office complex and hotel in Washington, DC, to steal campaign materials. Although no evidence tied the president to the scheme, he faced two years of congressional and public scrutiny as he and his advisors covered up his involvement. The House of Representatives prepared three articles of impeachment: obstruction of justice, misuse of power, and failure to obey subpoenas issued by the House Judiciary Committee. During congressional hearings, a Nixon aide testified that the Nixon administration possessed some 3700 hours of audiotapes of recorded White House conversations from February 1971 to July 1973. The government released all but 700 hours of tapes, withholding those for national security and privacy reasons.

Meantime, several members of the Nixon administration were indicted for obstruction of justice and conspiracy in regard to covering up the Watergate scandal. A federal district court in Washington, DC, demanded all audiotapes as part of their defense. The president declined to release them on the grounds that he enjoyed absolute executive privilege in conversations with his advisors. Otherwise, presidents would fail to hear candid and confidential advice. The federal prosecutor challenged that position, and the matter became the case of *United States v. Nixon*. Ruling eight to zero – Justice William Rehnquist recused himself because he had served in the Nixon Justice Department – the Court held that presidents enjoyed limited, not absolute, executive privilege. Nixon had to relinquish the tapes in the interest of due process. The defendants who had served in his administration had a right to a fair trial with all the evidence present. To avoid impeachment, Nixon resigned on August 9, 1974.

Congress made its first major attempt in years to rein in the president's warmaking authority by passing the War Powers Resolution (WPR) in 1973. The measure drew a delicate line balancing the power of Congress to declare war against the president's role as commander in chief. It required him to withdraw troops after 60 days if Congress declined to authorize their deployment. Nixon vetoed the resolution. He argued that it diminished the president's power to protect the nation. His successors agreed, declaring that the WPR unconstitutionally undermined their ability to protect national security. The Supreme Court never adjudicated its constitutionality. Many commentators claim that its constitutionality will never be litigated in that it poses a political question that the president and Congress must work out. After the fall of the Soviet Union and the end of the Cold War in 1991, presidents have argued that the United States must have flexibility to move American troops wherever they may be needed.

In 1978, Congress further attempted to curb the president when it passed the Foreign Intelligence Surveillance Act (FISA). The law created a special court staffed by 12 federal judges. Its "sole purpose" ensured that all domestic intelligence surveillance, including wiretaps, only uncovered intelligence to combat espionage and terrorism undertaken by foreign enemies of the United States. The law was a reaction to complaints that the FBI had spied on those who opposed the Vietnam War and on leaders of the civil rights movement.

Re-emergence of a Powerful Executive

During the two Reagan administrations in the 1980s, the theory of the unitary executive once again emerged. As a staunch anti-communist, Ronald Reagan wanted desperately to combat the influence of the Soviet Union around the world. In Latin America, he believed that a Soviet stronghold gripped the island of Cuba and its leader, Fidel Castro. When it appeared that the Soviets, through their Cuban puppets, were attempting to spread communism into Latin America, especially through Nicaragua and its Sandinista communist regime, he secretly sent millions of dollars to the Contras, the Sandinista's conservative enemies operating out of Honduras. He instructed the CIA to train and assist them. When Congress finally stopped financial support of the Contras, Reagan continued to send aid in what became the Iran–Contra scandal in 1986.

This complicated set of affairs had its origins in the Iranian revolution in 1979 when Islamic militants overthrew the Shah of Iran and seized the US embassy in Tehran, the capital. The rebels held seven Americans hostage. A year later, war broke out between Iran and Iraq. Reagan thought he could use the war as leverage on the Iranians to free the American hostages and find a way to send funds to the Contras fighting the Sandinistas in Nicaragua. Soon, 1500 missiles reached Iraq to be used against Iran, and several hostages were released. In addition, $8 million of the $12 million in arms sales was transferred to the Contras. When the story reached the public, the president claimed he remembered little of what went on. Reagan was never indicted for disobeying Congress, but eight members of his administration were and six were convicted. Reagan's successor, George H.W. Bush, pardoned all of them.

Another important step in the unitary executive during the Reagan years was the increased use of presidential signing statements. Since Monroe's administration, presidents have signed bills and then issued an accompanying statement expressing their understanding of the laws and how they intended to enforce them. Two young members of the Reagan administration, John G. Roberts Jr. and Samuel Alito who later joined the Supreme Court, argued that signing statements enhanced presidential power. President Reagan issued statements concerning 95 provisions in various bills, while George H.W. Bush issued 232 and Bill Clinton 140. In addition, the military budget grew during Reagan's two administrations. The budget deficit increased from 2 to almost 4 percent of the gross domestic product. The national debt rose from about $3 trillion to $4 trillion. Still, when President Reagan left office in 1989, he had the highest approval rating of any exiting president since Franklin Roosevelt.

Meantime, Wyoming Representative Richard B. ("Dick") Cheney condemned the War Powers Resolution as an infringement on presidential power and demanded Congress repeal it. He favored strong unilateral presidential authority in military and national security affairs. When he became secretary of defense in the George H.W. Bush administration, he oversaw the US Marines' invasion of Panama in 1989, without congressional authorization, to arrest the authoritarian President Manuel Noriega with the goal of protecting American security interests in the Panama Canal Zone and restoring democracy.

Another goal was to end Noriega's alleged involvement in illegal drug trafficking from South America to the United States. American forces secretly brought Noriega to the United States where he was convicted and sentenced to 15 years in federal prison. Congress never invoked the WPR because the operation lasted less than 60 days. Noriega completed his sentence in 2007 and was extradited to France on murder charges. He died 10 years later.

A more significant moment came the following year after Iraqi forces invaded Kuwait in the Middle East. US officials feared that American Middle Eastern sources of oil were endangered. President Bush and Secretary Cheney assembled an international military coalition that included members of the United Nations and the Arab League. A United Nations Security Council resolution authorized the use of force as an incentive to Iraqi President Saddam Hussein to withdraw his troops. Cheney opposed asking Congress to invoke the WPR. Instead, the president asked Congress for an authorization to use force, and Congress complied. American and coalition military buildup in Saudi Arabia amounted to well over 900,000 troops, 73 percent of whom were Americans. The coalition consisted of some 34 nations, including Britain, France, Italy, Spain as well as Saudi Arabia, Syria, and the United Arab Emirates. It was the largest military coalition since World War II, though American objectives were limited. The fighting ended in approximately six weeks with the defeat of Iraq. Kuwait was liberated, but Iraqi President Saddam Hussein remained in power.

In December 1992, again without congressional approval, the Bush administration intervened in Somalia in West Africa in a humanitarian effort to help thousands of starving Somalis. President Bill Clinton, who defeated Bush the previous November, continued the effort. American forces were soon drawn into intra-clan battles. At the same time, the United States attempted to help Somalia develop a democratic order. Clinton never once even winked toward the WPR. He claimed that American troops were not involved in sustained combat. Nation building failed as the Somalis, who once welcomed Americans, soon brutally attacked and killed them in the streets of Mogadishu, the capital. Clinton withdrew all troops by the end of 1993. In addition, while ignoring Congress, he ordered air strikes when the states of the former Yugoslavia erupted into fighting, and Serbian forces massacred thousands of Kosovo Muslims. He directed the firing of several hundred cruise missiles into Afghanistan and the Sudan after al-Qaeda, an anti-American Islamist organization led by Osama bin Laden from Saudi Arabia, bombed US embassies in East Africa.

Clinton continued to flex executive muscle despite his impeachment by the House in 1998 for perjury and obstruction of justice in a sex scandal involving a White House intern. The Senate failed to convict him. For example, in 1993 he proposed a tax increase/spending reduction bill, known as the Omnibus Budget Reconciliation Act. It was designed to reduce the national debt and led to the first federal budget surplus five years later. No House or Senate Republican voted for it. As a law affecting the budget, it could avoid a Senate filibuster, which would take 60 votes to halt debate and start the voting, in a procedure known as the budget reconciliation process. Vice President Al Gore supplied the winning margin in the Senate as it passed 51 to 50.

The exception during these years was trade, when the president and Congress worked cooperatively together. Beginning with President Reagan, the United States began negotiations with Canada to allow goods to flow without tariffs between the two countries. The two nations signed an agreement in 1988. President Bush followed by opening talks with Mexico, and in 1994 the North American Free Trade Agreement, known as NAFTA, passed the House by a vote of 234 to 200, and the Senate, 61 to 38. At the time, it was the largest trade bloc in the world based on the three nations' gross domestic product. It was superseded in 2020 by the United States-Mexico-Canada Agreement.

Most actions by Reagan, Bush, and Clinton demonstrated, however, that both Republicans and Democrats believed strongly in the theory of the unitary executive when presidents acted alone to protect American interests without congressional or judicial oversight.

The welfare state republic witnessed the phenomenal growth of entitlement programs like Social Security, Medicare, and Medicaid. President Roosevelt enjoyed huge electoral victories in 1936 and 1940 as well as large majorities of his party, the Democrats, in Congress. His New Deal legislation became the basis of the contemporary welfare state in America. These programs continued under both Republican and Democratic administrations even when presidents staunchly criticized their costs and effects. The costs of the programs have contributed to the growth in the nation's debt.

It was also a period of expanding civil liberties in the realm of free speech, a free press, religious liberty, voting, and privacy. The Supreme Court confirmed many of these rights and liberties. The justices adopted several tests to determine whether government action led to the establishment of religion. Some believed in the strict separation of church and state while others followed an approach that accommodated religious expression in the public square. Still others tried to judge whether government action forced or coerced youngsters into hearing prayers that they may wish not to hear while still others tried to unveil whether government-sponsored religious activities actually endorsed a religion or excessively entangled it with religion.

Much of the Court's expansive views of civil rights and liberties resulted from the Court's incorporation of the Bill of Rights into the Fourteenth Amendment and their application to the states. Under the Warren Court and its successors, the justices incorporated 16 provisions of the Bill of Rights and applied them to the states: all through the liberty component of the Fourteenth Amendment's due process clause. The Court also applied several civil liberties protections to the states that were not addressed in the Bill of Rights. These included the judge-made exclusionary rule and the right to privacy, but also the right to an impartial jury and a jury trial in all criminal cases involving a prison term.

The period also included the dramatic expansion of presidential power in the realms of military and national security affairs. The United States entered World War II after the 1941 attack on the US naval base on Pearl Harbor and then undertook wars in the Far East twice: Korea in 1950 and Vietnam after 1961. In addition, Republican and Democratic presidents deployed American troops abroad on several occasions with no declaration of war by Congress. Despite the attempt by Congress in 1973 to stop presidents from acting alone in sending troops abroad, the WPR has failed. Presidents, no matter their political party, ignore it.

The world began to face new challenges with the demise of the Soviet Union and its allied bloc after 1991. Acts of extreme aggression by rootless terrorist organizations like al-Qaeda, beginning in 1993, caused presidents to deal with a new phenomenon: stateless terrorism. This new development increased presidential power in an increasingly dangerous world.

Part 5

The Executive Republic, 1995–2021

The executive republic continued the trend to increase the power of the president that had been developing since the Reagan administration. It was a reaction to the severe decline in presidential authority that developed in the wake of the aftermath of the Vietnam War and the Watergate scandal ending the Nixon administration. President Bill Clinton unilaterally undertook highly controversial military action in the Middle East, Africa, and in the Balkans. For example, in 1995, he sent the Air Force under NATO auspices to bomb Balkan Serb targets, and, three years later, he ordered a four-day bombing campaign against Iraq's military installations.

President George W. Bush faced the difficult challenge of how to respond to the 2001 terrorist attacks on the World Trade Center in New York and the Pentagon in Washington, DC, which included the downing by passengers of an airliner in Pennsylvania. With a vague congressional authorization, he sent American troops along with those of other nations into Afghanistan, leading to the longest war in American history, which ended in 2021. Two years later, after claiming that Iraqi President Saddam Hussein harbored hundreds of weapons of mass destruction, Bush deployed American forces into that nation to overthrow the regime: again, the congressional authorization was weak and open ended. He denied that terrorist or suspected terrorists deserved protection under the Geneva Conventions and opened a detention camp on the United States naval base in Guantánamo Bay,

American Constitutional History: A Brief Introduction, Second Edition. Jack Fruchtman.
© 2022 John Wiley & Sons, Inc. Published 2022 by John Wiley & Sons, Inc.

Cuba. His thinking, as well as that of his vice president, Dick Cheney, was that they would be beyond the reach of the federal courts. It turned out they were wrong.

President Barack Obama, without congressional authorization but under NATO auspices, launched massive bombing raids on Libya in 2011. Members of both parties in the House and Senate complained that he needed their authorization, but he declined to seek it. He used attacks by unmanned drones to kill suspected terrorists, including in at least two instances American citizens who he thought engaged in attacks against Americans.

President Donald J. Trump stated that presidential authority was unlimited. A lifelong real estate developer and television reality personality, he was the first president to take office with no previous experience in government or the military. His campaign and election were overshadowed by accusations of sexual assault, which he firmly and consistently denied. The charges stimulated a backlash among many women who claimed they too suffered sexual discrimination, sexual assault, and even rape, leading to the organization of the #MeToo movement in many parts of the United States and later the world. Another organization, Black Lives Matter (BLM), developed in 2013 after the acquittal of a white vigilante who murdered an unarmed young African American. The movement promoted peaceful protests to raise awareness about police officers who used deadly force against African Americans. In 2020, as president, Trump faced widespread BLM demonstrations after police killed a handcuffed African American, George Floyd, in Minneapolis. The demonstrations were soon global in scope.

President Trump became the first president to be impeached twice by the House of Representatives. The first time occurred in 2019 after he pressured a foreign leader to investigate a political rival, Joe Biden, who was running against him in his re-election bid. No Republicans joined the effort in the House and the Senate declined to convict him. He remained in office but faced a second impeachment at the beginning of 2021 when he incited an insurrection against the US Capitol. At the time, Vice President Mike Pence was leading the electoral count resulting from the 2020 presidential election. The count stopped when insurgents took over the building, wrecked offices, and threatened members of Congress and the vice president. This time, 10 Republican members joined the Democrats to impeach the president, but the Senate again declined to convict him.

As president, Joe Biden reversed several policies his predecessor implemented by executive order by signing his own orders. He also promised to combat climate change, which Trump called a hoax. He increased the distribution of vaccines to slow the progress of the coronavirus pandemic, known as Covid-19, which broke out globally in 2019. He took steps to re-engage the United States in diplomacy and to cooperate with America's allies. He submitted legislation to Congress to stimulate the economy and fix the failing infrastructure plaguing the United States.

The Supreme Court narrowed the interstate commerce power of Congress. Chief Justice William Rehnquist had long argued that Congress's commerce clause power was limited to the standard set out in 1937 in the *Jones & Laughlin* steel case when the Court ruled that Congress possessed "the power to control" activities that have "a substantial relation to interstate commerce." The result was that Court overturned several federal criminal laws. Rehnquist's successor as chief, John G. Roberts Jr. (2005–present), did not have the same interest in limiting federal commerce power except in the major case involving the 2010 Patient Protection and Affordable Care Act (ACA, also known as Obamacare). He ruled that Congress had no authority to use its interstate commerce to pass the law but upheld the law based on Congress's tax and spending power.

The period was also one when some conservative leaders argued that fewer governmental regulations and lower taxes would stimulate the economy. In the aftermath of the New Deal, some argued that government had grown too big, taxes were too high, and regulations were too intrusive. The welfare state republic, they argued, departed from free market principles. Social welfare programs with entitlements like Social Security, Medicare, and Medicaid were expensive when government dealt with poverty and illness. Despite the criticism aimed at them by free market advocates, these programs remained intact in the twenty-first century. No attempt to eliminate them or downsize government succeeded. In fact, government attempted to stimulate the economy in 2020–2021 during the worldwide Covid-19 pandemic.

Most presidential administrations, Democratic or Republican, presided over the increased size of the bureaucracy and the national debt. The only exception occurred during the Clinton administration because of government surpluses. As the costs of entitlement programs rose, the administration of George W. Bush persuaded Congress to reduce federal income taxes, add a prescription drug plan to Medicare, and incur the costs of two wars in Afghanistan and Iraq after the September 11, 2001, terrorist attacks in the United States. When Congress passed the Tax Cuts and Jobs Act at the end of 2017, the national debt grew even larger. It turned out the tax reductions for corporations and the wealthiest Americans failed to lead to greater investment and higher employment.

The Covid-19 pandemic led to a government-prompted shutdown of the economy when many governors issued "stay-at-home" orders to reduce contagion of the disease in the states. From March 2020 to April 2021, total congressional spending amounted to $5.2 trillion with the national debt swelling to $28 trillion. While polls showed that over 60 percent of the American people supported the spending, economists determined that the costs amounted to 24 percent of gross domestic product (GDP), the highest since World War II. The federal deficit for fiscal year 2021 reached $3 trillion, though some economists predicted it would taper off the following year.

Presidents Bush, Obama, and Trump made several new appointments to the Supreme Court. With the death of Chief Justice Rehnquist in 2005, Bush nominated John G. Roberts Jr. One year later, Sandra Day O'Connor retired, and Bush nominated Samuel A. Alito Jr. In 2009, President Obama chose Sonia Sotomayor, the first Latina, to succeed David Souter, and the next year, Elena Kagan took the place of 90-year-old John Paul Stevens after his retirement. In February 2016, Justice Scalia suddenly died. President Obama nominated a moderate replacement, Chief Judge Merrick B. Garland of the US Court of Appeals for the District of Columbia, to replace him. Senate majority leader Mitch McConnell (R-KY) declined to hold a hearing, claiming that because it was an election year, the choice should be left "to the American people." Once the Senate reconvened in January 2017, Garland's nomination expired. Garland later became President Biden's attorney general.

As president, Donald Trump was highly successful in reframing the federal judiciary. The Senate, which has the authority to confirm or reject a president's judicial nominees, approved the vast majority of those whom Trump wanted. These included three Supreme Court justices, 54 judges of the United States Courts of Appeal, and 174 district court judges. All were conservative in terms of politics, culture, religion, and economics. One of his first nominees was Tenth Circuit Court Judge Neil M. Gorsuch to replace the deceased Justice Scalia. Gorsuch followed Scalia's judicial philosophy of originalism. One year later, Justice Kennedy retired, and his former law clerk, Judge Brett M. Kavanaugh of the DC Circuit, took his seat after a heated nomination hearing involving his qualifications and claims that he sexually assaulted young women while in high school and college. He too proclaimed that, like Scalia, he was an originalist. Justice Ruth Bader Ginsburg died in September 2020, and Trump nominated Seventh Circuit Court Judge Amy Coney Barrett to succeed her. Barrett, who clerked for Justice Scalia, announced that she too is an originalist. With these presidential successes, political and social conservative justices dominated the Court in the executive republic. In the meantime, the court's number of signed opinions declined. In the October 2019 term, which ended in June 2020, the court released 53 opinions in argued cases. A year later the number was 54. By contrast, the year before William H. Rehnquist became chief justice in 1986 and announced he planned to reduce the caseload, the Court disposed of 161 cases by full opinion. In the 2020–2021 term, the Court ruled unanimously or near unanimously on 66 percent of the cases but only 12 percent by a bare majority. With the new conservative majority, cases decided six to three, or five to three with Justice Barrett recused, amounted to 15 percent.

The Court incorporated two provisions of the Bill of Rights and applied them to the states through the due process clause of the Fourteenth Amendment: in 2010, in *McDonald* v. *City of Chicago*, it applied the Second Amendment's individual right to bear arms and in 2019, in *Timbs* v. *Indiana*, it applied the Eighth Amendment's prohibition on excessive fines.

On taking office, President Joe Biden appointed a 36-member, bipartisan commission to study the makeup of the Court. Its duty was to make recommendations in these areas: increasing the number of justices, establishing term limits, requiring a supermajority to overturn an act of Congress, and limiting the Court's jurisdiction.

14

Federal Commerce Power and Economic Regulation

The Constitution in Article I, Section 8, bestows on Congress the power "to regulate commerce among the states." The courts have long interpreted this phrase to mean that Congress may set the rules and regulations whenever goods and services pass through more than one state. In 1824, in the first major commerce clause case before the Supreme Court, Chief Justice Marshall explained that Congress's interstate commerce power is "complete," "unlimited," and "plenary … as absolutely as it would be in a single government." In other words, he distinguished the interstate from intrastate movement of goods. The United States controlled the former, the states the latter. Over a hundred years later, another chief justice, Charles Evans Hughes, set out the modern version of Marshall's ideas when he noted that Congress's interstate commerce power extended only to activities that had "a substantial relation to interstate commerce." Based on this principle, Congress has enacted legislation affecting the manufacturing, production, and transportation of goods and services passing through interstate commerce. Moreover, the clause has also become the foundation for Congress to approve all civil rights bills for almost 60 years.

American Constitutional History: A Brief Introduction, Second Edition. Jack Fruchtman.
© 2022 John Wiley & Sons, Inc. Published 2022 by John Wiley & Sons, Inc.

Narrowing Federal Commerce Power

From the time he was named to the Court in 1972, William Rehnquist sought to narrow federal interstate commerce power in areas that did not touch on the economy or commerce. In 1995, he finally had his chance in a case involving high school senior Alfonzo Lopez who brought a .38 caliber handgun to school in San Antonio, Texas. Local law enforcement authorities charged Lopez with violating a state law prohibiting firearms on a school campus. They had to drop the charges as a matter of federal preemption after the United States intervened and accused him of violating the federal Gun-Free School Zones Act of 1990, which made it a crime to carry a gun within 1000 feet of a school. Once convicted, Lopez claimed that Congress had gone beyond its interstate commerce power to pass a criminal law that had nothing to do with commerce or the economy. The US Circuit Court of Appeals for the Fifth Circuit agreed and reversed his conviction. The justices then, by a vote of five to four, affirmed that decision.

Using language directly taken from *Jones & Laughlin*, Chief Justice Rehnquist noted that Congress failed to show during congressional hearings that guns in schools had "a substantial relation to interstate commerce." In *United States* v. *Lopez*, he ruled that congressional committees found only anecdotal evidence that guns in schools had a negative impact on economic activity. Congress cited the connection between gun violence and insurance costs. Moreover, Congress presumed that guns deter people from traveling to certain neighborhoods where stores and shops might financially suffer (Box 14.1). Without a showing of direct, particularized evidence, Congress had no authority to pass the law. Voting with him were Justices O'Connor, Kennedy, Scalia, and Thomas. Thomas argued that an originalist approach leads to the eighteenth-century understanding of commerce as encompassing only selling, buying, bartering, and transporting. The law had nothing to do with an enterprise like carrying a gun.

Five years later, the chief justice continued his quest to promote states' rights over Congress's commerce power. The Court dealt with a violation of Section 13981 of the federal Violence Against Women Act of 1994, which provided that a person convicted of a violent crime against a woman may have to pay compensatory and punitive damages. After a freshman at Virginia Polytechnic Institute and State University (Virginia Tech) sued two student football players for

Box 14.1 *United States* v. *Lopez* (1995), excerpts

The possession of a gun in a local school zone is in no sense an economic activity that might, through repetition elsewhere, substantially affect any sort of interstate commerce. Respondent was a local student at a local school; there is no indication that he had recently moved in interstate commerce, and there is no requirement that his possession of the firearm have any concrete tie to interstate commerce.

To uphold the Government's contentions here, we would have to pile inference upon inference in a manner that would bid fair to convert congressional authority under the Commerce Clause to a general police power of the sort retained by the States. Admittedly, some of our prior cases have taken long steps down that road, giving great deference to congressional action. The broad language in these opinions has suggested the possibility of additional expansion, but we decline here to proceed any further. To do so would require us to conclude that the Constitution's enumeration of powers does not presuppose something not enumerated, and that there never will be a distinction between what is truly national and what is truly local. This we are unwilling to do.

United States v. *Lopez* 1995 /
U.S. Department of Justice / Public domain

allegedly raping her, her civil suit eventually went to the Court. In *United States* v. *Morrison*, Rehnquist posed the question of whether a substantial relationship existed between the crime of rape and interstate commerce. His answer was no. This time, Congress had assembled piles of evidence regarding the impact on interstate economic activity of violent acts against women. "In contrast with the lack of congressional findings that we faced in *Lopez*," wrote Rehnquist, the law here was "supported by numerous findings regarding the serious impact that gender-motivated violence has on victims and their families." But just because Congress concluded that violence was connected to commerce, it "does not make it so." Rehnquist invalidated the provision to sue in federal court.

After Rehnquist's death in 2005, John Roberts became the first chief to have clerked for a sitting chief justice. From 1980 to 1981, he served as Rehnquist's law clerk. During his confirmation hearings, he argued that a judge enjoyed a modest role, like a baseball plate umpire calling balls and strikes. Moreover, he said he hoped to develop a consensus on the Court so that the justices would arrive at more unanimous or near-unanimous decisions. Roberts also declared that the principle of precedent or *stare decisis* was essential to the integrity of the Court. A judge applies this principle to uphold a ruling formulated in an earlier case to maintain consistency and stability in the law. His tenure, however, demonstrated that he sometimes supported overruling precedent and he often tolerated bare majority decisions on controversial topics. When Sandra Day O'Connor retired in 2006, the swing vote on a Court split between four conservatives and four moderate liberals fell to Anthony Kennedy. In his first year as the swing vote, Kennedy voted with the majority 11 out of 16 times, which was more than any other member of the Court. A year later, the Court split five to four 24 times on controversial issues; Kennedy voted with the majority in all of them.

The debate over government's size, its regulatory authority, and high taxes intensified when new elements arose in American politics, especially the Tea Party movement. This loosely organized group, which bloomed after Barack Obama's presidential election in 2008, took its name from the 1773 Boston Tea Party when American rebels protested British taxes by tossing a shipload of imported tea into Boston harbor. The acronym also inspired the slogan, "Taxed Enough Already." The Tea Party promoted three goals: a smaller federal government with citizens paying fewer taxes; a decrease in government expenditures to eliminate the national debt; and a restructuring of government entitlements like Social Security, Medicare, and Medicaid. Some conservative voters first articulated many of these ideas during the Reagan administration but gained traction after Barack Obama became president in January 2009.

In 2007, after subprime mortgages issued by banks and mortgage companies became due, thousands of Americans homeowners suddenly found that they had to pay an entire mortgage after only a few years of signing. The ensuing downturn in the economy led many companies to lay off thousands of employees nationwide. Government at the local, state, and federal level reduced their staffs by thousands. With little money circulating through the economy, many industries faced decreasing revenues as sales plummeted. The Bush and Obama administrations undertook several steps to restore economic stability as well as the confidence of the American people. The Bush Treasury Department and Federal Reserve persuaded Congress to create the Troubled Asset Relief Program (TARP) to relieve big banks of "toxic" or subprime mortgages, which were detrimental to the economy. Under Obama, a Democratic-controlled Congress, with the support of just three Republican senators and no Republican House members, passed a $787 billion stimulus package that sent millions of dollars to the states for public works projects. It also invested billions of dollars in the automobile industry, especially General Motors, when it faced bankruptcy. The economic principle lay in the theory that when private enterprise was incapable of investing in growth, the US government was the sole entity with the means to bring about a recovery.

Healthcare Reform

The White House also undertook a major effort to reform the healthcare system with two goals: to lower healthcare costs and to insure as many as 45 million Americans who lacked health insurance. A national health insurance policy had been on the federal agenda since the end of World War II.

In 2010, again with Democratic majorities in both houses, Congress passed the Patient Protection and Affordable Care Act (ACA or Obamacare) to provide universal health insurance through private industry with government regulatory oversight. The Senate passed the bill by the process known as budget reconciliation, which avoids the filibuster requiring 60 votes to move forward. It allows the Senate to pass a law that implements changes in budget policy by a simple majority vote. Senators voted on the measure without debate or amendment. The healthcare program mirrored one designed in 1989 by the Heritage Foundation, a conservative research institute. According to its authors, Stuart M. Butler and Edmund Haislmaier, "Every resident of the US must, by law, be enrolled in an adequate health care plan to cover major health care costs ... The requirement to obtain basic insurance would have to be enforced ... If the family did not enroll in another plan before the first insurance coverage lapsed and did not provide evidence of financial problems, a fine might be imposed." In 2006, Republican Governor Mitt Romney of Massachusetts guided a health insurance program into place in his state based on the Heritage proposal. It was the first of its kind in the nation. The Heritage Foundation and Romney openly opposed the ACA: Heritage because of too many regulations; Romney because he thought healthcare was a state, not a federal, matter.

The new law included many facets. First, the private health insurance industry remained market driven: insurance firms, not government, covered the uninsured. Second, the plan prohibited companies from denying insurance to those with pre-existing illnesses. Third, children attending school or college could remain on their parents' plans until they were 26 years old. And, fourth, the law expanded the eligibility threshold that a state had to meet to remain qualified for Medicaid funds or lose its Medicaid funding. The ACA also contained the individual mandate, which meant that in 2014 all Americans must obtain health insurance or pay a penalty based on their income. The uninsured would have to pay the penalty to the Internal Revenue Service (IRS) at the time federal taxes were due in April each year.

Several challenges to the law occurred from 2012 to 2021, and not all were based on the commerce or tax and spending clauses.

Twenty-six state attorneys general challenged the law. They claimed Congress had exceeded its interstate commerce power. One case reached the Supreme Court in March 2012. By then, the National Federation of Independent Business and several individuals also challenged the act's constitutionality, especially the individual mandate. Twelve federal circuit courts of appeal heard the challenges. The Obama administration persuaded nine that the individual mandate was constitutional but failed in the other three. In Florida, the US Court of Appeals for the Eleventh Circuit held that the individual mandate violated Congress's interstate commerce power but declined to rule on whether the rest of the act could stand without the mandate.

At the same time, the court upheld the Medicaid requirements. The federal government appealed concerning the mandate, and Florida concerning Medicaid. The National Federation of Independent Business argued that the entire law must fail. One issue that the Eleventh Circuit had not dealt with was impact on the law of the 1793 Anti-Injunction Act. This eighteenth-century measure prohibited challenges to a federal tax until someone actually paid it. The US Court of Appeals for the Fourth Circuit had held that no one could challenge the ACA until after April 15, 2014, when individuals without health insurance were due to pay the penalty to the IRS.

The Supreme Court agreed to hear *National Federation of Independent Business* v. *Sebelius* on four grounds: whether the individual mandate exceeded Congress's authority under its interstate commerce and taxing power; whether the rest of the act could be salvaged if the individual mandate were eliminated; whether the case was premature under the Anti-Injunction Act of 1793 because no individual had yet paid the penalty; and whether the Medicaid requirements could withstand judicial scrutiny. The Court scheduled an extraordinary three-day session in March 2012 to hear oral arguments. Its decision split three ways.

Chief Justice Roberts initially voted to overturn the law and join four justices who comprised the eventual dissent. After he changed his mind, he prepared an opinion that Justices Ginsburg, Breyer, Sotomayor, and Kagan joined in part. He ruled that Congress, under its taxing and spending powers, possessed the authority to impose a tax on those who failed to purchase health insurance. "The Affordable Care Act's requirement that certain individuals pay a financial penalty for not obtaining health insurance may reasonably be characterized as a tax. Because the Constitution permits such a tax, it is not our role to forbid it, or to pass upon its wisdom or fairness." Individuals without insurance paid the penalty to the IRS as part of their income taxes each year on April 15. Roberts then dealt with the dissent's argument that Congress had referred to the exaction as a penalty, not a tax. By pure legerdemain, he argued that Congress's decision to call it a penalty was based on its members' political timidity to levy taxes on Americans. Thus, for purposes of the Anti-Injunction Act, which prohibited a challenge to the case until 2014, it was not a tax, but a penalty. From the perspective of the Taxing Clause, however, it was a tax. In other words, Roberts had it both ways, something that infuriated the four dissenting justices.

Meantime, the chief justice rejected the government's argument that Congress could impose the individual mandate under its interstate commerce power. Congress could regulate interstate commerce, he ruled, if that commerce already existed. Universal healthcare created a new market. Congress could not create commerce to regulate it. He rejected the argument that the health insurance and medical industry constituted pre-existing markets. Instead, "the individual mandate … does not regulate existing commercial activity. It instead compels individuals to *become* active in commerce by purchasing a product, on the ground that their failure to do so affects interstate commerce." Like his predecessor, William Rehnquist, Roberts declined to expand the meaning of the commerce clause to cover mandated healthcare insurance. The chief justice also decided two other issues. First, he ruled that the Court did not need to reach the severability question because he declined to strike down the individual mandate. And, second, he held as constitutional the Medicaid extension but only in part. Congress could not withdraw all of a state's Medicaid funding if that state rejected the expansion.

Justice Ginsburg, joined by Sotomayor and Breyer, concurred and dissented in part. She agreed that Congress had the power to tax those who declined to buy health insurance. At the same time, she added that Congress could also use its interstate commerce power to create the individual mandate. As far as she was concerned, John Marshall's dictum was correct concerning the expansive power that Congress possessed to regulate interstate commerce. The health insurance business and the financial problems surrounding the millions throughout the nation who did not possess it was an interstate not an intrastate problem.

In a rare jointly signed dissent, Scalia, Kennedy, Thomas, and Alito expressed annoyance at Roberts's argument regarding the penalty/tax Americans had to pay if they failed to purchase health insurance. Congress called it a penalty, they argued, so it must be a penalty. Echoing the rhetorical style of Antonin Scalia, the joint dissenting opinion concluded that "what the Government would have us believe in these cases is that the very same textual indications that show this is *not* a tax under the Anti-Injunction Act show that it *is* a tax under the Constitution. That carries verbal wizardry too far, deep into the forbidden land of the sophists."

In 2014, the Court reviewed a challenge by a closely held family corporation that declined to provide contraception to its female employees. The Department of Health and Human services added this requirement to its regulations as a matter of implementing the ACA. Wealthy, evangelical Christian family-owned Hobby Lobby, a national arts and crafts chain, objected to the requirement by filing suit in district court, arguing that the federal Religious Freedom Restoration Act exempted them from the requirement. In a five to four decision, the Court in *Burwell v. Hobby Lobby Stores* ruled that for purposes of the contraception mandate, a corporation may be considered a "person." Writing for the Court, Justice Alito held that the government had placed "a substantial burden" on religious liberty. In a heated dissent, Justice Ginsburg contended that "in a decision of startling breadth, the Court holds that commercial enterprises, including corporations, along with partnerships and sole proprietorships, can opt out of any law (saving only tax laws) they judge incompatible with their sincerely held religious beliefs."

The following year, another challenge focused on four words in the ACA: "established by the State." The program allowed the states to set up marketplaces called exchanges. People could go online to purchase insurance through these exchanges. For those unable to afford the cost of insurance, the government provided subsidies by means of tax credits. But nearly half the states declined to create an exchange, so the United States created a federal exchange. The question in *King* v. *Burwell* was whether the subsidies were available to those applying for health insurance on a federal exchange because the law explicitly identified only those exchanges "established by the State." In a six to three decision, Chief Justice Roberts held that the phrase "established by the State" is "ambiguous" because "it could also refer to all exchanges – both State and Federal – for purposes of the tax credits." Dissenting along with Justice Thomas and Alito, Antonin Scalia wrote, "The Court holds that when the Patient Protection and Affordable Care Act says, 'Exchange established by the State,' it means 'Exchange established by the State or the Federal Government.' That is of course quite absurd, and the Court's 21 pages of explanation make it no less so … So it rewrites the law to make tax credits everywhere. We should start calling this law SCOTUScare."

Although Republicans in Congress voted numerous times to repeal Obamacare, they failed each time. By mid-2021, some 23 million Americans had health insurance through the ACA with 54 percent of the American people saying they favor the program. The 2017 Tax Cuts and Jobs Act reduced the mandate amount to $0. Several Republican governors and state attorneys general then filed suit in federal court claiming that the entire act was unconstitutional because the mandate was zero. In *California* v. *Texas*, the Court ruled, by a seven to two vote, that the plaintiffs lacked standing to challenge the individual mandate because they had not shown a past or future injury fairly traceable to the defendants' conduct. The opinion by Justice Breyer, stated that "to find standing here to attack an unenforceable statutory provision would allow a federal court to issue what would amount to an advisory opinion without the possibility of any judicial relief." He did not address the merits of the case, that is, the validity of the mandate or the severability of the mandate from the rest of the law.

15

Civil Liberties and Judicial Doctrines

Americans experienced changes in civil liberties during the executive republic, involving religion, campaign financing, gun ownership, and privacy. Americans also witnessed the continued blossoming of the doctrine of originalism in the opinions by Antonin Scalia and Clarence Thomas and then by Neil Gorsuch, Brett Kavanaugh, and Amy Coney Barrett. Originalism holds that the only legitimate way to interpret the Constitution is to determine the original understanding or meaning of each provision at the time the drafters wrote and ratified it. Its opposing ideology, the doctrine of the living constitution, promotes the idea that as times change, the justices' duty is to modify the meaning of constitutional provisions. The tension between these two interpretative approaches during this era affected civil liberties.

The court's conservative majority expanded the rights of corporations, unions, and super-Political Action Committees (super-PACs) to engage in political campaigns. The Court made clear by bare majorities that a contribution to a political campaign is guaranteed by the First Amendment as expressive conduct and an expression of political rights. In 2014, in *McCutcheon* v. *Federal Election Commission*, the Court held that federal law could not limit the aggregate amount of money that an individual could contribute to all campaigns in a two-year period. In a five to four decision, Chief Justice Roberts wrote that no evidence demonstrated that corruption or the appearance of corruption existed when an individual gave money to as many candidates

American Constitutional History: A Brief Introduction, Second Edition. Jack Fruchtman.
© 2022 John Wiley & Sons, Inc. Published 2022 by John Wiley & Sons, Inc.

throughout the nation as he wished. Justices Ginsburg, Breyer, Sotomayor, and Kagan dissented.

Donald Trump, more than any president in history, vocally and online criticized the Court and any federal or state judge who ruled in ways with which he disagreed. In 2018, a federal judge, whom President Obama appointed, issued a temporary restraining order to halt the administration's plan to end asylum for immigrants crossing from the southern border if they did not arrive through a port of entry. President Trump complained that the judge made the ruling only because he was an "Obama judge." In an extraordinary rebuke for a chief justice, Chief Justice John Roberts wrote that "we do not have Obama judges or Trump judges, Bush judges or Clinton judges. What we have is an extraordinary group of dedicated judges doing their level best to do equal right to those appearing before them. The independent judiciary is something we should be thankful for."

One of John Roberts's goals when he became chief justice was to increase the number of unanimous or near-unanimous opinions. An example occurred during the October 2019 term when the Court decided unanimously that state electors in presidential elections must support the candidate to which they pledged their support if that candidate wins the state's popular vote. Writing for the Court in *Chiafalo* v. *Washington*, Justice Kagan rejected the arguments presented by elector Peter Chiafalo and two others, who had declined to vote for Hillary Clinton in the 2016 election after she won the popular vote. They are known as "faithless electors." The state fined them $1000 each. The Court held that "a State may enforce its pledge law against an elector." It ruled that "a State may also penalize an elector for breaking his pledge and voting for someone else other than the presidential candidate who won his State's popular vote."

Religious Establishments

The First Amendment begins with two religion clauses that often conflict with each other: the (anti)-establishment and religious liberty provisions. One person may argue that a government benefit to a religious institution violates the establishment clause, while another may argue that the denial is an infringement on religious liberty. As a result, it is sometimes difficult to distinguish when the Court is dealing with an establishment or religious liberty issue. As outlined above, the Court has developed several means to deal with these issues, such as neutrality, coercion, and endorsement. With the lead taken by Chief Justice Roberts after 2005, the Court's conservative majority increasingly pressed for increased accommodation of religion in the public sphere.

In 1997, the four moderate liberals – Souter, Stevens, Ginsburg, and Breyer – were still in the minority when Sandra Day O'Connor constitutionalized her endorsement test. The case involved remedial education concerning the Elementary and Secondary School Act of 1965, which required the states to provide remedial education for disadvantaged children. When a New York law allowed public school teachers to go into the parochial schools for this purpose, the Court held in 1985 in *Aguilar* v. *Felton* that public school teachers working in parochial institutions constituted "excessive entanglement" with religion – the third prong of the 1971 *Lemon* test – and held the program unconstitutional. After that ruling, states set up trailers to allow disadvantaged students at parochial schools to receive remedial education outside the schools. The Court in *Agostini* v. *Felton* overruled *Aguilar*.

Writing for the Court, Justice O'Connor argued that the states had erected many constraints on what public school teachers could and could not do in parochial schools, including restrictions on teaching religion. Remedial education was not, however, a matter of government endorsement of religion. "This carefully constrained program … cannot reasonably be viewed as an endorsement of religion," she wrote. But in dissent, Souter objected: "The state is forbidden to subsidize religion directly and is just as surely forbidden to act in any way that could reasonably be viewed as a religious endorsement." This program endorsed religion when it crossed the line separating church from state.

By 2002, the Court affirmed its endorsement of religious accommodation. For the first time, the justices held as constitutional a funding program concerning parochial schools. The question asked whether students attending parochial schools may constitutionally use state-funded school vouchers (tuition assistance) to pay part of their parochial school tuition. In 1995, the state of Ohio seized control of the Cleveland public schools when a federal court declared that they were in a "crisis of magnitude." In 1996, Ohio established a voucher program for inner-city students called the Pilot Project Scholarship Program. Families could receive tuition assistance of up to $2250 per student to attend any school of their choice, including a participating private parochial school.

By the academic year 1999, 96 percent of the students who chose to attend a private school with a voucher enrolled in a parochial school. Did the program have a "secular" purpose in providing an education to inner-city children in a school system that was financially and educationally failing? In *Zelman* v. *Simmons-Harris*, the Court collapsed the first two parts of the *Lemon* test into one: a program's secular purpose must neither inhibit nor advance religion. And it kept the third one intact: there must be no excessive entanglement of government with religion, that is, no endorsement of religion. If the schools, especially those with religious affiliation, were the primary beneficiaries of the program, Ohio may have breached the "excessive entanglement" test. There would be no violation if the parents benefited by giving them greater choice concerning where their children went to school. A bare majority of five justices concluded that parents of the schoolchildren, not the schools, received financial assistance to pay tuition to the schools their children attended. The program only incidentally advanced the religious mission of the school. They could choose to send their children to one of the public, charter, or magnet schools. Chief Justice Rehnquist held that the funding program was not only religiously neutral and assisted poor children, but the schools themselves never directly received funds. It was a matter of true private choice.

Three years later, the Court again narrowly split in two establishment clause decisions released on the same day. The question was whether the placement of the Ten Commandments on public property violated the principle of the separation of church and state. In 1980, in *Stone* v. *Graham*, the Court overturned a Kentucky law requiring the display of the Ten Commandments in all public-school classrooms. Now, in 2005, the justices had two opportunities to review the placement of the Ten Commandments on public property.

In the first case, *Van Orden* v. *Perry*, the issue was whether the Ten Commandments could be displayed on the grounds of the Texas State Capitol. In the 1950s and 1960s, the Fraternal Order of Eagles, a civic organization, began to erect granite Ten Commandment monuments in hundreds of public places, including in the front of courthouses and parks. The organization's founders wanted to demonstrate America's reliance on the biblical foundations of America to combat juvenile delinquency. The monument stood next to 21 other historical markers and 17 statues in the 22-acre public park that surrounded the Capitol building. Thomas Van Orden, a homeless lawyer, passed the monument every day on his way to the law library in the Capitol. One day, he decided to file suit. Writing for an all-conservative, five-justice majority, Chief Justice Rehnquist found that had the commandments stood alone, the display would have violated the establishment clause. Its message was, however, diluted when it appeared along with the other historical markers and statues. "We cannot say that Texas' display violates the First Amendment."

On the same day that the Court decided *Van Orden*, it ruled on another Ten Commandments display in *McCreary County v. American Civil Liberties Union of Kentucky*, but with a different outcome. The problem was that county officials took three attempts to dilute their displays. In McCreary County, the first showed the Ten Commandments alone, and the second modified it to include eight smaller, historical documents containing religious references as their sole common element. Only the third attempt, entitled "The Foundations of American Law and Government Display," consisted of nine framed documents of equal size, including the *Star Spangled Banner*'s lyrics and the Declaration of Independence accompanied by statements about their historical and legal significance. Justice Souter stated that it was impossible to distance the final message from the officials' initial motivation when they erected the monument. The county's purpose "needs to be understood in light of context; an implausible claim that governmental purpose has changed should not carry the day in a court of law any more than in a head with common sense." Justice Scalia's dissent demonstrated his adherence to originalism. "Those who wrote the Constitution believed that morality was essential to the well-being of society and that encouragement of religion was the best way to foster morality." The Court's attempt to "sandblast" the Ten Commandments from the public sphere defied the original meaning of the First Amendment's establishment clause.

Religious Liberty

Conservative justices continued their drive to allow for the accommodation of religion in public places like schools, and to protect against implementing policies, such as contraception provided through medical insurance, that conflict with their religious faiths. The Court increasingly sided with religious petitioners in the twenty-first century. In 2003, the Court tackled the question of the constitutionality of a postsecondary school scholarship program in Washington State that excluded students studying "devotional theology." In a seven to two decision in *Locke* v. *Davey*, Chief Justice Rehnquist held that, based on the state constitution, "given the historic and substantial state interest at issue, we … cannot conclude that the denial of funding for vocational religious instruction alone is inherently constitutionally suspect." Justices Scalia and Thomas dissented.

In its October term 2013, the Court ruled in *Town of Greece* v. *Galloway* that the recitation of prayers before town council meetings was appropriate even when the town mainly allowed Christian prayers with references to Jesus Christ. Justice Kennedy, writing for a bare majority, rejected the argument that the town had effectively endorsed Christianity as its official religion. He noted that prayers before legislative sessions were for legislators and did not force anyone else to follow the faith of the prayer giver. Justices Breyer, Ginsburg, Sotomayor, and Kagan dissented.

When the Trinity Lutheran Church in Missouri operated a licensed preschool and day care center, it applied for a state-funded grant to resurface its playground from the Missouri Department of Natural Resources, which provided recycled tires for this purpose. Because the state constitution provides that "no money shall ever be taken from the public treasury, directly or indirectly, in aid of any church," the department denied the application. Trinity Lutheran appealed and, in 2017, Chief Justice Roberts disagreed, writing for a seven to two majority in *Trinity Lutheran Church of Columbia* v. *Corner*. The department, he ruled, failed to acknowledge that "the exclusion of Trinity Lutheran from a public benefit for which it is otherwise qualified, solely because it is a church, is odious to our Constitution all the same, and cannot stand." Justices Sotomayor and Ginsburg dissented.

In 2020, the Court confronted several cases involving religious liberty issues. *Espinoza* v. *Montana Department of Revenue* focused on whether a person who contributes to a state scholarship program for private secular or parochial schools is eligible for a tax credit. In this case, three mothers applied for the tax credit for their children to attend a Catholic school but were denied because the state constitution "bars government aid" to any school "controlled in whole or in part by any church, sect, or denomination." Some 37 state constitutions have provisions like this one, known as a Blaine amendment after Representative James G. Blaine's 1875 attempt to amend the federal constitution with such language failed. Historians argue that these provisions were regarded as anti-Catholic measures. Montana's provision was adopted in 1972. In a five to four decision, the conservative majority, in an opinion by Chief Justice Roberts, ruled that "a State need not subsidize private education. But once a State decides to do so, it cannot disqualify some private schools solely because they are religious." By the time the court decided the case, the state had ended tax breaks for nonsectarian schools.

The question left unanswered in *Espinoza* was whether a state unconstitutionally barred students from receiving funding when they attend schools that provide religious instruction as part of the curriculum but offers it to those who attend secular schools. The Court agreed to hear arguments just on this question during its 2021–2022 term in *Carson v. Makin*.

Two other cases, both decided in 2020, concerned a judge-made doctrine known as "the ministerial exception" and the requirement that employers provide contraception in accordance with the Affordable Care Act (Obamacare). The justices decided both by the same seven to two majority.

In the first, *Our Lady of Guadeloupe School v. Morrisey-Berru*, Justice Alito expanded and redefined the meaning of the ministerial exception first described in *Hosanna-Tabor Evangelical Church and School v. Equal Employment Opportunity Commission*. In that 2012 case, Chief Justice Roberts held for a unanimous Court that federal employment discrimination laws do not apply to religious organizations when they choose their religious leaders. In the present case, the Court extended the doctrine to cover teachers in parochial schools who have no religious training. Writing for the Court, Justice Alito wrote, "Although these teachers were not given the title of 'minister' and have less religious training" than the teacher in *Hosanna-Tabor*, "we hold that their cases fall within the same rule that dictated our decision in *Hosanna-Tabor*. The religious education and formation of students is the very reason for the existence of most private religious schools, and therefore the selection and supervision of the teachers upon whom the schools rely to do this work lie at the core of their mission."

In the second case, *Little Sisters of the Poor Saints Peter and Paul Home v. Pennsylvania*, the Court reviewed a challenge to a 2017 Trump administration's rule that expanded exemptions from the ACA regarding the birth-control mandate (see Box 15.1). The new rule allowed private employers to decline to provide certain kinds of contraception if they held religious or moral objections to the mandate. The Third Circuit overturned the rules, but the Supreme Court, in an opinion by Justice Thomas, reinstated them as a matter of religious liberty and moral objection.

In June 2021, the Court decided, in *Fulton* v. *the City of Philadelphia*, a challenge to the Philadelphia Department of Social Services' foster care program that the department stated was unavailable to agencies that do not comply with city's equal employment law. The department claimed that Catholic Social Services failed to certify same-sex couples as foster parents. CSS and others challenged the policy as a violation of the free exercise clause of the First Amendment. The case lined up as a confrontation between the First Amendment's religious liberty clause and the Fourteenth's equal protection clause.

Catholic Social Services also asked the Court to reconsider *Employment Division* v. *Smith* (1990), which ruled that a neutral or generally applicable law may burden religious practices, rituals, and beliefs. Because the case involved a fundamental right (religious liberty), the justices used the strict scrutiny test to determine the outcome. In an opinion by Chief Justice Roberts, the Court unanimously ruled that the same-sex requirement issued by Philadelphia's Social

---

Box 15.1 *Little Sisters of the Poor Saints Peter and Paul Home* v. *Pennsylvania*

After two decisions from this Court and multiple failed regulatory attempts, the Federal Government has arrived at a solution that exempts the Little Sisters from the source of their complicity-based concerns–the administratively imposed contraceptive mandate. We hold today that the Departments had the statutory authority to craft that exemption, as well as the contemporaneously issued moral exemption. We further hold that the rules promulgating these exemptions are free from procedural defects. Therefore, we reverse the judgment of the Court of Appeals.

Justice Clarence Thomas
Little Sisters of the Poor Saints Peter and Paul Home v. *Pennsylvania* /
U.S. Department of Justice / Public domain

Services "cannot survive strict scrutiny, and violates the First Amendment." He wrote that the city's standard foster care is not generally applicable as required by *Employment Division*, which he declined to overrule. In this case, the First Amendment trumped the Fourteenth.

The Court also reviewed in 2021 several emergency measures related to restrictions California imposed on church services during the Covid-19 pandemic. While allowing film studios, restaurants, and other establishments to remain open to some indoor activities, the state prohibited or limited indoor church services and in-house prayer services. The Court ruled six to three in *South Bay United Pentecostal Church* v. *Newsom* and five to four in *Tandem* v. *Newsom* that the state's efforts were discriminatory and could not ban or limit indoor religious services.

Campaign Finance and Speech Rights

The Court also dealt with the First Amendment's impact on campaign financing, especially by corporations and labor unions. Congress first restricted corporate and union contributions to federal elections in 1907 with the passage of the Tillman Act, which was strongly supported by President Theodore Roosevelt. These limitations were upheld as recently as 2003 when the Supreme Court decided *McConnell* v. *Federal Election Commission*, which ruled on various provisions of the Bipartisan (or McCain–Feingold) Campaign Reform Act of 2002. The Court concentrated on the measure's Sections 203 and 441b, which addressed corporate and labor union campaign financing. *McConnell* was largely based on a 1990 decision in *Austin* v. *Michigan Chamber of Commerce* when the Court outlawed corporate funding of campaign advertisements in state elections. Justice Thurgood Marshall ruled that restrictions aimed at "the corrosive and distorting effects of immense aggregations of wealth that are accumulated with the help of the corporate form" in political campaigns were perfectly constitutional: they have "little or no correlation to the public's support for the corporation's political ideas."

The Court initially heard arguments in *Citizens United* v. *Federal Election Commission* in its 2008 October term. At issue was whether a conservative, nonprofit, political organization's distribution of a 90-minute film called *Hillary: The Movie* attacking Senator Hillary Clinton's candidacy for president, violated the McCain–Feingold Act or whether its distribution was protected by the First Amendment. When the case was first argued, the issue was narrow: whether a small nonprofit corporation could broadcast a film concerning a presidential candidate within the prohibited period that McCain–Feingold identified as 30 days before a primary and 60 days before a general election. The Court asked for re-arguments the following September after hearing Citizens United's opinion that if the government could ban a movie like *Hillary*, it could also ban a book financed by a corporation or labor union. On re-argument, the Court asked the parties to address not the initial narrow question, but two broader ones: should the Court overrule the part of *McConnell* that addressed the facial validity of McCain–Feingold and should it entirely overrule *Austin*.

Voting five to four along ideological lines, the conservative majority overruled *Austin* and overturned Sections 203 and 441b of McCain–Feingold. Justice Kennedy, who wrote the opinion for the Court, held that the criminal penalties that restricted corporate spending on "electioneering communications within 30 days of a primary election and 60 days of a general election" had a chilling effect on speech. The First Amendment required the law to treat corporations like natural persons in regard to campaign finance. "The Court has recognized that First Amendment protection extends to corporations," and "we now conclude that independent expenditures, including those made by corporations, do not give rise to corruption or the appearance of corruption." Justice Stevens, writing for three others in dissent, was persuaded that money did promote access and access led to influence and possible corruption: the larger the amounts, the greater the influence.

In June 2012, the Court rejected an opportunity to revisit *Citizens United* when a Montana state law, which had been on the books for a hundred years, restricted corporate campaign financing. In *American Tradition Partnership* v. *Bullock*, the Court declared that "the question presented in this case is whether the holding of *Citizens United* applies to the Montana state law. There can be no serious doubt that it does. Montana's arguments in support of the judgment below either were already rejected in *Citizens United*, or fail to meaningfully distinguish that case." Four justices, led by Stephen Breyer, objected.

In an important 2021 free speech decision involving schoolchildren, the Court heard arguments in *Mahanoy School District* v. *B.L.* (initials are used because the student is a minor). It involved a Pennsylvania high school student, Brandi Levy, who posted negative and lewd attacks on her school and coaches on social media after she became angry when she failed to make varsity cheerleading. She posted on Snapchat while off-campus on a weekend, condemning her school and cheerleading coaches. Although her post automatically disappeared after 24 hours, more than 250 people saw it and one reported it to school officials. Her coach then suspended her from the junior varsity squad for the whole of her sophomore year. The question for the Court was whether school administrators may discipline off-campus student speech. In an eight to one decision, the justices ruled that the First Amendment protected Brandi's speech, despite its vulgarity. Writing for the Court and using her initials, Justice Breyer stated that "it might be tempting to dismiss B.L.'s words as unworthy of the robust First Amendment protections discussed herein. But sometimes it is necessary to protect the superfluous in order to preserve the necessary." He did not determine the limits school authorities have to punish student speech made outside of schoolgrounds. Justice Thomas dissented alone: arguing from an originalist position, he stated that public schoolchildren have long been subject to "strict discipline" imparted by their teachers.

The Right to Bear Arms

If the Court granted greater freedom for campaign financing and schoolchildren, the same was true for the right to bear arms. The Second Amendment reads, "A well-regulated militia, being necessary to the security of a free state, the right of the people to keep and bear arms shall not be infringed." The Court, throughout its history, rarely confronted the question of whether the wording of the amendment protected and guaranteed an individual right of gun ownership or a collective right for the purpose of forming a militia, a citizen armed force. Americans in the eighteenth century distrusted standing professional armies and relied on a citizen army or militia of able-bodied men to defend the community. The Second Amendment pro-moted gun ownership for this purpose. Its language and the historical record surrounding its crafting and adoption were, however, ambig-uous. The resulting debate long centered on the meaning of the right of gun possession as an individual or collective right.

This question emerged in the late twentieth and twenty-first centuries' debate on the limits of gun control and gun safety laws. Could the government require buyers of firearms to obtain permits? Must a purchaser wait a length of time before taking possession of them? Must owners register their guns? Could government prohibit minors, convicted felons, and the mentally disturbed from owning guns? Could government ban entire categories of guns or the size of magazines? In 1939, in *United States* v. *Miller*, Justice James McReynolds ruled for a unanimous Court that a sawed-off shotgun was inappropriate for military use and thus could not "contribute to the common defense." McReynolds did not consider whether the amendment guaranteed an individual the right to own a gun or reserved only to a collective body like a militia or the National Guard. Nearly 70 years later, in 2008, the Court addressed this very issue in *District of Columbia* v. *Heller*.

The case involved a Washington, DC, law that banned handgun possession by making it a crime to carry an unregistered firearm. It required residents to keep lawfully owned firearms unloaded and disassembled or bound by a trigger lock or similar device. Dick Anthony Heller, a security guard, tried to register a handgun to protect himself at home. After the DC government rejected his application, he sued the city to stop it from enforcing the ban on handgun registration, the licensing requirement insofar as it prohibited carrying an unlicensed firearm in the home, and the disassembly or trigger lock requirement that prohibited the use of functional firearms in the home. Justice Scalia, with four conservative justices joining him in an originalist decision, reviewed why the first federal Congress included the Second Amendment by determining the meaning of the amendment's words. The first prefatory clause guaranteed the creation of a militia. The decisive second clause concerning the right to bear arms demonstrated that the framers conferred "an individual right to keep and bear arms" for self-defense. In contrast, four dissenters, led by Justice John Paul Stevens, argued from an originalist position as well: for them, the framers of the amendment designed it as a community not an individual right to forestall the development of a professional standing army. A citizen militia required that every able-bodied male own a firearm for the sole purpose to defend the nation (Box 15.2).

Two years later, the Court revisited the issue. The same five justices overturned a Chicago ban and held that the Second Amendment applied to the states through the Fourteenth Amendment's due process clause. In *McDonald* v. *City of Chicago*, Justice Samuel Alito agreed

Box 15.2 *District of Columbia* v. *Heller* (2008), Justices Antonin Scalia and John Paul Stevens, excerpts

We find that the [Second Amendment] guarantee[s] the individual right to possess and carry weapons in case of confrontation. This meaning is strongly confirmed by the historical background of the Second Amendment. We look to this because it has always been widely understood that the Second Amendment, like the First and Fourth Amendments, codified a *pre-existing* right. The very text of the Second Amendment implicitly recognizes the pre-existence of the right and declares only that it "shall not be infringed." Justice Antonin Scalia

The Second Amendment was adopted to protect the right of the people of each of the several States to maintain a well-regulated militia. It was a response to concerns raised during the ratification of the Constitution that the power of Congress to disarm the state militias and create a national standing army posed an intolerable threat to the sovereignty of the several States. Neither the text of the Amendment nor the arguments advanced by its proponents evidenced the slightest interest in limiting any legislature's authority to regulate private civilian uses of firearms. Specifically, there is no indication that the Framers of the Amendment intended to enshrine the common-law right of self-defense in the Constitution.

Justice John Paul Stevens
District of Columbia v. *Heller* 2008 /
U.S. Department of Justice / Public domain

that the amendment protected an individual's right to own firearms, but he now expanded it to every state, county, and municipality. The decision marked yet another moment when the Court applied one of the rights in the first 10 amendments to the states.

In his last major opinion before his retirement, John Paul Stevens attacked Alito's reasoning. Stevens argued that the Court should allow the states the right to experiment, as Justice Louis D. Brandeis suggested in 1932 in *New State Ice Co.* v. *Liebmann*. Brandeis had written that "it is one of the happy incidents of the federal system that a single courageous state may, if its citizens choose, serve as a laboratory and try novel social and economic experiments without risk to the rest of the country." Stevens thought the states were "capable of safeguarding the interest in keeping and bearing arms."

Meantime, the Court accepted a case, *New York State Rifle & Pistol Association* v. *Bruen*, presenting the most important open question concerning gun rights, namely whether a person with a gun permit can constitutionally carry a concealed weapon outside the home for self-defense purposes. The justices plan oral arguments in the term beginning in October 2021. Most observers predicted that the conservative majority of Chief Justice Roberts and Justices Thomas, Alito, Gorsuch, Kavanaugh, and Barrett will rule to allow gunowners to carry their concealed weapons outside their homes.

The Right to Privacy

In 1997, the Court decided two issues regarding privacy rights: whether the Constitution permitted physician-assisted suicide for terminally ill patients and whether it allowed for late-term abortions after viability when a fetus may live outside the womb naturally or with artificial support.

For the first, in a pair of cases, *Washington* v. *Glucksberg* and *Vacco* v. *Quill*, a unanimous Court upheld laws in Washington and New York State prohibiting physicians from prescribing lethal drugs to terminally ill patients. Meantime, in 1994, Oregon became the first state to legalize assisted suicide when voters approved a ballot measure enacting the Oregon Death With Dignity Act (ODWDA). The law required terminally ill patients to make the request to their physician and to undergo psychological counseling if they suffered from depression or other emotional disorder. They also had to obtain a second opinion to confirm the attending physician's diagnosis that a patient's illness was terminal. Physicians could prepare the prescription but could not administer the drugs. The patient alone decided when and whether to take them.

Shortly thereafter, the Department of Justice decided that Schedule II of the Controlled Substances Act (CSA) conflicted with the ODWDA: that section concerned drugs available only by a physician's written prescription. In 2001, US Attorney General John Ashcroft issued an Interpretative Rule that declared that using controlled substances to assist suicide was not a legitimate medical practice under Schedule II. A physician, a pharmacist, and some terminally ill residents challenged the Ashcroft Rule. By the time the case reached the Supreme Court, Alberto Gonzales had succeeded Ashcroft as US attorney general, and the case took his name in its title. In 2006, the Court ruled in *Gonzales* v. *Oregon* by a vote of six to three that the attorney general had no authority to prohibit doctors from prescribing regulated drugs for use in physician-assisted suicide under a state law permitting the procedure. Justice Kennedy argued that if the attorney general could issue rules concerning the use of drugs by a physician, "he could decide whether any particular drug may be used for any particular purpose, or indeed whether a physician who administers any controversial treatment could be deregistered."

The following year, the Court dealt with the second privacy case when it upheld a federal law known as the Partial-Birth Abortion Ban Act that had allowed late-term abortions (generally after 20 weeks of a pregnancy) only when the life, but not the health, of the woman was at risk. In 2000, in *Stenberg* v. *Carhart*, the Court overturned a similar state law in Nebraska, because it failed to provide a health exception. After Congress passed the law banning such procedures, the same physician who challenged the Nebraska law, Dr. Leroy Carhart, now opposed the federal measure. Writing for five justices in *Gonzales* v. *Carhart*, Justice Kennedy upheld the federal law on the grounds that no medical evidence revealed that a woman needed a late-term abortion for health reasons. Besides, "it seems unexceptionable to conclude some women come to regret their choice to abort the infant life they once created and sustained. Severe depression and loss of esteem can follow."

In writing for four justices in dissent, Justice Ginsburg attacked Kennedy for viewing women through Justice Bradley's lens in the 1883 Myra Bradwell case. Bradley had argued that men were women's protectors, because the ladies occupied a secondary position in society. "This way of thinking reflects ancient notions about women's place in the family and under the Constitution," Ginsburg argued. Plenty of medical evidence supported the dangers to women's health in some late-term pregnancies. As a result, "the Court offers flimsy and transparent justifications for upholding a nationwide ban" on late-term abortions. The Court had clearly drawn the line on a woman's right to an abortion in this case.

Some states placed restrictions on abortion clinics, requiring their physicians to have admitting privileges in a nearby hospital and to have medical standards that were the same as ambulatory surgical centers. In Texas, because of a law like this one, the number of clinics declined from 42 to 19. When a challenge reached the Court in *Whole Women's Health v. Hellerstedt*, the justices in 2016 ruled five to three that these restrictions placed an undue burden on a woman's right to an abortion. Justice Breyer, writing for the Court, noted that "we have found nothing in Texas's record evidence that shows that … the new law advanced Texas's legitimate interest in protecting women's health." Because the decision came while the Court lacked a ninth vote due to Scalia's death, a new case involving the same question from Louisiana arrived at the Court in 2020, *June Medical Services v. Russo*. In a five to four ruling, Chief Justice Roberts held that the precedent set in *Whole Women's Health* required the same outcome and the law was over-turned. It was the first time the chief justice joined the majority to uphold abortion rights.

The Court agreed to hear a challenge to a Mississippi law in its October 2021 term prohibiting abortions after 15 weeks of a preg-nancy. In *Dobbs v. Jackson Women's Health Organization*, the justices planned to examine whether "all pre-viability prohibitions on abortion are unconstitutional." Pre-viability has been a key component of the Court's jurisprudence from *Roe v. Wade* to the present: it protects a woman's right to obtain an abortion before the fetus can survive outside her womb. The Court must decide whether the law creates an undue burden on a woman seeking an abortion. With President Trump's successful addition of Justices Gorsuch, Kavanaugh, and Barrett, anti-abortion groups hoped the Court would use this case to overrule *Roe*. A decision is expected in the spring of 2022.

16

The Struggle for Equal Rights and Criminal Justice

The executive republic also witnessed changes in affirmative action, same-sex relationships, and voting rights. During this 25-year period, because conservative justices dominated the Court, some observers predicted that their decisions would end affirmative action, prohibit same-sex protections, and weaken voting rights. In fact, the Court upheld affirmative action programs and expanded same-sex relationship guarantees. The justices, however, reviewed the Voting Rights Act of 1965 and with a bare majority decided that Congress had failed to update where discriminatory practices in voting took place in the United States. In fact, Congress had not updated its list of states, counties, and municipalities where voter discrimination took place since 1972. The result was that a major section of the VRA, called preclearance, was declared unconstitutional until Congress acted: this section required the listed states and subdivisions to first gain Justice Department approval for any changes in their voting procedures, such as moving a polling place or requiring voter identification. As of 2021, Congress still had not acted, although some members of Congress introduced several proposals to restore the preclearance provision. In 2021, the latest such proposal was the John Lewis Voting Rights Act, named for the civil rights leader and member of the House of Representatives who died in 2020.

American Constitutional History: A Brief Introduction, Second Edition. Jack Fruchtman.
© 2022 John Wiley & Sons, Inc. Published 2022 by John Wiley & Sons, Inc.

Affirmative Action and Education

The Court returned to affirmative action in public higher education in 2003 in two University of Michigan cases. The justices focused on the admissions programs at the university's undergraduate college and its law school. The outcomes of the two cases were very different. Writing for a six to three majority, Chief Justice Rehnquist found in *Gratz* v. *Bollinger* that the undergraduate admissions program amounted to a numerical quota, which the Court had banned in *Bakke* in 1978. The admissions office admitted applicants if they reached a minimum of 100 points on a scale that included their standardized test scores, grade point average, extracurricular activities, being the children of alumni, and other factors. Among those was a 20-point award for membership in an underrepresented racial or ethnic minority group. "Unlike Justice Powell's example [in *Bakke*], where the race of a 'particular applicant' could be considered without being decisive," the program's "automatic distribution of twenty points has the effect of making 'the factor of race … decisive.'" Under the strict scrutiny test, the program was not narrowly tailored to achieve the compelling interest of diversity.

Meantime, a bare majority concluded that the law school admission program in *Grutter* v. *Bollinger* used race only as one factor among many. For five justices, it was therefore constitutionally sound, again according to principles laid out in *Bakke* following the model of the Harvard Plan. Here, Sandra Day O'Connor used the strict scrutiny test to rule that the law school's use of race as one factor among many in admitting students achieved the compelling interest of creating a diverse student body in a narrowly tailored manner. She also noted that in her opinion, affirmative action programs would end in 25 years, marking what would be the fiftieth anniversary of the *Bakke* decision. All four dissenting justices filed opinions.

In 2013, the Court reviewed, but did not rule on, yet another affirmative action case involving a higher education admissions program. The University of Texas's admissions program considered race as one factor among many when determining a candidate's qualifications. In *Fisher* v. *University of Texas at Austin*, Justice Kennedy's opinion for the Court stated that, before he and his colleagues ruled on the program's constitutionality, the Fifth Circuit Court of Appeals must first determine whether the program was "narrowly tailored" to achieve the university's goal of creating a diverse student body. Only Justice Ginsburg dissented.

On reconsideration, the Fifth Circuit again issued a summary judgment in favor of the University. Fisher again appealed to the Supreme Court, but without Justice Scalia, who died in February of 2016, and without Justice Kagan, who recused herself. She was the Solicitor General of the United States when the case first reached the Supreme Court. By a vote of four to three, the Court affirmed the Fifth Circuit's decision. Kennedy wrote the opinion of the Court and for the first time he voted to uphold an affirmative action program. He noted, that "as this Court's cases have made clear … the compelling interest that justifies consideration of race in college admissions is not an interest in enrolling a certain number of minority students." Rather, a university may institute a race-conscious admissions program as a means of obtaining "the educational benefits that flow from student body diversity."

A challenge to an affirmative action program with an unwieldy title reached the Court in 2014: *Schuette* v. *Coalition to Defend Affirmative Action, Integration and Immigration Rights and Fight for Equality By Any Means Necessary (BAMN)*. The justices decided that a constitutional amendment, added by referendum in Michigan, could ban affirmative action in public university admissions. The amendment was adopted after the 2003 decision in *Gratz* v. *Bollinger* when the Court ruled that the University of Michigan improperly used race as one factor among many in rejecting Jennifer Gratz's application for undergraduate admission (the Harvard Plan, upheld in *Bakke*, 1978). Gratz then became the chief promoter of the amendment. In a bare majority of five to four, Justice Alito held that the amendment expressed the will of the people of Michigan and did not violate the equal protection clause. Such issues, he wrote, should be left to the political process.

Finally, the Court in 2021 considered whether to hear oral arguments in a challenge to Harvard University's race-conscious admission program, which allegedly discriminated against Asian Americans. The litigants in *Students for Fair Admissions* v. *President and Fellows of Harvard College* asked the Court to overturn the program on two grounds: it violated Title VI of the Civil Rights Act of 1964, which forbid racial discrimination in any program receiving federal funds; the justices should overrule the *Grutter* decision, which affirmed the race-conscious admission program at the University of Michigan School of Law. The justices planned to decide on whether to hear the case during the October 2021 term.

The Court also resolved the issue of forced school desegregation at the elementary and secondary level. Led by Chief Justice Roberts, the

Court in a 2007 five to four decision overturned a Seattle school board's attempt to ensure diversity among its high school students. The plan was undertaken, not by court order, but voluntarily by school officials. In *Parents Involved in Community Schools* v. *Seattle School District No. 1*, Roberts ruled that the placement of children based on race violated the equal protection clause. "The way to stop discrimination on the basis of race," he wrote, "is to stop discriminating on the basis of race," echoing a 1979 statement by William Van Alstyne, professor of law at Duke.

However, the decision did not establish a precedent, because Justice Kennedy, who supplied the fifth vote, concurred rather than joining the majority. He left the door slightly ajar for racial balancing because racial diversity was "a compelling educational goal" and "a school district may pursue" it. Kennedy offered some advice to school boards on how to achieve a constitutionally approved program of desegregation: "strategic site selection of new schools; drawing attendance zones with general recognition of the demographics of the neighborhoods; allocating resources for special programs; recruiting students and faculty in a targeted fashion; and tracking enrollments, performance, and other statistics by race."

Same-Sex and Transgender Rights

In same-sex marriage and other gay rights cases, Justice Kennedy until his 2018 retirement led the Court in asserting the rights of same-sex couples. In 2003, he ruled for a six to three majority in *Lawrence* v. *Texas* that two consenting adults of the same sex enjoyed a privacy right to engage in sodomy in the privacy of their own home. John Lawrence and Tyron Garner were arrested when police in Houston entered their bedroom after receiving reports of a man "going crazy" with a gun in the house. In reviewing the Texas anti-sodomy law, Kennedy held that the men "were free as adults to engage in the private conduct in the exercise of their liberty under the due process clause of the Fourteenth Amendment." He overruled the 1986 *Bowers* v. *Hardwick* decision when Justice Byron White determined that the Constitution conferred no "fundamental right upon homosexuals to engage in sodomy." Kennedy argued that this position "failed to appreciate the extent of the liberty at stake."

In the spring of 2013, the Court decided two cases concerning gay and lesbian rights. The first attacked Proposition 8 (also known as Prop 8), a California ballot initiative passed by referendum in 2008 that amended the state constitution, stating that "only marriage between a man and a woman" is valid or recognized in California. In the first, a private organization, which had initially promoted the measure, defended it. Writing for a bare majority in *Hollingsworth* v. *Perry*, Chief Justice John Roberts, joined by Justices Scalia, Ginsburg, Breyer, and Kagan, ruled that "no matter how deeply committed petitioners may be to upholding Proposition 8 or how zealous [their] advocacy, that is not a 'particularized' interest sufficient to create a case or controversy under Article III." They were a private party and "we have never before upheld the standing of a private party to defend the constitutionality of a state statute when state officials have chosen not to," the chief concluded, and "we decline to do so for the first time here."

The second involved a challenge to Section 3 of the Defense of Marriage Act (DOMA) that President Bill Clinton signed into law in 1996. The provision denied federal benefits, including those involving inheritance and approximately a thousand other federal statutes and regulations, to people in same-sex marriages even if a state recognized those marriages. The United States, under President Obama, declined to defend the DOMA provision. Instead, the Republican leadership of the House of Representatives defended the law. *United States* v. *Windsor* focused on whether Edith Windsor, the surviving spouse of a same-sex marriage, must pay federal inheritance taxes after her deceased spouse left her a bequest. Section 3 of DOMA required the federal government to treat same-sex couples as unmarried. As a result, the Internal Revenue Service sent Windsor a $363,000 inheritance tax bill. She was ineligible for the federal estate tax exemption for surviving spouses. After the IRS denied her request for a refund, she appealed to federal district court. Her claim was based on the doctrine of reverse incorporation, the very principle that Chief Justice Earl Warren created in the 1954 *Bolling* v. *Sharpe* desegregation case and Justice Ginsburg, as an attorney, used in the 1973 *Frontiero* v. *Richardson* decision: the application of the equal protection clause of the Fourteenth Amendment to the United States government through the liberty component of the Fifth Amendment's due process clause. Windsor argued that the United States had deprived her of the equal protection of the laws as applied to the United States.

The district court granted standing to the Republican House leadership as "an interested party" and then ruled that Windsor was entitled to a refund, because DOMA denied her equal protection. The US Court of Appeals for the Second Circuit affirmed. In June 2013, Justice Kennedy, writing for a bare five to four majority, agreed with the lower courts' ruling. To deny Windsor the benefits that other married couples possessed violated the equal protection clause. He especially focused on the animosity against the gay community that stimulated the passage of discriminatory laws like DOMA.

In 2015, the Court ruled five to four in *Obergefell* v. *Hodges* that same-sex marriage was guaranteed by the Constitution's Equal Protection and Due Process Clauses. Ruling five to four, Justice Kennedy emphasized his notion of the living constitution (Box 16.1). For him, the right to marry is a fundamental right. On the same grounds, he ruled that all states must recognize same-sex marriages performed in other states. "It is now clear that the challenged laws burden the liberty of same-sex couples, and it must be further acknowledged that they abridge central precepts of equality … Especially against a long history of disapproval of their relationships, this denial to same-sex couples of the right to marry works a grave and continuing harm. The imposition of this disability on gays and lesbians serves to disrespect and subordinate them. And the Equal Protection Clause, like the Due Process Clause, prohibits this unjustified infringement of the fundamental right to marry."

Box 16.1   *Obergefell* v. *Hodges* (2015), Justice Kennedy's living constitution and Justice Scalia's originalism, excerpts

The nature of injustice is that we may not always see it in our own times. The generations that wrote and ratified the Bill of Rights and the Fourteenth Amendment did not presume to know the extent of freedom in all of its dimensions, and so they entrusted to future generations a character protecting the right of all persons to enjoy liberty as we learn its meaning.

Justice Anthony Kennedy

When the Fourteenth Amendment was ratified in 1868, every State limited marriage to one man and one woman, and no one doubted the constitutionality of doing so. That resolves these cases.

Justice Antonin Scalia
Obergefell v. *Hodges* 2015 /
U.S. Department of Justice / Public domain

All four dissenters filed opinions, a rare move. The lead one by Chief Justice Roberts noted that "if you are among the many Americans – of whatever sexual orientation – who favor expanding same-sex marriage, by all means celebrate today's decision. Celebrate the achievement of a desired goal. Celebrate the opportunity for a new expression of commitment to a partner. Celebrate the availability of new benefits. But do not celebrate the Constitution. It had nothing to do with it." When he read his dissent from the bench the day the decision was announced, Court observers noted it was the first time he had a read a dissent aloud. Also dissenting, Justice Scalia wrote that only the people should decide this issue, not five unelected judges. It appeared at the time that same-sex marriage was a settled matter, but some commentators began to wonder after the confirmation of conservative Justices Gorsuch, Kavanaugh, and Barrett.

The *Obergefell* case involved constitutional interpretation. In the October 2019 term, the court engaged in statutory interpretation to determine whether Title VII of the Civil Right Act of 1964 protected gay, lesbian, and transgender people against employment discrimination. Historically, courts have interpreted the law as only guaranteeing non-discrimination based on male and female sex characteristics. The Court heard three cases together: *Altitude Express Inc.* v. *Zarda*; *R.G. and G.R. Harris Funeral Homes* v. *EEOC*; and *Bostock* v. *Clayton County, Georgia*. The transgender case involved Aimee Stephens who worked at a funeral home. When she came to work as a transwoman, her supervisor fired her, telling her that it would violate "God's commands" if he allowed her "to deny [her] sex while acting as a representative of [the] organization." The other two cases involved gay men whose employers fired them because they were openly gay.

In a landmark decision, Justice Neil Gorsuch ruled that discrimination "on the basis of sex" outlawed by Title VII of the Civil Rights Act of 1964 included these three groups of people. He wrote that "an employer who fires an individual for being homosexual or transgender fires that person for traits or action it would not have questioned in members of a different sex. Sex plays a necessary and undisguisable role in the decision, exactly what Title VII forbids. Those who adopted the Civil Rights Act might not have anticipated their work would lead to this particular result … But the limits of the drafters' imagination supply no reason to ignore the law's demands. When the express terms of a statute give us one answer and extratextual considerations suggest another, it's no contest. Only the written word is the law, and all persons are entitled to its benefit."

Chief Justice Roberts joined the decision along with four liberal Justices Ginsburg, Breyer, Kagan, and Sotomayor. Justice Alito, in dissent, argued that only Congress had the authority to update the meaning of Title VII: "There is only one word for what the court has done today: legislation. The document that the court releases is in the form of a judicial opinion interpreting a statute, but that is deceptive."

Voting Rights

The Court in 2013 dealt with two election challenges. In *Arizona v. Inter Tribal Council of Arizona*, the Court ruled on both constitutional and statutory grounds that the federal National Voter Registration Act (NVRA) of 1993 preempted Arizona's 2004 law that required prospective voters to prove they were US citizens when voting by providing copies of passports, birth certificates, driver's licenses, or naturalization papers. The act, also known as the "motor voter law," because the application form is available in motor vehicle offices, was designed to increase access to registration. Writing for a seven to two majority, Justice Scalia held that the Elections Clause in Article I, Section 4, empowered Congress to preempt all state elections laws. Congress may prescribe all federal and state election rules regarding "the times, places, and manner" of all federal and now state elections. Under the NVRA, Congress required the states to "accept and use" a federal form to register voters who must declare – but not prove – under penalty of perjury, that they were US citizens. The state law conflicted with the federal law and could not stand.

The second case involved a challenge to two sections of the Voting Rights Act (VRA) of 1965, which Congress passed to end racial discrimination in voting, especially in the South. Section 4 laid out a formula to determine whether states and localities discriminated in their voting procedures. If they did, they fell under the requirements of Section 5. By 1972, Section 4 identified 9 states, mostly southern, 12 cities, and 57 counties with histories of voting discrimination. Subject to Section 5, these jurisdictions were required to gain permission from either the US Department of Justice or the district court for the District of Columbia if they wished to make any electoral changes, including minor ones such as moving a polling place from one location to another or changing the size or shape of electoral districts. Critics of Section 5 claimed that the law undermined the principle of state equality and that it was "a badge of shame" for them to have to ask federal permission, or "preclearance," before they made any changes to voting procedures.

A challenge to the VRA arose in 2010 in *Northwest Austin Municipal Utility District No. 1* v. *Holder*. The Court declined to rule on its constitutionality at that time, but dealt only with the statutory issue: did the act cover utility districts? Writing for the Court, Chief Justice Roberts ruled that it did, but added that "things have changed in the South. Voter turnout and registration rates now approach parity. Blatantly discriminatory evasions of federal decrees are rare. And minority candidates hold office at unprecedented levels." With that sentiment in mind, officials in Shelby County, Alabama, claimed that Congress should not have included the county when it overwhelmingly reauthorized the act for 25 years in 2006. The racial makeup of the county's voting registration had drastically changed since the act originally passed. While preclearance may have been necessary in 1965, it no longer was. Many minority voters were registered, voted, and held public office in numbers far greater than 45 years before. The district court and the United States Court of Appeals for the District of Columbia upheld the 2006 reauthorization, and Shelby County appealed.

In *Shelby County* v. *Holder* (2013), Chief Justice Roberts, writing for Justices Scalia, Kennedy, Thomas, and Alito, agreed that the information regarding voting violations in the named jurisdictions was outdated. "In 1965, the states could be divided into two groups: those with a recent history of voting tests and low voter registration and turnout, and those without those characteristics ... Congress based its coverage formula on that distinction. Today the nation is no longer divided along those lines, yet the Voting Rights Act continues to treat it as if it were." He acknowledged that the formula worked well for several years, but it was now time to update the formula. Congress last revised the data in 1972. Voting in the South did not reflect "current conditions," Roberts declared. In Alabama, in 1965, 69 percent of all eligible white voters were registered to vote whereas only 19 percent of black voters were. In 2004, the numbers dramatically changed: 74 percent for whites versus 73 percent for blacks. He attributed this change to the VRA but contended that Congress must update the formula to require preclearance, thus overturning Section 4 but leaving the rest of the act intact (Box 16.2).

> **Box 16.2** *Shelby County* v. *Holder* (2013), excerpts
>
> Striking down an Act of Congress "is the gravest and most deli-
> cate duty that this Court is called on to perform." *Blodgett* v.
> *Holden* (1927) (Holmes, J., concurring). We do not do so lightly.
> That is why, in 2009, we took care to avoid ruling on the consti-
> tutionality of the Voting Rights Act when asked to do so, and
> instead resolved the case then before us on statutory grounds.
> But in issuing that decision, we expressed our broader concerns
> about the constitutionality of the Act. Congress could have
> updated the coverage formula at that time, but did not do so. Its
> failure to act leaves us today with no choice but to declare Section
> 4(b) unconstitutional. The formula in that section can no longer
> be used as a basis for subjecting jurisdictions to preclearance. ...
>
> Our country has changed, and while any racial discrimination
> in voting is too much, Congress must ensure that the legislation
> it passes to remedy that problem speaks to current conditions.
>
>
>
> Chief Justice John G. Roberts Jr.
> *Shelby County* v. *Holder* 2013 /
> U.S. Department of Justice / Public domain
>
>

The John Lewis Voting Rights Advancement Act, named for the late
Democratic Georgia representative and civil rights activist, was introduced each year beginning in 2019. Its goal was to restore Section 4 by
creating a new formula to identify discriminatory actions in the states,
municipalities, and counties and to reestablish Section 5's preclearance
by the Justice Department. Although the House passed it, the Senate
had not as of December 2021.

Section 2 of the VRA was not at issue in any of these cases. It allows
plaintiffs to file lawsuits after they witnessed racial discriminatory effects
in voting procedures. This section was challenged in 2021 in *Brnovich*
v. *Democratic National Committee*. The suit challenged two provisions
of Arizona law: one allows election officials to discard votes when they
were cast at the wrong precinct and the other prohibited "ballot harvesting," which permits party officials to deliver absentee or mail-in
ballots to polling places. The penalty for violating the second provision
was a two-year prison term and a fine of $150,000. Exceptions to ballot

harvesting included family members, caregivers, mail carriers, and election officials. The DNC claimed the provisions had a disproportionate effect on minorities' voting rights, the standard by which Section 2 should be judged. In *Brnovich*, the Court ruled six to three, in an opinion by Justice Alito, that the laws did not violate Section 2 of the Voting Rights Act or exhibit racial discrimination.

Meantime, after President Trump claimed he would have won the 2020 presidential election but for voter fraud, several states put new practices into law. The Brennan Center for Justice at New York University School of Law counted nearly 400 proposals in 48 states restricting voting rights. These included hardening voter identification procedures, restricting early voting hours and days, closing or moving polling places, and other factors. Democrats in the House in 2021 passed the For the People Act. Designed to expand access to voting, it aimed to reduce the influence of large amounts of money in campaigns, especially when the sources of funding were unknown, and strengthen ethics rules for public servants. In June 2021, all Republican senators killed it by voting against debating it. President Biden's attorney general, Merrick Garland, pledged to make voting rights a key element of the Department of Justice.

Capital Punishment and Criminal Justice

The Court also ruled on the government's authority to execute those found guilty of capital crimes. Two cases in the early twenty-first century focused on a person's state of mind and level of maturity when committing a capital crime. The first, *Atkins* v. *Virginia* in 2002, asked whether a state could execute a person judged to be "mentally challenged" (at the time, the justices used the term "mentally retarded"). Six justices answered no. Writing for the Court in overruling the 1989 decision in *Penry* v. *Lynaugh*, Justice John Paul Stevens noted that an increasing number of states outlawed the execution of the mentally challenged so that a national consensus had emerged opposing it. Moreover, retribution, the primary reason for capital punishment, was inappropriate for the mentally challenged because they possess "lesser culpability" than those not so challenged. The key precedent Stevens cited was a noncapital case *Trop* v. *Dulles* (1958), which involved the loss of US citizenship by a combat soldier who had deserted during World War II. The principle in that case focused on whether Americans could lose their citizenship because of "the evolving standards of decency that mark the progress of a maturing society." The Court had answered no.

In 2005, in *Roper* v. *Simmons*, for the same two major reasons – the growth of a national consensus and reduced mental culpability – the Court ended executions of those who committed a capital crime before they turned age 18. Ruling five to four, with Justice Kennedy writing for the Court, the majority again used the *Trop* principle to argue that a national consensus had developed among the states to oppose the execution of people who committed capital crimes when they were minors. Kennedy noted that juveniles under 18 were incapable of behaving like adults. They were far more vulnerable to negative influences than were adults due to peer pressure and besides "the character of a juvenile is not as well formed as that of an adult." After 1990, the United States was the only Western democracy that executed juveniles, putting it in the company of Iran, Pakistan, Saudi Arabia, Yemen, Nigeria, the Democratic Republic of Congo, and China. And yet, "each of these countries has either abolished capital punishment for juveniles or made public disavowal of the practice. In sum, it is fair to say that the United States now stands alone in a world that has turned its face against the juvenile death penalty."

As a result of *Roper*, the justices tackled the thorny problem of life without parole (LWOP) sentences for juvenile offenders. With Kennedy leading the way, the Court in 2012 banned mandatory LWOP sentencing for juveniles in *Miller* v. *Alabama*. Two years later, in *Montgomery* v. *Louisiana*, the justices extended this ruling to make such sentencing even rarer by proclaiming that the sentence must be reserved for "those whose crimes reflect permanent incorrigibility." After Kennedy's retirement in 2018, replaced by Brett Kavanaugh and with the addition of Amy Coney Barrett, the Court changed course. In 2021, in a case involving the murder of a grandfather by his fifteen-year-old grandson, Brett Jones. the Court ruled that the judge's discretion allowed him to avoid making a factual determination that the defendant was "permanently" incorrigible. Kavanaugh thus upheld Brett's life-without-parole sentence in *Jones* v. *Mississippi*.

In 2015, the Court reviewed a challenge to a method of execution and the rights of a prisoner to be free of pain when put to death. After Oklahoma adopted lethal injection as its preferred method of execution, it settled on a three-drug protocol of (1) sodium thiopental (a barbiturate) to induce a state of unconsciousness, (2) a paralytic agent to inhibit all muscular-skeletal movements, and (3) potassium chloride to induce cardiac arrest. In an earlier case, *Baze* v. *Rees* (2008), the Court held that this protocol does not violate the Eighth Amendment's prohibition against cruel and unusual punishments. Anti-death-penalty advocates then pressured pharmaceutical companies to prevent sodium thiopental and, later, another barbiturate called pentobarbital from being used in executions. Unable to obtain either sodium thiopental or pentobarbital, Oklahoma used a 500-milligram dose of midazolam, a sedative, as the first drug in its three-drug protocol. Dentists often use it to put patients to sleep before pulling their teeth.

Oklahoma death-row inmate Richard Glossip and others claimed that the use of midazolam violated the Eighth Amendment. They argued that they would feel pain associated with administration of the second and third drugs. The federal district court held that the prisoners failed to identify a known and available alternative method of execution that presented a substantially less severe risk of pain. The court also ruled that the prisoners failed to establish a likelihood of showing that the use of midazolam created a demonstrated risk of severe pain. The United States Court of Appeals for the Tenth Circuit affirmed.

In *Glossip* v. *Gross*, the prisoners appealed to the Supreme Court, which, voting five to four, upheld the Court of Appeals' decision on two grounds. Justice Alito agreed with the district court that "first, the prisoners failed to identify a known and available alternative method of execution that entails a lesser risk of pain, a requirement of all Eighth Amendment method-of-execution claims." And second, "the district court did not commit clear error when it found that the prisoners failed to establish that Oklahoma's use of a massive dose of midazolam in its execution protocol entails a substantial risk of severe pain." Justice Breyer couched his passionate dissent in living constitutionalist language: he echoed Thurgood Marshall and William Brennan who argued that it was time for the Court to prohibit the death penalty in all cases. In a concurrence responding to him, Justice Scalia as an originalist wrote, "The framers of our Constitution disagreed bitterly on the matter. For that reason, they handled it the same way they handled many other controversial issues: they left it to the People to decide. By arrogating to himself the power to overturn that decision, Justice Breyer does not just reject the death penalty, he rejects the Enlightenment."

Congress in 2018, with bipartisan support, passed the First Step Act, a major step toward criminal justice reform. The law was designed to reduce the federal inmate population and recidivism. While its main impact lowered mandatory minimum sentences for low-level crimes, mainly minor drug offenses, it left mandatory sentences in place for other criminal offences. In mid-2020, over 160,000 federal prisoners resided in all facilities, the highest of any country in the world. The United States holds approximately 20 percent of the world's prisoners despite it having 5 percent of the world's population. Conservatives and progressives agreed that the legislation was the beginning of a larger movement toward criminal justice reform, but Congress failed to pass additional measures.

The Supreme Court was also active in criminal justice reform. Only two states, Louisiana and Oregon, allowed convictions without a unanimous jury. Evangelisto Ramos was convicted of murder on a 10 to 2 vote in 2016 and sentenced to life without parole. On appeal, he argued that his conviction required a unanimous jury. In 2020 in *Ramos v. Louisiana*, the Supreme Court agreed in a six to three decision. Writing for the Court, Justice Neil Gorsuch overturned an earlier decision, *Apodaca v. Oregon* (1972), which held that federal, but not state, prisoners must have unanimous juries to be convicted: "there can be no question either that the Sixth Amendment's unanimity requirement applies to state and federal criminal trials equally … So if the Sixth Amendment's right to a jury trial requires a unanimous verdict to support a conviction in federal court, it requires no less in state court." A 2021 decision in *Edwards v. Vannoy* determined, six to three, that the *Ramos* ruling was not retroactive.

17

The Continued Growth of Executive Power

The most notable transformation in this period was the continued rapid expansion of presidential power, a process that had been underway since Ronald Reagan was president. Some of the expansion was due to the increased use of executive orders, which had been in place since the Washington administration. They do not require the consent of Congress. A president's executive order may be easily overturned by a successor. Increased executive authority occurred despite the outcome of the highly controversial 2000 and 2016 presidential elections when both Democratic candidates, respectively, won the popular vote but lost the electoral vote. In the first, the contest depended on the outcome in Florida, which led to lawsuits and a Supreme Court decision in *Bush* v. *Gore*. The Court stopped the vote recount, and the bare margin of victory in the electoral count went to Republican George W. Bush, 277 to 266.

In 2016, Donald J. Trump defeated Hillary Clinton by an electoral vote of 304 to 227, but Clinton received 2.86 million more popular votes than Trump. These elections marked the fourth and fifth time in US history when a candidate with the second highest popular vote won the presidency: the others were in 1824, 1876, and 1888. The outcomes damaged neither the presidency nor, in *Bush* v. *Gore*, the Court's stature, because the focus quickly shifted to executive and military authority after the September 11, 2001, terrorist attacks on the United States in New York and Washington, DC, and other pressing issues

American Constitutional History: A Brief Introduction, Second Edition. Jack Fruchtman.
© 2022 John Wiley & Sons, Inc. Published 2022 by John Wiley & Sons, Inc.

facing the American people, including the outbreak in 2020 of the worldwide Covid-19 pandemic.

Foreign Terrorist Attacks and the Bush Administration

The Constitution divides military power between Congress and the president to ensure that neither one acts alone to take the nation into war: only Congress can declare war while the president controls the armed forces. Yet, presidents have sometimes acted alone, or they have asked Congress for vague "authorizations" to use military force. An authorization passed in 2001 allowed President George W. Bush to send American troops into Afghanistan to find and destroy al-Qaeda, the perpetrators of the September 11 attacks. Congress passed another a year later authorizing the president to send troops to invade Iraq. President Bush and Vice President Dick Cheney adhered to the theory of the unitary executive, which had its roots in the Washington administration. A result was that the administration ordered federal agents and the military to send hundreds of suspected terrorists captured in these two conflicts to a detention camp on the US Naval Base in Guantánamo Bay, Cuba. The president argued that the incarceration of terrorist suspects in a federal prison was dangerous to the American people. If detained offshore, they would be beyond federal court authority: Guantánamo Bay was a no-man's-land, "the legal equivalent to outer space," as one unnamed official was said to have commented. It opened in January 2002.

The Bush administration designated all detainees "illegal enemy combatants," a phrase reminiscent of the World War II *Quirin* decision. The president proclaimed that Guantánamo Bay was beyond the sovereign territory of the United States and that prisoners captured in Iraq and Afghanistan were stateless enemies. The plan was to hold them there without formal charges until the end of the "war on terrorism." The official position was that terrorists were linked to no nation and thus not covered by the Geneva Conventions or laws of war. To extract information from the detainees without causing death, federal agents established two programs.

The first consisted of "enhanced" or "harsh" interrogation techniques. In 2007, Bush authorized American military and civilian intelligence officers to use these techniques, including waterboarding, which meant interrogators would force a suspect to lie on his back while pouring water over a cloth covering his mouth and nose to produce a sensation of drowning. The goal was to force him to provide information. Experts debate whether the suspect will be forced to tell the truth or make up stories to stop the procedure. Agents could force a detainee to stand for long hours with his back and heels against a wall. They could drape a detainee with a hood for long hours and subject him to loud noises, leading to sleep deprivation. They could withhold food and drink from him for long periods and humiliate or embarrass him for personal or religious purposes: force him to stand naked before female soldiers or bring growling German Shepherd dogs very close to his face.

A second program involved "extreme rendition," which involved sending suspected terrorists secretly abroad to countries that engaged in torture during interrogations. These countries were primarily in the Middle East and Eastern Europe. Although some members of the Bush administration objected, namely Secretary of State Colin Powell and Attorney General John Ashcroft, they remained publicly silent. The administration claimed that US officials never sent suspected terrorists to a country that engaged in torture.

A major enhancement of presidential authority occurred on October 18, 2001, when Congress passed the USA Patriot Act. The title is an acronym for "Uniting and Strengthening America by Providing Appropriate Tools Required to Intercept and Obstruct Terrorism." It was designed to identify and arrest suspected terrorists residing in the United States. The Senate overwhelmingly passed the law with one negative vote and the House with only 66 nays. It dramatically increased executive authority in terms of searches and seizures and the deportation or detention of suspected terrorists. The act authorized the FBI to implement roving wiretaps on suspected terrorists, register all keystrokes by suspects using a computer, and undertake "sneak-and-peek" searches to search private property without the permission of the owner and without a warrant. The FBI could also investigate any American citizen suspected of terrorism or associated with a terrorist organization. The Bureau could seize suspected terrorists' bookstore sales receipts and library records without informing them in advance. The Department of the Treasury was empowered to keep under surveillance banking and non-banking institutions and to seize medical and other electronic records of any individual. Foreigners living in the United States, who were suspected of terrorism or suspected of having any association with terrorism, could be detained or deported.

After the September 2001 attacks, joint action by the president and Congress led to the reorganization of intelligence operations. In 2002, Congress created a new cabinet-level Department of Homeland Security. It encompassed the Coast Guard, the Transportation Safety Agency, and the Immigration and Customs Enforcement (formerly the Immigration and Naturalization Service). Congress had not created a new executive department since 1979 when it established the Department of Education. Two years later, the National Commission on Terrorist Attacks upon the United States, also called the 9/11 Commission, recommended the appointment of a director of national intelligence. The director was to coordinate information among all agencies charged with protecting the nation. Bush signed four executive orders implementing the recommendation, and Congress solidified it with the Intelligence Reform and Terrorism Prevention Act of 2004.

During his two administrations, President Bush signed nearly 300 executive orders. Presidents act alone when they issue such orders, which bypass treaty requirements and diminish congressional oversight. A controversial executive order in 2007 stated that the Geneva Conventions did not apply to detainees held in Guantánamo because they neither wore national uniforms nor were agents of a recognized foreign government. In addition to issuing executive orders, presidents have also prepared signing statements since James Monroe's presidency. These documents indicate his interpretation of a federal law after he signed it, or it may record a president's thoughts concerning its enforcement. Others addressed his legal, constitutional, and administrative concerns. George W. Bush issued more signing statements than any previous president: 161 concerning over 1000 provisions of law. His most controversial one explained why he declined to enforce a law banning torture of detainees after he signed it.

In 2003, the public learned that harsh interrogation techniques may have involved some form of torture (Box 17.1). The day after signing the Torture Ban into law in 2005, Bush issued a signing statement, which stated that he would not enforce the ban if he determined that a threat of terrorism required harsh interrogations or torture to protect the nation.

The Bush administration acted alone in approving policies that involved the National Security Agency. The goal was to locate terrorists through the interception of telephone calls made in the United States to people overseas suspected of terrorism. In December 2005, the *New*

Box 17.1 William J. Haynes, II, General Counsel of the Department of Defense, "Military Interrogation of Alien Unlawful Combatants Held Outside the United States," March 14, 2003, excerpt

Torture is not the mere infliction of pain or suffering on another but is instead a step well removed. The victim must experience intense pain or suffering of the kind that is equivalent to the pain that would be associated with serious physical injury so severe that death, organ failure, or permanent damage resulting in a loss of body function will result. If that pain or suffering is psychological, that suffering must result from one of the acts set forth in the statute. In addition, these acts must cause long-term mental harm. Indeed, this view of the criminal act of torture is consistent with the term's comment meaning. Torture is generally understood to involve "intense pain" or "excruciating pain," or put another way, "extreme anguish of body or mind."

York Times revealed the program in news articles. After an outcry by civil liberties groups and members of Congress, a new law, the Protect America Act of 2007, permitted the administration to continue to monitor phone calls and e-mail messages, including those of US citizens, if the target was a suspected terrorist living abroad.

Wars in Afghanistan and Iraq

The United States invaded Afghanistan in 2001 to track down the leaders of al-Qaeda who planned and implemented the September 11 attacks. Two years later, American forces attacked Iraq. The initial goal was to capture or kill Osama bin Laden, the son of a prominent, wealthy Saudi billionaire and the leader of al-Qaeda, which in Arabic means "the base," and others responsible for the attacks. These included the then-current theocratic rulers of the Islamic Emirates of Afghanistan, known as the Taliban or "brothers," who believed that Islamic law had to govern all political decision-making and social mores. Bin Laden, whom the Taliban sheltered and whose philosophy he followed, spearheaded the 1998 bombing of US embassies in the East African nations of Tanzania and Kenya. He opposed Middle Eastern dictatorships and US support of those governments. He dedicated his life to eradicating all American influences in the Middle East.

After the American invasion, US forces captured several hundred combatants, including members of the Taliban and al-Qaeda as well as many "others." These "others" included those whom anti-Taliban tribal allies such as the Northern Alliance transferred to American troops who paid a bounty of $5000–25,000 for every "terrorist" brought to them. The Pakistani government or the Northern Alliance turned over to the Americans nearly 50 percent of those captured in the "war on terrorism." Most American troops did not know anything about these prisoners, where they came from, or what they were doing when captured. Many prisoners challenged their detention in federal court. Four major cases eventually reached the Supreme Court. The Bush administration lost all of them.

The first involved a US citizen, Yaser Esam Hamdi, whom the Northern Alliance captured during fighting in Afghanistan allegedly holding an AK-47. The United States denied him due process rights. In 2004, the Supreme Court, in an opinion by Sandra Day O'Connor, ruled in *Hamdi* v. *Rumsfeld* that due process demands that a US citizen detained in the United States as an enemy combatant must be given a meaningful opportunity to contest the factual basis for his detention in an appropriate tribunal. Although courts defer to the executive branch in a time of war, she declared, "we have long since made clear that a state of war is not a blank check for the president when it comes to the rights of the Nation's citizens."

On the same day, the Court decided a companion case involving the habeas corpus rights of foreign detainees held in Guantánamo Bay. The White House maintained that the Court's precedent in the 1950 *Eisentrager* case, involving German prisoners of war, meant that foreign enemy combatants held outside US sovereign territory enjoyed no habeas relief in federal court. In a six to three decision in *Rasul* v. *Bush*, the justices held that it was not the territory that determined whether a detainee or prisoner enjoyed habeas rights, but the custodian. The custodian here was the United States. While Guantánamo was beyond US sovereignty, the United States enjoyed complete jurisdiction over its naval base. The district court, therefore, had the authority "to hear petitioners' habeas corpus challenges to the legality of their detention at the Guantánamo Bay Naval Base."

Two years later, in its third major case, the Court rejected the Bush administration's argument that Salim Ahmed Hamdan had committed conspiracy "to commit ... offenses triable by military commission." Hamdan, a Yemeni national and Osama bin Laden's driver and bodyguard, was detained in 2001. He argued that a military commission lacked authority to try him because no federal law or the common law of war supported conspiracy as an illegal act of war. Writing for the Court in 2006 with four others in *Hamdan* v. *Rumsfeld*, Justice Stevens ruled that Hamdan's military commission lacked "power to proceed because its structure and procedures violate[d] both the [Uniform Code of Military Justice] and the Geneva Conventions." Moreover, conspiracy was "not an offense that by ... the law of war may be tried by military commission."

After *Hamdi*, the Defense Department, under the president's order, established Combatant Status Review Tribunals to determine whether individuals detained in Guantánamo were truly "enemy combatants." In 2005, Congress tried to stop all habeas appeals by enacting the Detainee Treatment Act (DTA), which withdrew all habeas actions except in the United States Circuit Court of Appeals for the District of Columbia. A year later, Congress passed the Military Commissions Act (MCA) to overcome the problems that Justice Stevens cited. For the first time since the war on terrorism began, Congress authorized the executive department to design military tribunals. Section 7 of the act ended federal habeas suits, asserting that no detainee accused of terrorism could submit a petition "relating to any aspect of the detention, transfer, treatment, trial, or conditions of confinement."

Finally, in 2008, the last major lawsuit reached the Court. Lakhdar Boumediene, an Algerian, and several others were turned over to US authorities in 2002 by Bosnian police. Denying he was a member of al-Qaeda or the Taliban, Boumediene sought a writ of habeas corpus. Anthony Kennedy, in a five to four decision in *Boumediene* v. *Bush*, held that the procedures in place that allowed for DTA review were inadequate for true habeas corpus review. Detainees must be able to appeal to a federal court.

The White House identified 14 "high value" al-Qaeda detainees incarcerated in Guantánamo Bay, all of whom were allegedly involved in the September 11 attacks. The government wanted to try the suspected mastermind, Khalid Sheikh Mohammed, along with others who were leaders and planners of the attacks. News reports suggested that the government subjected him to waterboarding over 183 times. No civilian court would allow evidence because they were tortured. The government chose to try them by military commission but, by June of 2021, military commissions had tried only a few Guantánamo detainees with just eight convictions: of these, six were by plea deals. At the same time, federal civilian courts convicted between 150 and 220 individuals charged with terrorism. The number varies depending on whether the defendants were true terrorists, including an American, John Walker Lindh, who was sentenced to 20 years in prison. In 2019, he gained supervised release for his final three years of imprisonment.

Obama and Unilateral Executive Action

Executive authority continued to expand after the 2008 presidential election. President Barack Obama at first openly rejected the expansive power of the executive that Bush and Cheney claimed under the Constitution, especially regarding national security, military affairs, and foreign relations. As a candidate, he noted that "the president does not have power under the Constitution to unilaterally authorize a military attack in a situation that does not involve stopping an actual or imminent threat to the nation." Once in the Oval Office, he adopted many of the Bush administration's positions, especially regarding the war on terrorism. In 2011, he ordered a Navy Seals team to capture or kill bin Laden once his hideout was discovered in Abbottabad, Pakistan. The team shot bin Laden to death and his body was buried at sea. Obama's attempt to close the detention center in Guantánamo Bay, Cuba, failed after Congress declined to find prisons for the remaining detainees.

Obama fully adopted the theory of the unitary executive in 2011 when he ordered US airstrikes against Libya. That year, several Middle Eastern dictatorships erupted into revolution and several authoritarian regimes collapsed in what the media called the Arab Spring. In Libya, the people rebelled against Muammar Gaddafi, the longtime dictator. Western nations launched a humanitarian effort to help the population. The North Atlantic Treaty Organization (NATO) and the United Nations (UN) authorized the use of airstrikes on government targets by member nations, including the United States, Britain, and France. Obama agreed to inform Congress of all US military actions. In June 2011, he ignored requests by Congress to invoke the 1973 War Powers Resolution, arguing that the mission involved no ground forces, and the overall authority placed the mission under the auspices of NATO and the UN.

Other examples of Obama's use of the unitary executive power were targeted killings of suspected terrorists abroad, whether foreign nationals or US citizens. He authorized more targeted killings than any previous administration. Drone airstrikes began under the Bush administration but reached their height under Obama. Sometimes they killed civilians, including women, children, and the elderly. No one knows the precise number of civilians killed in these attacks. The administration authorized drones to fire lethal rockets at militants, including Taliban and al-Qaeda forces, and bomb terrorist sites in a 50-mile radius inside Pakistan. American citizens living abroad were subject to attack if they were identified as "a senior operational leader of al-Qaeda" or a group associated with al-Qaeda and if they posed an "imminent threat" to the United States (Box 17.2).

Box 17.2   Jeh Johnson, General Counsel, Department of Defense, February 22, 2012, excerpt

I want to spend a moment on what some people refer to as "targeted killing" ... In an armed conflict, lethal force against known, individual members of the enemy is a long-standing and long-legal practice. What is new is that, with advances in technology, we are able to target military objectives with much more precision, to the point where we can identify, target and strike a single military objective from great distances. ...

Under well-settled legal principles, lethal force against a valid *military* objective, in an armed conflict, is consistent with the law of war and does not, by definition, constitute an "assassination."

As I stated at the public meeting of the ABA Standing Committee on Law and National Security, belligerents who also happen to be US citizens do not enjoy immunity where non-citizen belligerents are valid military objectives. Reiterating principles from *Ex Parte Quirin* in 1942, the Supreme Court in 2004, in *Hamdi* v. *Rumsfeld*, stated that "a citizen, no less than an alien, can be 'part of or supporting forces hostile to the United States or coalition partners' and 'engaged in an armed conflict against the United States'."

In late 2010, an unmanned drone unleashed a rocket attack in Yemen that killed Anwar al-Awlaki, a US citizen and Muslim clergyman. American officials claimed that he had helped al-Qaeda in the Arabian Peninsula plan attacks on the United States. Also killed in the attack was another American citizen, Samir Khan, an al-Qaeda propagandist. Al-Awlaki's 16-year-old son, who was born in Denver, was killed two weeks later. In 2013, al-Awlaki's father filed wrongful death suits against specific members of the Obama administration in a civil action, holding them personally responsible for the deaths of al-Awlaki and his grandson. Under US law, Anwar al-Aulaqi – the father – could not successfully sue either the military or the Central Intelligence Bureau because of the state secrets privilege. The Court wrote the privilege into the Constitution in *United States* v. *Reynolds* in 1953. In most actions, the act leads a judge to dismiss the case for lack of evidence. Al-Aulaqi then sued individual members of the government under a 1971 Supreme Court decision (*Bivens* v. *Six Unknown Named Agents of the Federal Bureau of Narcotics*) that allows suits to name individual officials in cases of alleged wrongdoing. The Court dismissed the case in 2014. The Court heard a new challenge to the state secrets privilege in the term beginning in October 2021, *FBI* v. *Fazaga*.

The Obama administration also prosecuted government whistleblowers at a far greater rate than those undertaken by all previous presidential administrations. Thomas Drake, a senior executive at the NSA in 2010 discovered misspent funds in "Trailblazer," a government program involving spying on American citizens. Because Drake believed that Americans had a right to know about government wrongdoing, he recounted his findings to a *Baltimore Sun* reporter. A federal grand jury then indicted him for violating the 1917 Espionage Act, although the government eventually allowed him to plead guilty to one misdemeanor count. He received no jail time. CIA agent Jeffrey Sterling was charged with violating the Espionage Act for passing classified information concerning Iran's nuclear program to a *New York Times* reporter. Convicted in federal district court, he was sentenced to three and a half years imprisonment in 2015 and released in 2018.

A highly publicized and controversial criminal case involved US Army Private Bradley Manning, who leaked national security documents and videotapes while stationed in Iraq to WikiLeaks, an international website whose chief operator, Julian Assange, then posted secret and classified information to inform people about government wrongdoing. WikiLeaks immediately posted the largest cache of secret and restricted documents in US history. Like Drake, Manning was indicted for violating the Espionage Act of 1917. In 2013, he was sentenced to 35 years in prison, the longest in a leak case, and dishonorably discharged from the Army. While incarcerated, he underwent a sex change operation and changed her name to Chelsea Manning. President Obama commuted her sentence in 2017.

Two years later, Edward Snowden, a National Security Agency (NSA) contractor, sent hundreds of thousands of telephone and e-mail documents, which the United States routinely collected on every person living in the country, to the press. Snowden illegally downloaded them while working as a cybersecurity analyst at Booz Allen Hamilton, a company that provided management and technological services to the Department of Defense. He escaped to Hong Kong and eventually traveled to Russia, which granted him political asylum (Box 17.3). Snowden claimed that Americans had a right to know that the government spied on them. The Russian government refused requests of the State Department to extradite him to the United States to stand trial for violating the Espionage Act.

Box 17.3   Edward Snowden, arriving in Moscow to seek political asylum in Russia, July 1, 2013, excerpt

One week ago I left Hong Kong after it became clear that my freedom and safety were under threat for revealing the truth … For decades the United States of America has been one of the strongest defenders of the human right to seek asylum.

Sadly, this right, laid out and voted for by the United States in Article 14 of the Universal Declaration of Human Rights, is now being rejected by the current government of my country. The Obama administration has now adopted the strategy of using citizenship as a weapon. Although I am convicted of nothing, it has unilaterally revoked my passport, leaving me a stateless person. Without any judicial order, the administration now seeks to stop me exercising a basic right. A right that belongs to everybody. The right to seek asylum.

The press later revealed that the NSA not only followed terrorist suspects, but also used the program to identify people involved in nuclear proliferation, espionage, and cyberattacks, in other words, those involving attacks on computer programs. Some civil libertarians questioned the secret Foreign Intelligence Surveillance Act (FISA) court and how its work had to be more transparent. The press revealed that Snowden trained himself to become competent in stealing the material from the NSA to reveal it to the world. News reports showed that, from 2011 to 2012, the NSA's own audit uncovered over 2700 illegal surveillance violations on American citizens, including unauthorized interceptions of telephone calls and e-mail messages. Congress has made many attempts to reform how the FISA court operated. In 2016, the FISA court allowed the FBI to investigate Russian attempts to sway the presidential election of that year.

In 2011, President Obama signed an extension of several provisions of the USA Patriot Act but after the act expired in 2015, Congress passed a new law, the USA Freedom Act, which allowed the telephone companies rather than the NSA to collect and store phone records. NSA officials were now required to ask the FISA court to approve a warrant to force the companies to release telephone records. It restored roving wiretaps and wiretapping of lone wolf suspects. Congress reauthorized it in 2020 until 2023.

In 2014, the United States confronted a new terrorist threat, known variously as the Islamic State in Iraq and Syria or the Islamic State in Iraq and the Levant, the latter term referring to most of the Middle East. Well-armed and astute in public relations, ISIS forces captured and held hostage several American and foreign journalists, demanding high ransoms or the release of prisoners suspected of terrorist activities. When their demands were not met, they beheaded their hostages, posting images of the executions on the Internet. Their actions also led to the rape, torture, and deaths of people who did not follow their version of Islamic law. In August, President Obama, acting unilaterally, ordered US airstrikes against ISIS targets and organized an international coalition to defeat it. Finally defeated in 2019, a remnant of the organization continued to undertake terrorist attacks against American forces and allies.

Obama also acted unilaterally on the US southern border. In 2012, he signed an executive order concerning some 800,000 young people whose parents brought them to the United States when they were children. The Deferred Action for Childhood Arrivals or DACA allowed so-called Dreamers to remain in the United States at work or in school, but they must reapply to receive a renewable two-year deferred action from deportation and other requirements. Two years later, the president, again by executive order, created a program for nearly 5 million undocumented immigrants who also would be free from the threat of deportation for three years. They could legally apply for work permits. In exchange, they had to pass background checks, pay taxes and a penalty, go to the back of the line in applying for citizenship, and learn English. Twenty-six states filed lawsuits against the president, accusing him of overstepping his constitutional authority. A district court agreed, and the Fifth Circuit Court of Appeals upheld that ruling. The Obama administration did not appeal to the Supreme Court, though he did not act to end the program.

Finally, Obama unilaterally entered into the Paris Climate Agreement in 2015 and the Trans-Pacific Partnership in 2016. With nearly every nation signing the climate agreement, the goal was to lower the global warming trend contributing to climate change. Obama achieved this by executive agreement so that the Senate would not have to ratify it as a treaty. The goal of the trade partnership was to lower tariff and non-tariff barriers to trade and create a mechanism to resolve trade disputes, primarily in the Far East. Donald Trump rescinded both with the stroke of a pen. President Joe Biden restored US membership in the climate agreement in 2021 but took no action on the Trans-Pacific Partnership.

Executive Authority under Trump

The Trump administration was one of the most divisive and controversial since the Civil War. Although he made numerous unilateral decisions, he promoted two major measures with congressional approval. The first in 2017 was the passage, by the Senate budget reconciliation process to avoid the filibuster, of the Tax Cuts and Jobs Act. It was a wholly partisan effort: like Clinton's 1993 tax cut and the 2010 Obamacare. No House or Senate Democrat voted for it. It vastly increased the federal deficit by at least $1 trillion. While it greatly aided the fortunes of corporations and wealthy individuals, it did not help the working or middle class. The second, as noted earlier, was the 2018 First Step Act, which was a rare bipartisan effort to reduce the size of the prison population and the recidivism rate (the rate at which former convicts return to prison after committing another crime). Liberal and conservative think tanks and political action committees supported it. Donald J. Trump spent the rest of his term doing what he wanted with Senate Republican acquiescence, to the consternation of their Democratic counterparts.

When he announced his candidacy in June 2015, President Trump claimed that the most serious problem facing the United States was "illegal immigration," namely the passage into the country of thousands of people who failed to possess the required documentation. He noted that "when Mexico sends its people, they're not sending their best ... They're bringing drugs. They're bringing crime. They're bringing rapists. And some, I assume, are good people." He seemed to want to end all immigration, illegal and legal, deporting record numbers of asylum seekers and undocumented immigrants. In December 2015, a US citizen of Pakistani descent and his wife, a green-card holder from Pakistan, killed 14 people and wounded 22 others in San Bernardino, California. Candidate Trump called for "a total and complete shutdown of Muslims entering the United States until our country's representatives can figure out what's going on." He assumed that all terrorist attacks in the US were conducted by foreigners, whereas in fact most were undertaken by native-born or naturalized Americans.

Trump's campaign motto, "Make America Great Again," became the hallmark of his goal of "America First." His words echoed those of the 1940 America First Committee that opposed US aid to its allies in World War II before the Japanese attack on Pearl Harbor in December of 1941. Its message contained isolationist, pro-Fascist, and anti-Semitic rhetoric. Trump's campaign and eventual electoral victory over the Democratic candidate, Hillary Clinton, attracted an array of voters who supported his platform, winning crucial states with a bare margin of victory. He lost the popular vote by 2.86 million votes but claimed without evidence that he would have won because millions of "illegal immigrants" voted for Clinton. As president, he claimed he possessed unlimited authority (see Box 17.4)

Box 17.4   Remarks by President Trump

More importantly, Article II allows me to do whatever I want.

Interview, ABC News, June 16, 2020

I have an Article II, where I have the right to do whatever I want as President.

Turning Point USA's Teen Student
Action Summit, 2019

On taking office, Trump issued several travel bans targeting people coming to the United States from Muslim countries, an order the Supreme Court later upheld after he broadened it to include more than Muslim countries. In *Trump* v. *Hawaii*, Chief Justice Roberts ruled for a bare majority that Article II delegated to the president the authority to target countries that do not properly scrutinize the backgrounds of those coming to the United States because they may be terrorists. As for the southern border of the United States, Trump promised to build "a big, beautiful wall" to shield the country from Mexico, and Mexico would pay for it "as sure as you're standing there, 100 percent." The Mexican government refused. Many segments of the existing wall were upgraded, but the administration only added several miles to the wall by transferring $2.5 billion in defense spending without congressional authorization. Congress had targeted the funds to upgrade military bases. The Sierra Club, an environmental group, attempted to stop the construction because of claimed damages to the environment and wildlife. The Supreme Court in an unsigned opinion in *Trump* v. *Sierra Club* removed the case from its docket in 2021 after President Joe Biden reversed several decisions by the Trump administration concerning construction of the wall.

To enhance his policy to halt immigration, the Trump administration created the Family Separation Policy to discourage undocumented migrants from entering the country. The program, known as "zero tolerance," meant that border patrol agents seized children from their parents and placed them in detention centers. It did not include a means to reunite the families. Several thousand children were separated, including many placed in cages. Despite a court order for the administration to end the program, it continued until President Joe Biden took office in 2021. The Biden administration attempted to locate the children's families.

Trump threatened to unilaterally withdraw the United States from the North Atlantic Treaty Organization, claiming that it was "obsolete." He never succeeded. He also threatened to attack the North Korean Communist regime with "fire and fury" unless that nation gave up its development of nuclear weapons. Trump told the United Nations in 2017 that if the United States "is forced to defend itself or its allies, we will have no choice but to totally destroy North Korea," referring to Leader Kim Jong-un as "Little Rocket Man." Less than two years later, Trump became the first president to step into North Korea when he met Kim without the usual advance planning. Trump believed he had Kim's commitment to a complete and total denuclearization of the Korean peninsula with the goal that North Korea would not develop nuclear weapons. Kim had no such intentions but was playing for time to develop them. North Korean resumed missile testing in 2020.

The Mueller Investigation and the First Impeachment

During the 2016 presidential campaign, 18 American intelligence agencies discovered that Russian agents attempted to interfere in the election to ensure a Trump victory because of the harsh tone Hillary Clinton used against Russia and President Vladimir Putin. A federal investigation sought to determine whether the Trump campaign had cooperated with these efforts. Eventually, the Justice Department chose former FBI director Robert S. Mueller III as special prosecutor to investigate whether the intelligence agencies' findings were based on solid evidence and whether the Trump campaign colluded with Russian operatives. After almost two years of inquiry and 34 indictments of Russians and Americans, Mueller released his report. Among those indicted were members of Trump's campaign, including his one-time campaign director, Paul Manafort, national security advisor Michael Flynn, and policy advisor Roger Stone. Also successfully prosecuted was Trump's personal lawyer Michael Cohen for lying to federal agents about hush money paid to two women with whom Trump allegedly had affairs. Mueller declined to indict the president, stating that sitting presidents, according to findings by the Justice Department, could not be indicted while in office. His report did not "exonerate" Trump or clear him of wrongdoing but concluded that Trump could be indicted once he left office (see Box 17.5). It listed several instances when Trump attempted to obstruct justice by undermining the credibility of the probe.

President Trump later unconditionally pardoned Manafort, Flynn, and Stone and denounced the Mueller investigation as a "hoax," "a witch hunt," and "a crooked scheme against us." He also attacked the news media for accurately reporting the inquest.

In July 2019, Trump's telephone call to the president of Ukraine led to his first impeachment by the House of Representatives in December 2019. During the call to Ukrainian President Volodymyr Zelensky, Trump asked Zelensky to investigate Joe Biden's role in demanding a new Ukrainian federal prosecutor. As vice president, Biden was assigned

Box 17.5   Department of Justice 2000 opinion on indicting sitting presidents

In 1973, the Department of Justice concluded that the indictment and criminal prosecution of a sitting President would unduly interfere with the ability of the executive branch to perform its constitutionally assigned duties and would thus violate the constitutional separation of powers. No court has addressed this question directly, but the judicial precedents that bear on the continuing validity of our constitutional analysis are consistent with both the analytic approach taken and the conclusions reached. Our view remains that a sitting President is constitutionally immune from indictment and criminal prosecution.

A Sitting President's Amenability to Indictment
and Criminal Prosecution 2000 /
U.S. Department of Justice / Public domain

to pressure the Ukrainians to clean up corruption by appointing an honest federal prosecutor. A properly run and corruption-free Ukraine could check Russian expansionism. But Trump suspected that the former vice president would become the Democratic candidate for president in 2020 and demanded the Ukrainians investigate him. A US intelligence investigation determined that Trump overstepped his authority when he asked a foreign government to investigate a former high federal official. The result was Trump's first impeachment by the House, although the Senate declined to convict him along party lines. (The second impeachment is reviewed in the epilogue.)

Trump also attempted to reframe the decennial census as required by Article I of the Constitution to determine the size of the nation's population and where people live. An accurate census allows Congress to equally distribute the number of House seats in each state and allocate federal funds to the states on an equitable basis. As the 2020 census drew near, the Department of Commerce announced that it would add a question about citizenship, which had not been on the census form since 1950. Following a 2019 lawsuit challenging the question, the Supreme Court in *Department of Commerce* v. *New York* ruled that the secretary's reason "appears to have been contrived." Trump then instructed the secretary to exclude undocumented immigrants from the census. New York and several states again challenged the order. The Supreme Court, ruling six to three in a *per curiam* decision, dismissed the lawsuit because it was not ripe for judicial determination. "Any prediction how the Executive Branch might eventually implement this general statement of policy is no more than conjecture at this time."

In 2017, Trump cancelled the DACA program, concerning undocumented children brought to the United States by their parents. In 2020 in three consolidated cases, the Supreme Court, in a five to four ruling, held that Homeland Security's procedures to end the program were illegal and it remained in place. In *Department of Homeland Security* v. *Regents of the University of California*, Chief Justice Roberts held that "we do not decide whether DACA or its rescission are sound policies," but "address only whether the agency complied with the procedural requirement that it provide a reasoned explanation for its action. Here the agency failed to consider the conspicuous issues of whether to retain forbearance and what if anything to do about the hardship to DACA recipients."

In the 2020 election year, Trump faced two of the gravest crises of his presidency: the Covid-19 global pandemic and the nationwide protests after police killed George Floyd, a Minneapolis Black man suspected of attempting to pass a counterfeit $20 bill at a convenience store.

First, after hitting hardest in Asia and Europe, the pandemic spread to the United States and eventually led to over 750,000 deaths in the US alone. Medical experts believe the number of deaths was higher because of incomplete death certificates. Trump initially suggested that the disease "miraculously goes away by April [2020]," which it did not. He left it to the governors to undertake critical testing and other medical matters. Fifty governors wound up competing and bidding against each other for medical supplies and medications, costing hundreds of thousands more dollars than had there been a federal response. In 2020, Congress passed several measures costing nearly $4 trillion to help small businesses, people out of work, hospitals, state and local governments, and the production of needed medical supplies.

In the meantime, Trump's company, the Trump Organization, and he himself faced prosecution after he left office concerning his personal and his company's financial records. The former president has long been involved in several civil suits, but he and his company never faced criminal charges. Former students sued him for fraud at Trump University, which was designed to teach real estate deals. In 2016, Trump paid $25 million to settle the lawsuit. Two years later, the New York State attorney general sued him for misusing money in his charity, and he was required to pay damages of $2 million and close the charity.

Cyrus Vance Jr., the Manhattan district attorney, served a subpoena, for tax records, on the president's accounting firm, Mazars USA. After Trump challenged the subpoena, the case, *Trump* v. *Vance*, went to the Supreme Court, where Chief Justice Roberts ruled, seven to two, that the president "is neither absolutely immune from state criminal subpoenas seeking his private papers nor entitled to a heightened standard of need." After Mazars turned over the documents, Vance convened a special grand jury to investigate whether the organization in its business dealings dealt in criminal activity, such as bank, tax, and insurance fraud, hush money paid to women on Trump's behalf, improper property valuations and employee compensation. In July 2021, a grand jury issued the first charges against the Trump Organization and its chief financial officer. The 15-count indictment related to tax fraud concerning unpaid taxes on benefits the company provided to its executives. Many observers expected more charges, ranging from hush money paid to women with whom Trump allegedly had sexual relations and real estate price manipulations on bank loan applications and tax returns.

During the executive republic, seven new justices joined the Court: John G. Roberts Jr., Samuel A. Alito Jr., Sonia Sotomayor, Elena Kagan, Neil M. Gorsuch, Brett M. Kavanaugh, and Amy Coney Barrett. By 2020, with a six to three conservative majority in place, commentators predicted the Court would produce few progressive decisions.

The executive republic contrasted with its predecessor, the welfare state republic when, in 1995, the Supreme Court narrowed Congress's power to regulate interstate commerce. Both the Rehnquist and Roberts Courts determined that Congress may pass laws affecting interstate commerce if a law has a substantial relationship to interstate commerce and the national economy. With bare majorities, Chief Justice Rehnquist made clear that federal laws fail when Congress does not directly link them to this principle. He was particularly concerned with conflicts that arose when federal and state laws achieved similar goals: carrying guns in school zones or civil lawsuits regarding rape.

Chief Justice Roberts argued that Congress may not create interstate commerce to regulate it when upholding the new national healthcare program based only on Congress's taxing power. He declined to affirm it on Congress's authority to regulate interstate commerce but did so on the grounds of Congress's tax and spending power.

At the same time, the Court expanded individual rights. The Court accepted the view that religion in public life may be accommodated without violating the establishment clause. It found that the Second Amendment right to bear arms constituted an individual right and applied the right to the states. It ruled that campaign financing was akin to free speech protected by the First Amendment and the same restrictions that apply to individual persons also apply to groups like corporations and unions. It held that the federal government and the states may not prohibit same-sex marriages and that the Civil Rights Act of 1964 protected lesbian, gay, and transgender individuals. In its October 2021 term, the Court anticipated hearing oral arguments in a major abortion case that may challenge its long-standing 1973 *Roe v. Wade* decision.

Executive power grew in the wake of the September 11, 2001, terrorist attacks and continued to expand into the presidency of Donald J. Trump. The controlling idea of the Clinton, Obama, and Trump administrations was the theory of the unitary executive. Under George W. Bush the United States entered two major wars in the Middle East, forced hundreds of suspects into indefinite detention in Guantánamo Bay, engaged in extreme rendition by sending suspects abroad to be interviewed by regimes that allowed torture, and undertook a series of harsh interrogation techniques of suspected terrorists. The Obama administration undertook unilateral action in Libya, increased the number of unmanned drone strikes on suspected terrorists even if they were Americans, and prosecuted several so-called whistleblowers of classified or secret national security information under the 1917 Espionage Act. Finally, the Trump administration continued the trend of unilateral action in its restrictive immigration and climate change policies and even sought to fulfill his personal goals in dealing with Ukraine, which led to his first impeachment, and then in provoking an attack on the US Capitol, which culminated in his second one. To forestall leaks to the media about these actions, he asked the Department of Justice to seize communication records of several reporters and at least two members of the House of Representatives.

Epilogue

The 2020 Presidential Campaign and Its Aftermath

President Trump filed for re-election five hours after he took the oath of office on January 20, 2017. He continued to hold campaign rallies around the country throughout his term, although he stopped doing so when the 2020 Covid-19 pandemic required several state governments to mandate the closure of businesses and a lockdown for residents. He renewed rallies in June 2020 with one in Tulsa, Oklahoma, despite warnings from health officials. It was sparsely attended, and several people were infected, including the governor, Kevin Stitt. A few weeks later, Trump went to Arizona to hold a rally at a megachurch. Again, few people wore masks. The virus surged throughout the South and Southwest, including Oklahoma and Arizona, causing some governors to again lockdown businesses.

The Campaign and the Second Trump Impeachment

Although economic growth and declining unemployment in the United States began in 2009 under Obama's presidency as the nation emerged from the great recession, Trump based his reelection on his claim that he built a strong economy with low unemployment numbers. With the 2020 pandemic, however, unemployment reached a high of 14.8 percent as the economy declined because of government-required shutdowns of major consumer businesses.

American Constitutional History: A Brief Introduction, Second Edition. Jack Fruchtman.
© 2022 John Wiley & Sons, Inc. Published 2022 by John Wiley & Sons, Inc.

Twenty-nine candidates competed for the Democratic nomination for president in 2020, twenty-five of whom ran at the same time. Eventually, the race became one between former Vice President Joe Biden and Vermont Senator Bernie Sanders. The Democrats nominated Biden at a virtual convention due to the pandemic. Biden chose California Senator Kamala Harris as his running mate for vice president. She was at one time a 2020 presidential candidate. Biden outlined a series of economic and financial plans, which he called "Build Back Better" and which he hoped to work with Congress to pass should he win the election. These plans included one to stimulate the economy by spending $700 billion over several years on American products and research. Another was to eliminate carbon pollution produced by industry by 2035 at a cost of $3 trillion. He wanted to invest another $775 billion to protect older Americans and young children. He advocated a plan to combat economic inequality to help people of color, especially through small business opportunities for minority entrepreneurs. He supported a plan to create an emergency housing support program with a tax credit up to $15,000 for families to purchase their first home.

The Republicans renominated President Trump and Vice President Mike Pence. Unlike the Democrats, the Republicans did not have a new platform but reindorsed the 2016 version, word for word. That platform was dated insofar as it included more than three dozen condemnations of the "current" president, namely Barack Obama. It added that the party "has and will continue to enthusiastically support the President's America-first agenda." President Trump characterized Biden's plans as "socialism," although the former vice president was a longtime moderate Democrat. Without evidence, he contended that Biden had a "corrupt" relationship with China, although Trump had tried to consummate a comprehensive trade agreement with that country. Finally, Trump accused Biden of wanting to "let terrorists roam free" and abolish "the American way of life," without defining what he meant by those phrases.

In May 2020, protests broke out throughout the country after the police killing of George Floyd in Minneapolis. Most protestors were peaceful during daylight hours, but at night violence damaged or destroyed property and stores were looted. Only 8 percent of those on the streets committed violence and unrest, which was carried out mainly by white supremacist militia groups. Trump threatened to invoke the Insurrection Act of 1807, which states, in part, that "whenever the president considers that unlawful obstructions ... assemblages, or rebellion against the authority of the United States, make it impracticable to enforce the laws of the United States in any State by the ordinary course of judicial proceedings, he may call into Federal service such of the militia of any State, and use such of the armed forces, as he considers necessary to enforce those laws or to suppress the rebellion." Most commentators claimed that the conditions did not amount to an insurrection. Demonstrations continued throughout the summer of 2020 as police killings of African Americans persisted.

Six weeks before the election, Justice Ruth Bader Ginsburg died. President Trump a week later nominated Judge Amy Coney Barrett of the Seventh Circuit to replace her. Although Senate Majority Leader Mitch McConnell in 2016 refused to allow the Senate to review the credentials of a Supreme Court nominee during a presidential election year, the Republican-controlled Senate confirmed Judge Barrett's nomination one week before the presidential election. No Democrat voted for her, and Maine Senator Susan Collins was the only Republican to cast a negative vote.

The November 3, 2020, election resulted in Biden's victory with 306 electoral votes to 232 for Trump. Trump declined to concede, claiming widespread voter fraud, especially among mail-in ballots. His campaign filed several lawsuits in six battleground states like Pennsylvania that Biden won. Federal and state judges dismissed all of them, some 60 lawsuits, including one filed directly in the Supreme Court by Texas and joined by 17 other states. Campaign lawyers produced no evidence of fraud or irregularities. Trump also demanded recounts in four battleground states. Once completed, they confirmed Biden's victory.

On January 6, 2021, Congress met to count the electoral votes. The session is usually a routine affair. A few senators and representatives planned to object to the outcomes in six battleground states: Arizona, Georgia, Michigan, Nevada, Pennsylvania, and Wisconsin. The session was interrupted after President Trump and others incited an insurrection against the US Capitol. Thousands of pro-Trump protestors seized the building. The Capitol Police presence was too small to stop them, and the electoral count shut down as members of Congress fled for their lives. The insurrectionists wrecked offices, broke furniture, and stole materials or threw them around the offices. Some defecated on the floor and others occupied the Senate and House chambers. Five people, including a Capitol police officer, died in the attack. After the Capitol police, reinforced by state police and National Guardsmen from DC, Maryland, and Virginia, restored order, the mob was dispersed, and the count continued with objections from several Republican members of the House and Senate. Congress confirmed Biden's win, 306 electoral votes to 232. Police and FBI agents soon arrested several hundred insurgents who invaded the Capitol, and several faced criminal charges and possible imprisonment.

One week later, the House of Representatives, for the first time in its history, impeached a president for a second time. A single article of impeachment charged Trump with "inciting violence against the Government of the United States." The article also mentioned Trump's unfounded claims of election fraud and his attempts to pressure governors and secretaries of state to overturn election results in their states. Ten Republicans joined the Democrats to impeach the president in a vote of 232 to 197 in the House. Although Senate leaders sought a conviction to prevent Trump from holding a future federal office, the Senate failed to convict him because it required a two-thirds vote. As former president, throughout 2021, Trump continued to spread the fiction that the election was stolen from him by voter fraud.

The Biden Presidency, 2021

Because of Covid-19, the inauguration on January 20 was a slimmed-down affair with few observers and no parade on Constitution Avenue or celebratory balls. President Biden continued the trend of increasing executive authority by leading an activist federal government along the lines of Franklin Roosevelt and Ronald Reagan. Within days of taking office, he signed almost a hundred executive orders, almost half of which overturned those of his predecessor. Among those were several dealing with gun violence, such as tightening regulations regarding homemade guns and a device placed on pistols to transform them into short-barreled rifles. He invoked the Defense Production Act, which allowed him to use his unilateral authority during an emergency to help the states vaccinate their residents and to provide funds for personal protection equipment for healthcare workers.

Biden proposed and Congress passed the American Rescue Plan, which continued the effort to help those in need resulting from unemployment and displacement because of the coronavirus. It provided $1.9 trillion in new spending. While unilateral action was impossible, it passed the House, 220 to 211, with one Democrat and all Republicans voting against it. The Senate employed the same budget reconciliation procedure it successfully used to pass President Clinton's 1993 tax cut bill, President Obama's 2010 Affordable Care Act, and President Trump's 2017 tax reduction bill. It avoided the filibuster, requiring 60 votes to end debate, and the measure passed the Senate 50 to 49 with all Republicans opposed.

The president submitted to Congress a $2.3 trillion, later reduced to $1.7 trillion, infrastructure project, known as the American Jobs Plan, to reconstruct the nation's crumbling roads, bridges, ports, railways, and airports. He expanded the definition of infrastructure to go beyond steel and concrete projects to include upgraded electrical grids, to provide clean water and improved broadband access as well as to stabilize and strengthen the workforce. It was designed to transform the nation from its reliance on fossil fuels to move to green energy like solar and wind sources. Biden proposed paying for the program by raising the corporate tax, which had stood at 35 percent until 2017 when Congress reduced it. He wanted to increase it from 21 to 28 percent. A bipartisan group of Democrats and Republicans agreed on a $1 trillion plan in June 2021, and Congress passed it in November 2021.

Meantime, Democrats worked on a larger package that might pass by the budget reconciliation process to avoid a Senate filibuster. This bill combined the American Jobs Plan with another measure, the American Families Plan, with a cost of $3.5 trillion dollars over 10 years. With climate change reform, it also provided for free childcare and family leave as well as extending child tax credits to 2025. It included free universal preschool and two years of free community college education. These programs would duplicate those in Britain, France, Germany, Denmark, and Italy. Biden proposed to pay for them by raising taxes on individuals earning more than $400,000 per year and by taxing corporations that had avoided paying taxes in the past through loopholes and deductions. In August, the bill passed the House with only Democrats voting for it, 220 to 212.

President Biden unilaterally took steps to combat domestic terrorism and violence by militia groups. Trump's own Department of Homeland Security, in a 2020 study, concluded that white supremacists and other domestic violent extremists were "the most persistent and lethal threat" to the nation. These included groups like the Ku Klux Klan and with names like the Proud Boys, the Three Percenters, and the Oath Keepers. The Trump administration's "Homeland Threat Assessment" determined that groups like these were responsible for more fatal attacks in the United States than any other extremist organization. In June 2021, Attorney General Merrick Garland released the government's first National Strategy for Countering Domestic Terrorism.

Discussions began to overhaul the immigration system with pathways to citizenship for undocumented immigrants and to permanently establish the DACA program for undocumented children brought to the United States by their parents. The president increased the number of refugees entering the US from countries suffering civil strife or natural disaster from a Trump low of 15,000 per year to 62,500. The Department of Homeland Security began to reunite children separated from their families by the Trump administration in its effort to stem the tide of immigrants illegally entering the United States.

A Republic If You Can Keep It

James McHenry, a Maryland signer of the Constitution in 1787 – Fort McHenry in Baltimore is named in his honor – watched Benjamin Franklin as he left the convention after the final draft was adopted. A woman by the name of Mrs. Powel walked up to the great scientist and asked him what type of government the delegates had given Americans: a republic or a monarchy. Franklin's answer: "A republic, if you can keep it." Since the Constitution's ratification, Americans have been "keeping" their republic for over 235 years. As this book has explained, while it is not the same republic Franklin was talking about, nevertheless it is a republic. No one can accurately predict the future changes the Constitution will undergo. However, one thing is certain: it will change as the government and the American people deal with economic regulations, individual and civil rights, and executive power. The Constitution changes whenever the government confronts the various crises that inevitably arise. Policymaking will depend on who governs: Democrats, Republicans, conservatives, liberals, libertarians, or any combination of these.

Americans have relied on the Supreme Court as ultimate interpreter of the Constitution. Indeed, the justices themselves, whether liberal or conservative, agree that they are the court of last resort, the final arbiter of the meaning of the document. Several recommendations have emerged over the years concerning their tenure. Under Article III, justices serve "during good behavior," which since 1789 has meant until they resign, retire, or die. While Congress may also impeach justices and remove them from office, no justice has ever suffered that fate. As indicated earlier, the House impeached Justice Samuel Chase in 1804, but the Senate declined to convict him the following year. He remained in office until his death in 1811.

In April, 2021, President Biden appointed a 36-member bipartisan commission consisting of constitutional scholars and others to investigate whether changes should be made to the Supreme Court. These included several areas of inquiry that may lead to proposals: expanding the number of justices due to the increased workload, introducing term limits or mandatory retirement ages, stripping the Court's jurisdiction over certain topics, requiring a supermajority to overturn laws or actions, and creating a means by which Congress could reverse Court decisions.

Some constitutional scholars have become so frustrated about the Constitution that they suggest that it is too antiquated to be relevant in the twenty-first century, especially regarding the changes that have occurred since 1787. Amendments are difficult, if not impossible, to add to the document: it still takes two-thirds of both houses of Congress to pass an amendment and then three-quarters of the states to ratify it. Attempts to update it typically end in failure.

Some argue that it is time to ignore the Constitution, even disobey it. In part, this reaction responds to how presidents, Congress, and the justices of the Supreme Court have changed the document: presidents acting unilaterally; Congress moving into areas that some believe properly belong to state and local governments; justices making up doctrines and tests to deal with constitutional matters unanticipated over two hundred years ago. In part, this reaction responds to their frustration with a document written and ratified by a few propertied white men, many of whom condoned slavery. How could these men, they ask, have anticipated the world of the twenty-first century with its electronic and technological devices, a shrinking globalized economic and political system, and a fast-paced lifestyle, an international war on terrorism, climate change, and domestic violence? They answer simply that they did not and could not have foreseen these changes. All citizens, public officials, and the people, they say, should therefore ignore or disobey the Constitution.

The republic will continue to move through major changes, perhaps even violent ones like the January 6, 2021, insurrection. As former President Trump continues to assert that he won the 2020 election because of widespread fraud or rigged voting machines, the people may see the demise of the once-inviolable democratic norm that winners and losers alike honor the outcome of elections. Even so, the Constitution protects Americans' fundamental freedoms like free speech and religion, due process and habeas corpus rights, privacy, and separate branches of the government that, to achieve anything, must work together even when the political parties vigorously disagree. The history of the Constitution has demonstrated its adaptability as its evolution reflects the transformations of American society, culture, and politics.

Bibliography

Over the past several decades, numerous excellent studies have appeared on various aspects of American constitutional history. It is possible and practical to suggest only a few of them here. The United States Constitution may be found in several Internet sites, chief among which are the following: the United States Archives (www.archives.gov/exhibits/charters/constitution_transcript.html), and the National Constitution Center (constitutioncenter.org/constitution).

In addition, for all Supreme Court cases, there is the comprehensive FindLaw site (www.findlaw.com) and the Legal Information Institute at Cornell University (www.law.cornell.edu/supremecourt/text). Cases may be searched by a litigating party or citation number. As an example, the *Brown* desegregation decision is formally listed as *Brown* v. *Board of Education*, 347 US 483 (1954). The number 347 designates the volume number in *US Reports* and 483 is the first page number in the volume. In cases decided before 1874, another name may appear instead of "US." Until that year, a court reporter was assigned to report decisions. The reporter's name became the citation. Prior to 1816 when Congress officially created the Office of the Reporter, A.J. Dallas (usually cited as Dall.) and then William Cranch reported Supreme Court decisions. The well-known *Marbury* case is now often cited as *Marbury* v. *Madison* 5 US (1 Cranch) 137 (1803).

For an excellent source for news and commentary about the Court, see the Scotusblog site (www. scotusblog.com).

American Constitutional History: A Brief Introduction, Second Edition. Jack Fruchtman.
© 2022 John Wiley & Sons, Inc. Published 2022 by John Wiley & Sons, Inc.

Prologue

The most comprehensive contemporary histories of American constitutional development are two two-volume works: Edgar J. McManus and Tara Helfman, *Liberty and Union: A Constitutional History of the United States*, two vols. (New York, 2013), with a single-volume edition in 2014; and Melvin Urofsky and Paul Finkelman, *A March of Liberty: A Constitutional History of the United States*, two vols., third edn. (New York, 2011). Readers should anticipate Akhil Reed Amar's completion of a planned trilogy, of which the first published volume is *The Words that Made Us: America's Constitutional Conversation, 1760–1840* (New York, 2021). Those to follow include *The Words that Made Us Equal: American's Constitutional Conversation, 1840–1920*, and *The Words that Made Us Modern: America's Constitutional Conversation, 1920 to 2000*.

For one-volume studies, see Michael Stokes Paulsen and Luke Paulsen, *The Constitution: An Introduction* (New York, 2015), and Michael Les Benedict's *The Blessings of Liberty: A Concise History of the Constitution of the United States*, third edn. (Boston, 2016). Two classic treatments are Alfred H. Kelly, Winfred A. Harbison, and Herman Belz's *The American Constitution: Its Origins and Development*, two vols., seventh edn. (*New York*, 1991), first published in 1948 but useful until the last decade of the twentieth century; and Robert G. McCloskey, *The American Supreme Court*, revised by Sanford Levinson, sixth edn. (Chicago, 2016), first published in 1960 and focusing on the work of the Court. In addition, Peter Irons's *A People's History of the Supreme Court: The Men and Women Whose Cases and Decisions Have Shaped Our Constitution*, revised edn. (New York, 2006) focuses on the background of the people litigating before the Court. For a lively confrontation with constitutional ideas within a political context, see Mark A. Graber's *A New Introduction to American Constitutionalism* (New York, 2013). A review of the Supreme Court's institutional evolution is covered in Peter Charles Hoffer, Williamjames Hull Hoffer, and N.E.H. Hull, *The Supreme Court: An Essential History*, second edn. (Lawrence, KS, 2018).

A highly accessible series that covers the entire history of the United States from the European discovery to the present is the multi-volume *Oxford History of the United States*, which began publication in 1982. For important studies of constitutional evolution, see Bruce Ackerman's trilogy, all under the collective title, *We the People*. The first is *Foundations* (Cambridge, MA, 1988), then *Transformations* (Cambridge, MA, 1998), and finally *The Civil Rights Revolution* (Cambridge, MA, 2014). Akhil Reed Amar has also prepared two lively studies with polished arguments in *America's Constitution: A Biography* (New York, 2005), and *America's Unwritten Constitution: The Precedents and Principles We Live By* (New York, 2012). For a contrarian analysis, see Ian Millhiser, *Injustices: The Supreme Court's History of Comforting the Comfortable and Afflicting the Afflicted* (New York, 2015). The history of how Americans gradually expanded their liberty is set out in Eric Foner's *The Story of American Freedom* (New York, 1998), and Sean Wilentz's *The Rise of American Democracy: Jefferson to Lincoln* (New York, 2005).

Part 1: The New Republic, 1781–1828

Many excellent scholars have studied and analyzed the American founding period, especially the constitutional convention. For a fine account of the events from the imperial crisis to the Constitution and the rise of the judiciary, see Gordon S. Wood, *Power and Liberty: Constitutionalism in the American Revolution* (New York, 2021). The Continental Congress and the beginning of the Revolution are covered by Jack N. Rakove in *The Beginnings of National Politics: An Interpretative History of the Continental Congress* (Baltimore, 1979), and *Revolutionaries: A New History of the Invention of America* (Boston, 2010). One of the best one-volume treatments of the constitutional convention is Carol Berkin's *A Brilliant Solution: Inventing the American Constitution* (New York, 2002). The ratification process was a raucous, messy affair: see Pauline Maier's indispensable *Ratification: The People Debate the Constitution, 1787–1788* (New York, 2010). For those opposed to the Constitution and a strong central government, see Saul Cornell, *The Other Founders: Anti-Federalism and the Dissenting Tradition in America, 1788–1828* (Chapel Hill, NC, 1999).

The essential work on the struggle between Federalists and Anti-Federalists is by the players themselves: Alexander Hamilton, James Madison, and John Jay, *The Federalist Papers*, ed. Isaac Kramnick (New York, 1987); the Anti-Federalist response may be found in Herbert J. Storing, *The Complete Anti-Federalist*, seven vols. (Chicago, 1981). The debate within the states may be located in the monumental undertaking by John Kaminski and his colleagues, *The Documentary History of the Ratification of the Constitution*, 36 vols. to date, with a projected total of 42 vols. (Madison, WI, 1976–). The period after ratification was studied by Stanley Elkins and Eric McKitrick in *The Age of Federalism: The Early American Republic, 1776–1809* (New York, 1993).

On judicial review, see Keith E. Whittington, *Repugnant Laws: Judicial Review of Acts of Congress from the Founding to the Present* (Lawrence, KS, 2019).

Part 2: The Slave Republic, 1789–1877

David Brion Davis has succinctly studied American slavery in *Inhuman Bondage: The Rise and Fall of Slavery in the New World* (Oxford, 2006), and *The Problem of Slavery in the Age of Revolution, 1770–1823* (Ithaca, NY, 1975). Ira Berlin has produced masterful works, especially *Generations of Captivity: A History of African-American Slaves* (Cambridge, MA, 2003), and *Many Thousands Gone: The First Two Centuries of Slavery in North America* (Cambridge, MA, 1998). Mark Tushnet has reviewed the legal foundations of slavery in *The American Law of Slavery: 1810–1860* (Princeton, 1981). For the Jacksonian period and the nullification debate, readers should turn to Richard E. Ellis, *The Union at Risk: Jacksonian Democracy, States' Rights, and the Nullification Crisis* (New York, 1987), and Jon Meacham, *American Lion: Andrew Jackson in the White House* (New York, 2008).

Lincoln and the Civil War are analyzed in these important studies: Daniel A. Farber's *Lincoln's Constitution* (Chicago, 2003); Harold Holzer's *Witness to War: The Civil War, 1861–1865* (New York, 1982); Eric Foner's *The Fiery Trial: Abraham Lincoln and American Slavery* (New York, 2010); James Oakes's *The Crooked Path to Abolition: Abraham Lincoln and the Antislavery Constitution* (New York, 2021); and James M. McPherson's now-classic *Battle Cry of Freedom: The Civil War Era* (Oxford, 1988, second edn. 2003). See also, Noah Feldman, *The Broken Constitution: Lincoln, Slavery, and the Refounding of America* (New York, 2021).

The Reconstruction period is covered by Eric Foner in *Reconstruction: America's Unfinished Revolution, 1863–1877*, updated edn. (New York, 2014), and James M. McPherson and James Hogue in *Ordeal by Fire: The Civil War and Reconstruction* (New York, 1982; fourth edn. 2010). See also Eric Foner, *The Second Founding: How the Civil War and Reconstruction Remade the Constitution* (New York, 2019), and Henry

Louis Gates, *Stony the Road: Reconstruction, White Supremacy, and the Rise of Jim Crow* (New York, 2019); Ilan Wurman, *The Second Founding: an Introduction to the Fourteenth Amendment* (Cambridge, 2020).

Part 3: The Free Market Republic, 1877–1937

The emerging American economy in the second half of the nineteenth century is well documented by Morton Keller, *Regulating a New Economy: Public Policy and Economic Change in America, 1900–1933* (Cambridge, MA, 1990); Maury Klein, *The Genesis of Industrial America, 1870–1920* (Cambridge, MA, 2001); and Stephen Skowronek, *Building a New American State: The Expansion of National Administrative Capacities, 1877–1920* (New York, 1982). For the rise of the separate but equal doctrine, see C. Vann Woodward's classic *The Strange Career of Jim Crow* (New York, 1955; commemorative edn., 2002), and Steve Luxenberg. *Separate: The Story of* Plessy v. Ferguson, *and America's Journey from Slavery to Segregation* (New York, 2019).

Howard Gillman and Paul Kens, respectively, have studied the Supreme Court's support of corporate America in *The Constitution Besieged: The Rise and Demise of Lochner Era Police Powers Jurisprudence* (Durham, NC), 1993), and *Lochner* v. *New York: Economic Regulation on Trial* (Lawrence, KS, 1998). The impact of the Fourteenth Amendment on American law and society in terms of the application of the Bill of Rights to the states is dealt with by Richard C. Cortner, *The Supreme Court and the Second Bill of Rights: The Fourteenth Amendment and the Nationalization of Civil Liberties* (Madison, WI, 1981). For progressive ideas in American constitutional thinking, see Lewis L. Gould, *America in the Progressive Era, 1890–1914* (New York, 2001), and Sidney M. Milkis, *Theodore Roosevelt, the Progressive Party, and the Transformation of American Democracy* (Lawrence, KS, 2009).

Sally McMillen covers the nineteenth-century women's rights movement in *Seneca Falls and the Origins of the Women's Rights Movement* (New York, 2008). Geoffrey R. Stone's seminal work on free speech, especially during and after World War I, is *Perilous Times: Free Speech in Wartime from the Sedition Act of 1798 to the War on Terrorism* (New York, 2004). See also Christopher M. Finan's *From the Palmer Raids to the Patriot Act: A History of the Fight for Free Speech in America* (Boston, 2007). Thomas Healy analyzes the role played by Oliver Wendell Holmes in the World War I cases in *The Great*

Dissent: How Oliver Wendell Holmes Changed His Mind – and Changed the History of Free Speech in America (New York, 2013).

Part 4: The Welfare State Republic, 1937–1995

The struggle over New Deal legislation has been excellently covered by Eric Rauchway, *Why the New Deal Matters* (New Haven, 2021); James F. Simon, *The Antagonists: Hugo Black, Felix Frankfurter, and Civil Liberties in Modern America* (New York, 1989); James McGregor Burns, *Packing the Court: The Rise of Judicial Power and the Coming Crisis of the Supreme Court* (New York, 2009); Noah Feldman in *Scorpions: The Battles and Triumphs of FDR's Great Supreme Court Justices* (New York, 2010); Jeff Shesol, *Supreme Power: Franklin Roosevelt vs. the Supreme Court* (New York, 2010); and Ira Katznelson, *Fear Itself: The New Deal and the Origins of Our Time* (New York, 2013). For free speech and press issues, see Leonard W. Levy, *The Emergence of a Free Press* (New York, 1985); Anthony Lewis, *Freedom for the Thought That We Hate: A Biography of the First Amendment* (New York, 2010); and James C. Goodale, *Fighting for the Press: The Inside Story of the Pentagon Papers and Other Battles* (New York, 2013).

For the religion issues that developed in the mid-twentieth century, see Leonard W. Levy, *The Establishment Clause: Religion and the First Amendment* (New York, 1986); Peter Irons, *God on Trial: Dispatches from America's Religious Battlefields* (New York, 2007); and Garrett Epps, *To an Unknown God: Religious Freedom on Trial* (New York, 2001). On student speech, see Justin Driver, *The Schoolhouse Gate: Public Education, the Supreme Court, and the Battle for the American Mind* (New York, 2018).

On capital punishment, see David C. Baldus, George G. Woodworth, and Charles A. Pulaski Jr. *Equal Justice and the Death Penalty: A Legal and Empirical Analysis*, known as the "Baldus study" (Boston, 1990), and James S. Liebman, "A Broken System: Error Rates in Capital Cases, 1973–1995," Columbia Law School, known as the "Liebman study," which may be found online at https://scholarship.law.columbia.edu/cgi/viewcontent.cgi?article=2220&context=faculty_scholarship. For contemporary studies, see Evan J. Mandery, *A Wild Justice: The Death and Resurrection of Capital Punishment in America* (New York, 2013), and Michael Waldman, *The Second Amendment: A Biography* (New York, 2014).

For a concise commentary on the Warren Court, see Geoffrey R. Stone and David A. Strauss, *Democracy and Equality: The Enduring Constitutional Vision of the Warren Court* (New York, 2020). For a counterargument, see Adam Cohen, *Supreme Inequality: The Supreme Court's Fifty-Year Battle for a More Unjust America* (New York, 2020).

On the controversial issue of privacy, especially a woman's right to have an abortion, see especially Laurence H. Tribe, *Abortion: The Clash of Absolutes* (New York, 1990), and David J. Garrow, *Liberty and Sexuality: The Right to Privacy and the Making of Roe v. Wade* (New York, 1994). The growth of executive power, especially during national security crises, is covered in Louis Fisher's *Military Tribunals and Presidential Power: American Revolution to the War on Terrorism* (Lawrence, KS, 2005). For the Supreme Court in the first decade of the twenty-first century, there is Jeffrey Toobin's *The Nine: Inside the Secret World of the Supreme Court* (New York, 2007).

Part 5: The Executive Republic, 1995–2021

The literature on the civil rights movement is voluminous. Readers will find Taylor Branch's trilogy invaluable: *Parting the Waters: America in the King Years, 1954–63* (New York, 1988); *Pillars of Fire: America in the King Years, 1963–65* (New York, 1998); and *At Canaan's Edge: America in the King Years 1965–68* (New York, 2006). Branch published a synopsis in *The King Years: Historic Moments in the Civil Rights Movement* (New York, 2013). The major study of the iconic *Brown* v. *Board of Education* decision is Richard Kluger's *Simple Justice: The History of* Brown v. Board of Education *and Black America's Struggle for Equality* (New York, 1976; revised and expanded edn., 2004).

On the Court's mixed rulings on race, see Orville Vernon Burton and Armand Derfner, *Justice Deferred: Race and the Supreme Court* (Cambridge, MA, 2021).

Six important studies focus on the Supreme Court as led by Chief Justices Rehnquist and Roberts: Tinsley E. Yarbrough, *The Rehnquist Court and the Constitution* (New York, 2000); Mark Tushnet, *A Court Divided: The Rehnquist Court and the Future of Constitutional Law* (New York, 2005); Jan Crawford Greenburg, *Supreme Conflict: The Inside Story of the Struggle for Control of the United States Supreme Court* (New York, 2005); Marcia Coyle, *The Roberts Court: The Struggle for the Constitution* (New York, 2013); Jeffrey Toobin, *The*

Oath: The Obama White House and the Supreme Court (New York, 2012); and Mark Tushnet, *In the Balance: Law and Politics on the Roberts Court* (New York, 2013).

On doctrinal debates concerning originalism and the living constitution, see Antonin Scalia, *A Matter of Interpretation: Federal Courts and the Law* (Princeton, 1997); Ilan Wurman, *A Debt Against the Living: An Introduction to Originalism* (Cambridge, 2017); David A. Strauss, *The Living Constitution (Inalienable Rights)* (New York, 2010); Jack Balkin, *Living Originalism* (Cambridge, MA, 2011); and Erwin Chemerinsky, *We The People: A Progressive Reading of the Constitution for the Twenty-First Century* (New York, 2018).

The argument that presidents possess unitary executive power is engaged by Steven G. Calabresi and Christopher S. Yoo, *The Unitary Executive: Presidential Power from Washington to Bush* (New Haven, 2008); John Yoo, *The Powers of War and Peace: The Constitution and Foreign Affairs After 9/11* (Chicago, 2006); Michael A. Genovese, *Presidential Prerogative: Imperial Power in an Age of Terrorism* (Stanford, 2011); and Michael W. McConnell, *The President Who Would Not Be King: Executive Power under the Constitution* (Princeton, 2020). For an opposing view, see Saikrishna Bangalore Prakash, *The Living Presidency: an Originalist Argument against Its Ever-Expanding Powers* (Cambridge, MA, 2020). The Heritage Foundation's early support of the healthcare mandate now partially embodied in the Affordable Care Act may be found in Stuart M. Butler and Edmund F. Haislmaier, "A National Health System for America," *Critical Issues* (Washington, DC, 1989).

Several critiques of contemporary issues have been published. On terrorism, see Joseph Margulies, *Guantánamo and the Abuse of Presidential Power* (New York, 2006). For the religion clauses, see Howard Gillman and Erwin Chemerinsky, *The Religion Clauses: The Case for Separating Church and State* (New York, 2020) and Jack N. Rakove, *Beyond Belief, Beyond Conscience: The Radical Significance of the Free Exercise of Religion* (New York, 2020). Nadine Strossen has written *Hate: Why We Should Resist It with Free Speech, Not Censorship* (New York, 2020).

For the history and debate over the Second Amendment, see Noah Schusterman, *Armed Citizens: The Road from Ancient Rome to the Second Amendment* (Charlottesville, VA, 2020), and Adam Winkler, *Gunfight: The Battle over the Right to Bear Arms in America* (New

York, 2011). Alexander Keyssar studies the Electoral College in *Why Do We Still Have the Electoral College?* (Cambridge, MA, 2020), while Carol S. Steiker and Jordan M. Steiker investigates the death penalty in *Courting Death: The Supreme Court and Capital Punishment* (Cambridge, MA, 2016) as does Maurice Chammah in *Let the Lord Sort Them: The Rise and Fall of the Death Penalty* (New York, 2021). On abortion, see Mary Ziegler, *Abortion and the Law in America*: Roe v. Wade *to the Present* (Cambridge, 2020).

The Office of Legal Counsel in the Justice Department produced the document concerning the indictment of sitting presidents: see https://www.justice.gov/olc/opinion/sitting-president%e2%80%99s-amenability-indictment-and-criminal-prosecution. For the results of the Mueller investigation, see Peter Finn, ed., *The Mueller Report* (New York, 2019).

Epilogue

The most comprehensive critique of the Supreme Court remains David M. O'Brien's *Storm Center: The Supreme Court in American Politics*, twelfth edn. (New York, 2020).

Important studies of presidential judicial selections may be found in the classic work by Henry J. Abraham, *Justices, Presidents, and Senators: A History of the US Supreme Court Appointments from Washington to Bush II*, revised edn. (Lanham, MD, 2008), and David Alistair Yalof, *Pursuit of Justices: Presidential Politics and the Selection of Supreme Court Nominees* (Chicago, 1999). David N. Atkinson has inquired into why and under what circumstances justices retire or resign in *Leaving the Bench: Supreme Court Justices at the End* (Lawrence, KS, 1999), as did Artemus Ward, *Deciding to Leave: The Politics of Retirement from the United States Supreme Court* (Albany, NY, 2003).

The 2020 Department of Homeland Security's "Homeland Threat Assessment" may be found at https://www.dhs.gov/sites/default/files/publications/2020_10_06_homeland-threat-assessment.pdf. The Department of Justice's National Strategy for Countering Domestic Terrorism may be found at https://www.justice.gov/opa/speech/attorney-general-merrick-b-garland-remarks-domestic-terrorism-policy-address. For the Presidential Commission on the Supreme Court of the United States, see https://www.whitehouse.gov/pcscotus.

The argument for ignoring the Constitution in contemporary America may be found in Louis Michael Seidman, *On Constitutional Disobedience* (New York, 2013). Studies regarding the protests and violence in 2020 after police killings of African Americans may be found at https://acleddata.com/2020/09/03/demonstrations-political-violence-in-america-new-data-for-summer-2020, a joint project of Princeton University and the Armed Conflict Location and Event Data Project.

Index

American Constitutional History: A Brief Introduction, Second Edition. Jack Fruchtman.
© 2022 John Wiley & Sons, Inc. Published 2022 by John Wiley & Sons, Inc.

9 781119 734277